TITANIC

JAMES CAMERON'S
ILLUSTRATED SCREENPLAY

TITANIC
JAMES CAMERON'S
ILLUSTRATED SCREENPLAY

Over 300 photographs ◆ The annotated film script
In-depth interview with Writer, Director, Producer James Cameron

ANNOTATED BY RANDALL FRAKES

A HarperEntertainment Book
From HarperPerennial

Design by Joel Avirom, Jason Snyder and Meghan Day Healey.

FIRST EDITION

ISBN 0-06-095307-1

ACKNOWLEDGMENTS

RANDALL FRAKES: This book would not have been possible without the dedicated help and guidance of the creative crew at Lightstorm: Carol Henry, Geoff Burdick, Rae Sanchini, Al Rives, Mike Trainotti and Jane Gonsoulin, as well as Ed Marsh and Jon Landau (all of whom carried the ball when crisis struck); the book's designers Joel Avirom, Jason Snyder and Meghan Day Healey; the patient forbearance and taste of Joseph Montebello from HarperCollins; and of course, the man who reinvents the word genius on every project he tackles, James Cameron.

Special acknowledgment to photographer MERIE WALLACE for her extraordinary work.

INTRODUCTION

THIS BOOK IS A JOURNEY back to James Cameron's *Titanic*, a fascinating step-by-step examination of the creative evolution of one of the most successful and critically acclaimed films in history.

By now almost everyone knows the film grossed nearly 2 billion dollars at the worldwide box office and won a record-tying 11 Academy Awards. But few people know how, let alone why, the script's ending was changed; what scenes were deleted or added; how historical accuracy was maintained; or what inspired writer/director/producer James Cameron to write this sweeping romantic epic in the first place.

You are about to find out as you turn the pages. But first, a few words to help you on your journey...

As is his usual custom, Cameron first wrote a *scriptment*, a very long, detailed treatment in prose style of the story he wanted to film, with sections of dialogue interspersed throughout. After completing it on August 25, 1995, Cameron travelled to the site of the actual wreck of Titanic, nearly two and a half miles below the surface of the North Atlantic, using the Russian research vessel Keldysh and its two deep water manned submersibles to film the remains of the ship for the film's opening sequence.

Cameron completed the screenplay you are about to read on May 7, 1996. This draft became the *shooting script* and was used for casting, rehearsals and other production preparations. After additional footage of the modern "framing story" was shot off the shores of Halifax, Nova Scotia, the project shifted into production of the 1912 sequences at the new Twentieth Century Fox studio in Baja, Mexico, which was built especially for the filming of *Titanic*. The script was further refined by the interplay of actors, crew and director during this phase of production, known as *principal photography*. Further alterations and refinements were made during the post production editing phase, including changes suggested by the reactions of test screening audiences to interim cuts of the complete film.

Titanic: The Illustrated Screenplay was designed to give both students of film writing and fans of the movie a unique look at the evolution of *Titanic* from script to screen. The annotations accompanying the screenplay and the hundreds of images from the film serve to illuminate the differences between the written idea and the realization of that idea on celluloid. James Cameron's thoughts on *Titanic* are threaded throughout the book as well, indicating in his own words why certain additions, deletions and modifications were made.

For those unaccustomed to reading screenplays, definitions for a few commonly used terms may prove useful.

Ext.	*Exterior of a location*
Int.	*Interior of a location*
Cut to	*A major shift in pacing, time or location*
Dissolve	*A slow transition, blending from one scene to another.*
Tight	*Close shot*
V.O. (Voice Over)	*Dialogue or narration spoken by a character not shown on screen*
POV (Point of View)	*Shot from a particular character's position to indicate what they are seeing*
Flashback	*A jump back in time to reveal information necessary to an understanding of the current scene*
Tracking	*Moving the camera through a set or location to follow the action*

Randall Frakes

GOING BACK TO TITANIC

Interview with James Cameron

Randall Frakes: *What inspired you to write "Titanic"?*

James Cameron: There's no simple answer because there was no one thing. There was my desire to tell a love story. There was my love of history. And a perceived opportunity to do history in a way that is not usually done in films.

RF: *How so?*

JC: Filmed history is usually done in a way that creates a barrier of language, dress and moral attitudes. In most historical movies the differences between then and now are emphasized, instead of the universality. I've based my cinematic career on creating a sense of unity between the audience and the characters on the screen, through whatever means necessary. I wanted to try the same stylistic approach with an historical event and see if I could create that unity through recognizable emotions and situations. There was also my fascination with the event itself and my love of submersibles and diving and deep ocean technology.

RF: *All the stuff we saw in "The Abyss"?*

JC: Yes, and although that movie was done independently of "Titanic," making it led me to Robert Ballard, one of the leading oceanographers and users of deep ocean technology, both manned and unmanned. And he proved its worth to the world by using that technology to find the *Titanic* wreck in 1985. So you have a convergence of two things; my love and desire to demonstrate the power of that technology and my love of history. So here was an ideal opportunity to converge two areas of interest.

RF: *Why did you want to write a love story? Hadn't you already done several love stories?*

JC: I always jokingly say all my films are love stories, which is really true.

"The Abyss" is a classic love story. "True Lies" is a movie about a marriage in jeopardy. "Aliens" is about unconditional parental love. And "The Terminator" is a classic gothic love story. I can remember interviews with the press for every one of my movies where I kept saying "Yes, but . . . " That was my entire conversation. They wanted to talk about the visual effects, about morphing and CG animation, and I'm going "Yes, but . . . what we were really doing is a story about a family, or about unconditional love, or a gothic romance or . . . " And the press was treating me as if they've heard this line from every Hollywood producer who tries to justify their overblown, overproduced visual exercise. When, in fact, for me the "yes, but" was fundamental. The relationships and the characters are far more important than the visual effects. You remove the relationships and all you've got left is a nifty effects demo reel. If you remove the effects but keep the relationships, you'll still have an emotional experience. What do people remember about "The Abyss"? Lindsay drowning and being revived by Bud. There's no visual effects in that scene.

RF: *Pure drama.*

JC: Exactly. With "Titanic," I wanted to get all that stuff that was eclipsing the dramatic writing out of the way. So, from my perspective, writing "Titanic" was just doing what I was already doing, only doing it in a more obvious way. Although there are enormously complicated visual effects in "Titanic," they are mostly weighted toward the last hour. So if the whole movie that goes before that wasn't working, the audience would have left, and they certainly wouldn't be coming back to see it again and again. You've got a two-hour movie that's all about people, and then the effects movie starts.

RF: *There were sporadic flourishes of visual effects in the beginning. I'm thinking of the scene with the dolphins, and the kiss at the bow.*

JC: I don't think people really thought of those as visual effects scenes. They thought of them as real moments, no different from "Doctor Zhivago" when the refugee train breathtakingly plows through the snow. But you don't ask yourself whether it's a miniature train or a real train. It doesn't matter. I think in the first half of "Titanic" the visual effects are dramatically supportive in an unobtrusive way. The story doesn't have to stop for a moment while visual effects dance across the screen. The effects can have a lyrical story function. When Jack and Rose kiss at the bow, the effects are not only advancing the story, but are creating and sustaining an emotional state. And I think that happens rarely in visual effects films.

RF: *Can you give another specific example?*

JC: The morphing of Rose from a young girl to an old woman at the end of the scene where Jack is sketching her. There's an amazing sense of a connection of that character across time. Her emotional state at that moment—a trembling, anticipatory longing for Jack—carries over across the gulf of time to a moment when she's an old woman, and you can see her still experiencing that. To me that moment works on so many different levels, because it says to the audience, "That young girl is still alive inside that old woman. So the next time you see an old woman, see the young girl she used to be."

RF: *One of the more breathtaking emotional transitions in the script and film is the scene on the bow when Jack and Rose kiss. The bow fades seamlessly into the wrecked bow at the bottom of the ocean. Jack and Rose fade more slowly, like ghosts.*

JC: They're like these youthful spirits, somehow still alive and attached to the ship in the depths. I think the moment when Jack and Rose fade as the ship transforms into the wreck turned out to be a kind of effects epiphany, because it shows the power visual effects can have to merge concepts in poetic ways. It's too limiting to use effects only to create spaceships, monsters and fantastic otherworldly things.

RF: *Although the transition we're discussing was filmed as written, it is hard to imagine the emotional impact of the finished shot from the description.*

JC: Which addresses the limitations of screenwriting. In order to write it, I had to see it in my mind, know that it was technically possible, and create a kind of inter-language to help the reader imagine it the way I did. But you can't really do it with something that is just beyond most people's experience.

RF: *You can only approximate it.*

JC: Yes, because the exact thing that I imagined, crudely described, and then even more crudely interpreted by readers, surprises them when they see it on the screen. It's frustrating to try and create a subtle cinematic feeling, or mood...it's nearly impossible to adequately convey it with words. I do whatever I can think of to convey the percussiveness of the cutting, or the surprise of the next piece of action. I wrote what I call the "ode to the ship," the sequence where *Titanic* heads out to sea. The captain sips his tea. Jack sees the dolphins. The engine room bustles. In reading it over, I didn't realize there was a transition point where I was going into a musical/visual set-piece without dialogue. In reading it, I felt like I was waiting for something to happen. And it had already happened. So I literally put in a paragraph that basically says that this is a big sequence that is starting now. And I'm not sure if readers even really get that. But I tried to describe what the music will do. How do you describe music? You can't describe it any better than a visual thing. You can only describe the effect it is intended to have. Most writers don't make musical annotations in their scripts because they think it's pointless. It's a given that the proper music will be there. But I don't think it's pointless. If you're really intending to write something that is purely cinematic, you have to characterize it that way for the readers.

RF: *So they can have as close an approximation of the finished film as you can manage on paper?*

JC: And that may be writing out of the box, and frowned upon by purist screenwriters, but I don't care.

RF: *Speaking of writing out of the box, you also put parenthetical instructions to the actors at the top of their dialogue bites. A lot of screenwriters have all but eliminated them due to resistance from actors and directors who want room to interpret the lines.*

JC: The problem is that some lines don't make sense unless you parenthetically indicate the actor should play against the line. Or with a wink. Or throw the line away. The lines can play flat without extra notation. When people in the business read scripts, they tend to prioritize the dialogue over the prose description, even though they should know better. If a piece of action is integral to the dramatics of the moment, especially when it happens in the middle of the actor's lines, you're much better off putting it parenthetically in the middle of the dialogue. "He puts the cup down, cocks the gun, looks away" whatever, because those little time-sensitive details (and God is in the details in film-making) can be the difference between a hackneyed moment and a great one. And sometimes there's a very fine line between the moment being corny or powerful. I think "Titanic" walks that line a lot of the time. It doesn't walk it successfully for some people.

RF: *Did it walk successfully for you?*

JC: I wrote that script for a direct emotional response—something I felt we could get away with because the story was enveloped in this tragic situation.

RF: *And it's a period piece about young lovers who can be exuberant without looking too foolish.*

JC: I really think it's the fact that you know death and doom are coming. You know what is going to happen to the ship. There's a creeping dread that informs every moment, no matter how frivolous or innocent. Jack and Rose walking around talking endlessly about sweet nothings works partly because we know that possibly one of them will die and certainly that everything around them will be destroyed. So there's a morbid fascination as you're drinking in the visuals and seeing all the other people. You're going that's nice, that's great, but . . . it's all going to sink. There's a strange kind of cognitive dissonance that's going on in every moment, and that allows the script to be more melodramatic than most contemporary films can get away with.

RF: *The younger audience seems to have responded to an honest characterization of teenage emotions.*

JC: I was talking to people about writing "Titanic" and some said that a teenage love story can't be powerful because teenager emotions aren't real. They're just

puppy love or crushes. They're not developed or informed by the adult experience.

RF: *I think someone said that to Shakespeare when he was writing "Romeo and Juliet". Fortunately, he ignored them.*

JC: (laughs) He knew teenage emotions are the most intense you'll ever have in your life. Subsequently, they're always watered down and contaminated by experience, by knowing that relationships usually end, that there's a point at which you will find out too much about the other person to keep loving them so unconditionally, or that emotions can change, that love is not eternal. There's a feeling when you're sixteen or seventeen that you're on the verge of a discovery unlike anything in the history of the world, even though most people on the planet have already passed that marker. But it's happening to you, so it fills your universe. You only feel things *that* intensely when you're that age. So I think kids get "Titanic" innately. The movie will res-

JC: It's been a pattern in all my films that first there's a long, detailed treatment, more accurately called a scriptment, then a first draft script, then a week later, a shooting script—a leaned out, cut-downed version of the script.

RF: *Do you use outlines?*

JC: I write a short beat-by-beat outline, reducing the beats to one line representing a single scene. I then expand those single lines into two or three pages each for the scriptment.

RF: *Your scriptments are like densely packed mini-novels. Did you ever consider writing prose fiction?*

JC: I actually started out thinking that I would be a science fiction novelist. I was more interested in the novel as a form than in screenplays. You got me interested in writing screenplays.

RF: *When you begin a script like "Titanic," do you usually begin with an image, a set piece, a specific character, or a theme?*

JC: Yes.

RF: *(laughs) All of them?*

JC: Yes.

RF: *What was the major thing inspiring you while writing "Titanic"?*

JC: I was just moving toward an ending based on a story of tragic love, set against a tragic event that would combine to create an almost insurmountable field of emotional energy for the audience. Some people said that the fictional story would only detract from the real events. With all the great history and all the fascinating real characters, why waste screen time on that sappy love story? Considering there have been a dozen other films about the *Titanic* disaster, most of them dealing only with the historical situations, there would have been little reason for audiences to line up around the block for this version if that's all it had to offer. I always believed the real events and the fictional story could turbo-charge each other. Apart, they would not have been as powerful. The fact that you are perceiving the tragedy through the subjective vantage point of these two young people who you care about

onate for adults, if they are at all honest with themselves and were lucky enough to feel that deeply when they were young. The movie will at least make them long for the intensity of those emotions, if nothing else. And then you have the minority who either never felt things so intensely, or denied that intensity, put their feelings into a denial box, and have since developed a jaded view of the world. That twenty percent or so are not going to appreciate the film. Or they might be able to appreciate it for other reasons.

RF: *The history. The re-creation of the times. The action.*

JC: And they'll trivialize or make fun of the Jack and Rose part of the story because they don't feel it. Frankly, I doubt the film would have done the business it has if the Jack and Rose story was missing or reduced.

RF: *How many drafts do you usually write to get to shooting script?*

makes it a completely different type of experience than all of the other docu-drama-like films that have been made about *Titanic*. And conversely the love story, where you know one of them is doomed, in and of itself doesn't seem to have enough size to it, doesn't seem to take the passion and display it across a grand enough theme.

RF: *You have a lot of nuclear explosions in your movies up until "Titanic," then you have this sudden devastation of a micro-world.*

JC: That's right. For me, the sinking of *Titanic* is metaphorically the end of the world for the people in the context of the story. So in a way it's just another nuclear explosion, another cataclysmic situation where human beings have to come to terms with the fact that there are forces in the universe greater than they are.

RF: *You have been quoted in the past as saying that you did not enjoy the writing process. Did the writing of "Titanic" change your attitude in any way?*

JC: "Titanic" was more enjoyable to write simply because it had an underlying subject that was not of my creation. So for me it was an exploration. Every day of writing was an official day of research. You have total control in a fictional environment. With "Titanic," there were certain immovable historical "pylons." I could slalom through the pylons but I couldn't move any, once I determined which ones were historically accurate.

RF: *How did you determine that?*

JC: Consensus. Sometimes you have to deal with a vocal minority that gets on the map. A perfect example of that is *Titanic's* second officer Lightoller saying that the ship did not break apart when it sank. He was a vocal minority of one. But he created, almost single-handedly, the official line that the ship did not break up when it sank. Yet, if you look closely at the transcript of the American Senate inquiry, there are at least 12 people who said that they saw the ship break up. And yet, Lightoller's version became *the* version, because he was the officer, the one who should have been the most responsible. In fact, he was the one with the greatest reason to whitewash this situation.

RF: *By saying the ship didn't break up, could he have been helping Titanic's owners to block civil suits for negligence?*

JC: Lightoller was angling for his own ship to captain, and he bent over backwards to support the company. If he testified that the ship broke up before sinking, it would be additional besmirching of the White Star name. Not only did they hit an iceberg and sink, but in the process of sinking the ship *broke in half*. People might think it wasn't a very good ship in the first place.

RF: *They might also think twice before booking passage on Titanic's sister ship Olympic.*

JC: Right. So he had pressing reasons to whitewash, and yet his version became history . . . until the wreck was discovered in 1985 in *two pieces*. The 1953 "Titanic" and the 1958 "A Night to Remember" showed the ship sinking in one piece, in utter defiance of the fact that there were many survivors who saw it break up and said so.

So in piecing together this historical event, I took the immutable facts and then the eyewitness accounts (some of which agree, some of which don't) and I started to force an answer out of it. And there are some places where there's no alternative but to use conjecture, especially in dealing with what happened in the last fifteen minutes of the life of the ship. There are other places where things are pretty crystal clear, reinforced repeatedly by eyewitness accounts, such as the distress rockets going off. Everyone remembers those. So there are things that you know happened. But even when I knew what happened, it was still difficult to fix it in time.

RF: *Didn't you work from a detailed chronology of events?*

JC: Yes. One of my goals in writing "Titanic" was to create a very accurate timeline of actual events, then string all my fictional characters into history in the proper order. Even a relatively minor moment should happen at the correct time and place throughout the length of the ship. To do that, you have to know the order in which the boats were being launched, and what officer was in charge of what boat.

RF: *What happened to this accurate timeline when you started editing the movie?*

JC: I removed certain historical beats, but I never changed the order of the events. Some of the time happening between events may have gotten telescoped down because of scenes being removed, but there were no historical violations. There were a few minor liberties taken, such as the elevator Rose uses to go down to E deck and search for Jack. At that point in time, it probably wasn't flooding, or it may have been flooding a little later. It was just a more dramatic image. I know all the elevators' lifting equipment was up in the deck house, so it would have been possible for the elevators to function even if the decks were flooding.

RF: *How do you account for some of the radical differences in testimony between witnesses who had no special agenda?*

JC: The survivors were all on different parts of the ship. Where you were determined the kind of experience you would have. It's like "Rashomon," taken to the nth degree.

RF: *Which would have been another way to do "Titanic."*

JC: There are infinite ways to deal with a subject that complicated. It's like the Vietnam War. You could do a hundred films on that subject and each one would be different. But you ultimately circle the same themes, because of historical consensus. The public already has a consensus opinion of what Titanic means before the facts.

RF: *Such as . . .*

JC: Human nobility, tempting fate, arrogance and hubris, and to a lesser extent, the class inequities. You have to deal with those themes either supportively or do an alternative version but you can't *not* deal with it.

RF: *One of the effective tools of writers throughout the ages is developing unity of opposites. This is something you seem to get into every script. A perfect example is in "The Terminator", where you have a pregnant woman fighting a metal skeleton bent on her destruction. Birth and death.*

JC: That's right. And on a character level in "The Abyss" you have the blue collar tool pusher and the col-lege-educated engineer, and a very similar relationship between Jack and Rose in "Titanic." He's a street vagabond and she's refined. But he's the one with the knowledge and emotional leadership.

RF: *In your scripts you also have tonal opposites. In "Titanic," the power and optimism of Jack and Rose's simple love contrasts with a terrifying universe where a few errors of judgment can lead to chaos and disaster. The first half of the film is a statement of the transforming power of love, the second half is the universe testing that power.*

JC: Yes, it's fate and free will. Predestination and human choice were the underlying themes of both *Terminator* movies. In "Titanic," there's a moment on the deck of the ship where Rose kisses Jack and tells him when the ship docks she's going with him. She's made a decision that will, in a sense, destroy her world and lead her into his. And it's at that exact moment that the ship rams the iceberg. Then the predestined part of it starts to play out.

RF: *It's that old dance between what we want to do and what the universe let's us do.*

JC: It gets even more complicated when the lookouts in the crow's nest are diverted by Jack and Rose kissing. The distraction is just a few seconds, but critical, because they don't see the iceberg in time for the ship to avoid hitting it. Rose's moment of greatest free will is the moment that seals her fate, as well as everyone else's on the ship.

RF: *So you were consciously intending that Jack and Rose's embrace would distract the lookouts?*

JC: Yes. Considering the size of the iceberg, it's reasonable to presume that the lookouts were distracted by *something*.

RF: *Some theorists assume they were sleeping, or huddled below the cowling to keep warm.*

JC: Or they may have simply been looking to the right or left at another iceberg.

RF: *The surviving lookout testified later that they did not see any other icebergs.*

JC: How much of that is covering your ass? Is he going to stand up there and say he saw other icebergs but the guys on the bridge didn't slow the ship down? It's clear to me that everyone got together and compared their stories and White Star told them what to say, or what not to say. The lookout didn't want to lose his job. Wouldn't you lie to feed your family?

RF: *Could they have done anything differently to avoid the berg once they sighted it?*

JC: Murdoch was not well-trained in maneuvering the ship. They had sea trials, but only a few hours of simple turns. They didn't really practice emergency maneuvering procedures. They hadn't drilled on the fact that in order to maintain maximum steerageway during an emergency turn, you went full reverse on your port engine, and full forward on your starboard engine, and put your turbine engine at half or one third ahead so that it was still turning, maintaining water flow across the rudder, but not substantially adding to the speed of the ship. Then you turn hard-a-starboard.

RF: *Which turned the ship the opposite way?*

JC: Right. That was the way they did it in those days. If you wanted to turn to the left, you called for starboard, as in a sailing boat, where you put the tiller to the right, which put the rudder to the left, which created a turn to the left. Coming back to screenwriting, what do you do when you're going to be showing something on screen that half of the audience is going to assume is wrong because they know port from starboard? Ultimately, I felt it was more important to be correct.

RF: *As in your script, did Ismay really tell Smith to speed up?*

JC: In the D deck reception area, after lunch on Saturday, Ismay and Smith had a conversation that was observed by several people, during which Ismay was overheard to emphasize that he wanted to beat the

Olympic's record. It's not specifically known what the Captain's response was. You have an interesting thing going on here. The Captain is officially the employee of Ismay, but on the other hand he is the master of the ship and Ismay had no authority at sea. So it's a case of subtle pressure, but it's not really that subtle. He was the Captain's boss.

RF: *Although Smith was due to retire. He probably didn't acquiesce out of fear.*

JC: I think it was just a voice in his ear that slightly outweighed his inner voice, which might have preached more caution. But Smith probably would have gone about that fast anyway because such speed was not that unusual. The great irony of this is that if they had slowed down, many of the passengers would have complained. They had been sold on the idea that they would travel in style *and* speed. Everybody looks back with hindsight and ascribes blame here and there, but back then, the White Star officials *and* passengers were participating in a consensus reality that was built on sand. Our society is probably doing that about some other issue now. That is one of the more interesting messages that can be taken from "Titanic".

RF: *Why do you think Ismay pocketed the ice warning Smith gave him and carried it around all day?*

JC: If the Captain gave it to him, it was because he felt it was a valid warning. Maybe he was trying to get Ismay to back off the pressure. If Ismay stuck it in his pocket, it might be because he didn't want it displayed on the chart room wall where it could worry the officers. If he showed it to other passengers, it was to dispel any worry about the ice, a false bravado based on his experience that you drove on until you saw ice blocking your way and then slowed down and moved gingerly through it. If they had not struck the berg they would have seen more ice eventually and slowed down, because they were going into an ice field. They didn't know they were, but they should have because they got enough ice warnings to indicate that possibility. But they must have thought the bergs were isolated and not a true field.

RF: *Shortly after the sinking, author Joseph Conrad wrote an article in which he said if the ship had hit the iceberg dead on, it would not have sank, because of the design of the water tight compartments.*

JC: Not true. The ship hit the bottom approximately at the same speed it was traveling when it hit the iceberg. The bow did not accordion. The ship's structure failed 200 or so feet further aft, in front of the bridge. If the ship struck dead on, it would have failed at the same point, right in front of the bridge, and it would have sunk in less than 15 minutes, like the *Lusitania*, killing almost everyone.

RF: *In the two hearings on the sinking, there was little testimony about steerage passengers being prevented from coming on deck. Why did you portray the majority of steerage as being prisoners below decks?*

JC: I didn't portray them all below decks. You see most of them on deck, eventually. Certainly there were some who were held below. Just because third class passengers did not testify doesn't mean they didn't write letters later, or weren't interviewed later. Over the years, there has been enough testimony by steerage passengers indicating some were held below for a time. There's ROV footage of the wreck showing gates closed and still locked. There's testimony from steerage passengers who said they were actively held back by stewards who would not allow them to come through first and second class spaces. I think it was not so much an order that came down from the bridge as just a knee-jerk reaction from the crew reflecting the way things were done on the ship—the fact that it was important not to have panic, and the first class passengers should have first access to the lifeboats. There was even a thought, since the boats were stored in first class space, that the first class passengers had first rights. The funny thing is, at that time, most of the steerage passengers probably bought into that world view as well. Many did what they were told. Although there is the case of the strapping young Irish man who knocked down one of the gates.

RF: *The one who chased the steward who insulted him?*

JC: That's right. And he let a number of people through. Which is what the sequence with Jack leading the charge through the locked gate is based on.

RF: *Predominate theory now seems to be that "Autumn," a popular contemporary song, not the hymn, was the last number the band played.*

JC: The actual evidence in favor of "Autumn" is based on one person's testimony. But many people on deck and in the boats independently remember hearing "Nearer My God to Thee." Wallace Hartley had previously told a fellow band member on another ship that if he was ever on a sinking ship, he would play "Nearer My God to Thee." He also wrote a letter to his sister saying the same thing. That's the evidence in favor. The evidence against is Harold Bride, 21-year-old junior assistant Marconi operator, who was paid a large sum by *The New York Times* to tell his exclusive story. He's the only person who said he thought he heard "Autumn" and he had a reputation of being a young braggart who liked to elaborate stories. He may even have been underwater at the time because he was swept off the ship with collapsible B.

But even if the band *had* played "Autumn" it didn't have to be the *last* thing they played. If they played "Nearer My God to Thee," they played it for a different reason than they played everything else. You have to assume a psychological mechanism on the part of Wallace Hartley who looked around, realized they were doomed, and played something for himself. By this time, the music was failing to prevent panic. People were ripping off doors and throwing them in the water for floats. There was screaming and chaos. There was no longer any reason to "allay panic" or soothe the nerves, because people were going crazy. If they played "Nearer My God to Thee," it was because *they* wanted to play it for themselves. And if Hartley had told a former shipmate and his sister what he would do if he were on a sinking ship, I can't imagine him not doing it. So I think that the evidence for "Nearer My God to Thee" is the most compelling. And it became a myth that they played it probably because it was true.

RF: *But which version of "Nearer My God" did they play?*

JC: Now it gets complicated, because there are 3 versions! And then you have to guess which version Hartley would likely have chosen, based on his background. But that's not the version I used. I used the one I liked. The one I thought was most evocative. Whatever they played, the scene was constructed to show that the band, having served dutifully throughout the sinking, took the opportunity to play something that had meaning to them. So for them to just play another waltz would have had no dramatic significance.

RF: *What about the theory that the band did not continue to play just before the ship went down?*

JC: There's evidence to support they did and evidence to support they did not. You could tell the story of the noble band members that has a meaning to all human beings everywhere, and speaks to a higher part of ourselves that has to do with duty and selflessness and our ability to transcend imminent death. Or you could tell the story of the cowardly band members who threw their instruments down and tried to claw their way into a lifeboat. The latter has no value to anyone because it is not inspiring. So the legend that's come

down is not based so much on what the band actually did, but what we hope they would have done.

RF: *Has your facility with words helped you sell projects like "Titanic?"*

JC: It don't hurt. I think good writing is a lot more important than good pitching. But I do see a lot of successful screenwriters who are able to verbalize what they're going to do before the fact in a way that ignites the excitement of a bored studio executive. But I don't think of myself as a good pitcher; I've seen people who can do it ten times as well as I can. In fact, I remember being amazed the first time I saw someone do a really full-on dog-and-pony pitch. I thought, "Oh, *that's* what you're supposed to do. Boy, I'm sure glad I'm past that phase of my life, because I was really lousy at it."

RF: *How would you characterize the interaction between writing, directing, and editing your own films?*

JC: If I can take something out, I'll do it before I shoot it, because shooting is hard. When you're writing, shooting, or cutting you must always ask, "How is this making me feel? Am I moving toward or away from an understanding of what this character is feeling?" Because that's what it's really all about...getting inside the characters' heads and hearts. If I feel I'm moving away from that, I'll put more music in, or add a line of dialogue. Movie-making is a living organic process. The script is just the first step. I know writers hate that, but it doesn't bother me. A writer just can't think of everything sitting at a desk. You can't know who the creative forces will be and what they will bring to the filming of your script. Nine times out of ten, the actors do things at a very subtle, non-dialogue level that gives you collateral information. You no longer need two pages of dialogue to explain something. But sometimes the actors need that dialogue to fill in their comprehension of what is happening in the moment. Sometimes you cut those lines while shooting, sometimes in rehearsal. But it's always good to have written more so that everyone knows what the goals of the scene are.

RF: *Did the dives you made to the actual wreck change anything substantial as you went to script?*

JC: Structurally, no. Certainly it had the effect of making me more interested in the emotional story than the suspenseful sub-plot of the diamond. The dive had the biggest impact on the directing and editing process, which was to focus more on the emotional story.

RF: *Would you describe editing as an act of creative attrition?*

JC: It's more like sculpting. You're taking away material to create a final form. I had <u>much</u> more time to cut this film than any of my previous films. I watched some scenes over a thousand times, And every time, I would take out maybe four frames, or a four-second shot. Eventually, I got it down to its essence. Don't mourn the chips of marble on the floor, Don't mourn for the sculpture that could have been. Celebrate what is there.

RF: *Why did you cut down the opening scene?*

JC: I knew the exploration of the wreck was holding up the pace, and not getting me to what the story was really about. Yet, in and of itself, it was very interesting to me, because it was almost a documentary of the dives I had made to the wreck and I knew how accurate it was. But I knew it would be less interesting to the average viewer. So I had to come up with a way of editing the scenes that made sense, some kind of filter. I couldn't just hang on to every image I liked. What I felt I should try to create was a human connection with the people who were on the ship through images of the wreck. The thing that is personally fascinating to me about shipwrecks is the connection to the people who were there, whether they survived or they died. You go into this alien world in scuba gear, which is like a space suit, or in a submersible, which is essentially a spaceship. Then you encounter a very mundane human object in this alien place. A chair. A table. A photograph. It's a surreal juxtaposition. So I decided to focus on that. The shot with the reading glasses. The doll's

head. Those shots were left in while others were taken out because they didn't support that sub-text, which is only hinted at in the script. *Titanic* was a human story. It wasn't about the ship, or about this big piece of rusting junk. It's about the people. Yes, when you first approach the ship, you are impressed by the scale of the wreck, how the subs are dwarfed by it, so I kept those shots which sold that idea. The other shots which sold the suspense and the spookiness were, in a way, misleading. The more suspenseful the scene became, the more you felt you needed a resolution, an action catharsis. But the scene doesn't end that way. They don't discover a monster in the wreck, or get attacked, or fight their way out. They're not even really inside the ship. They've sent in a robot. So I had to clarify in my own mind what the ultimate goal of the scene was. To create a sense of human connection with *Titanic* as an event which really happened, with its wreckage lying around now in the present day, which you could visit in this

alien world. And to advance the plot by creating the mystery of what was in the safe.

RF: *Bill Paxton told me he modeled his character on you. Of course, as the writer of the piece, you're also Jack, and Rose, and Cal. You obviously are drawing from parts of yourself, but also other people you have known personally, or researched, like Beatrice Wood. Who is Brock mostly based on?*

JC: Brock is based on Mel Fisher, a treasure hunter who spent ten or fifteen years of his life searching for the wreck of the *Atocha*, which was a Spanish galleon that sank with tons of gold on board. He used up one set of investors, then another, and another. His son got killed when he was sucked into a big vacuum device they were using to scour the bottom. Basically, he gave up everything for this search. So, in Brock's speech in Scene 65, which was cut from the film, when he says he gave up everything to find the Heart of the Ocean, that was loosely based on a guy who had sacrificed years of his life to find the thing he was obsessed with. But from a personality standpoint and how he talks and deals with people, his social dynamic, he is loosely based on me.

RF: *Any parallels between Brock's expedition and making "Titanic"?*

JC: Sure. They were both complex technological challenges always on the verge of falling apart. Every time we shot Brock's scenes where he's talking to the investors on the phone, I always said he should call them Peter and Bill (Twentieth Century Fox executives Peter Chernin and Bill Mechanic). Of course, I didn't see the wreck the way Brock did. He was ready to tear that ship apart for money. He had no appreciation for the people on that ship. However, his quest to find that diamond and my quest to make that film were very resonant.

RF: *Why was the ending altered?*

JC: The scene was filmed as scripted and worked beautifully. But when I screened the entire film for the first time, I realized I didn't care about Brock and the diamond. I didn't want anything that stood between me and my continued immersion in the Jack and Rose story. I wanted to hold on to the memory of Jack, and not let

that slip away too much before the finale. And I knew that was all the audience was going to care about. They weren't going to have room in their hearts for Brock's epiphany.

RF: *Did any test screening audience see Brock's epiphany?*

JC: No one ever saw it except for the editors and myself, and the initial group that saw the first screening of the film on video. Because it was so obvious. It was obvious to me before that initial group said anything, and then they confirmed it.

RF: *Was that a function of the power of the Jack and Rose story going beyond what even you thought it would?*

JC: It's impossible to intellectually figure out the emotional and visceral response to a movie, until you've watched the movie. People call the screenplay a blueprint, but blueprints have to be followed almost exactly. A script is a proposal. It presents certain ideas. You go and film them with actors who bring those ideas to life. The music, lighting, editing and the director all bring added dimensions. Some scenes don't translate from page to screen as well as you hoped they would. Other scenes work better. See, audiences don't think in scenes. They think in a continuously dynamic and evolving force field of ideas and emotions. You have to make your editorial decisions based on that understanding of how films work. If you don't, you'll make some colossal mistakes. I see a lot of films, my own best efforts included, that have mistakenly been cut using intellectual film aesthetics as the prime motivation.

RF: *Any plans of releasing a longer version of "Titanic" on video?*

JC: I'm not sure I would do a separate version with additional footage. I might do a laser disc or DVD version with supplements that isolate deleted scenes and longer cuts of scenes for film students and fans. So many people ask me if there's going to be a director's cut. I tell them they've *already seen* the director's cut. I believe that the cut that played in theaters is the best cut of the film. The idea of a director's cut for home video comes from disgruntled directors forced by the studios to release a version of the film theatrically with which they were not happy. "Titanic" was one hundred percent my cut.

RF: *Tacked up on your computer monitor are handwritten Post-Its that say "break new ground" and "good enough isn't." Are these your personal mantras as a writer?*

JC: "Good enough isn't" is really pretty much what I live by as a director and a writer. And it makes everybody crazy, because that's the way I think. It's not about being a perfectionist, because perfection in a subjective art form like writing or filmmaking is a moving target. It's relative to the individual's perception. For me it's more a question of striving for excellence. If you don't try to push beyond mediocrity, then you're falling short of the potential that you've created by marshaling all these resources and talented people that you put in the cross-hairs of cinematic history every single second the camera is on. And I challenge any director to tell me that he doesn't strive for his own brand of excellence. I just admit it. I'm willing to steamroll obstacles to make things happen and some people think that's egocentric. It's not about my ego. It's about the film having taken on a life, having its *own* ego. And we all serve that. We serve that life.

RF: *Although it still has to be filtered through your subjective view of the universe.*

JC: Not always. Certainly when you're dealing with actors you're working in a consensus environment. They have to feel good about what they're doing, and they bring their own subjective view to it, and that's great. But when you're dealing with the nuts and bolts of production, you have to make a million decisions a day to move forward on a film. There's no time for those decisions to be made by consensus or committee.

RF: *Along those lines, as a writer, usually working alone, who do you answer to?*

JC: I answer to a kind of phantom audience I carry around with me all the time. They ultimately are the arbiter of what should and should not be in my films. I've been a card carrying member of that beer-drinking, drive-in-going audience, so I feel qualified to re-create it in my mind and play to it. And that's what every screenwriter does. He imagines the moment when the actors say the lines, the music comes up, and the audience is reacting. If you can't imagine that moment, you can't write a good screenplay.

TITANIC

A Screenplay

by

James Cameron

May 7, 1996

During post-production, Cameron decided he wanted to contrast the ship at the peak of her glory with the wreck's present sad condition on the ocean floor. To achieve this, he pulled images from the April 10th departure sequence (starting at Scene 38), and altered them visually, slowing shots down and applying an aged sepia newsreel look to the brief title sequence. (In point of fact, no real motion picture footage of *Titanic's* departure survives today.) He then mixed in music from Jack's death scene, letting it carry over into the original opening shots of the submersibles falling to the ocean floor. Combining these images of hope and joy with the poignant music created the audience's first emotional resonance with the past, and juxtaposed well with the visually striking shots of Brock's technological approach to the wreck site that followed.

CAMERON: "The "scriptment" [See Cameron interview, page ix] has a different opening scene altogether. We see an Irish worker painting the gold lettering TITANIC on the hull. Then the camera cuts wider, revealing how huge the ship is. The painter crosses himself with dread as he looks up at the finished word. I always felt that was a great way to begin the film. Later, however, I learned that the ship was built mostly by Irish Protestants, not Catholics, so it's a good thing I didn't shoot that opening."

Anatoly (Dr. Anatoly M. Sagalevitch)

1   BLACKNESS   1

Then two faint lights appear, close together... growing brighter. They resolve into two
DEEP SUBMERSIBLES, free-falling toward us like express elevators.

One is ahead of the other, and passes close enough to FILL FRAME, looking like a
spacecraft blazing with lights, bristling with insectile manipulators.

TILTING DOWN to follow it as it descends away into the limitless blackness below.
Soon they are fireflies, then stars. Then gone.

                                                                      CUT TO:

2   EXT./ INT. MIR ONE / NORTH ATLANTIC DEEP   2

PUSHING IN on one of the falling submersibles, called MIR ONE, right up to its
circular viewport to see the occupants.

INSIDE, it is a cramped seven foot sphere, crammed with equipment. ANATOLY
MIKAILAVICH, the sub's pilot, sits hunched over his controls... singing softly in
Russian.

Next to him on one side is BROCK LOVETT. He's in his late forties, deeply tanned,
and likes to wear his Nomex suit unzipped to show the gold from famous shipwrecks
covering his gray chest hair. He is a wiley, fast-talking treasure hunter, a salvage
superstar who is part historian, part adventurer and part vacuum cleaner salesman.
Right now, he is propped against the CO2 scrubber, fast asleep and snoring.

On the other side, crammed into the remaining space is a bearded wide-body named
LEWIS BODINE, who is also asleep. Lewis is an R.O.V. (REMOTELY OPERATED VEHI-
CLE) pilot and is the resident Titanic expert.

Anatoly glances at the bottom sonar and makes a ballast adjustment.

                                                                      CUT TO:

3   EXT. THE BOTTOM OF THE SEA   3

A pale, dead-flat lunar landscape. It gets brighter, lit from above, as MIR ONE
enters FRAME and drops to the seafloor in a downblast from its thrusters. It hits
bottom after its two hour free-fall with a loud BONK.

                                                                      CUT TO:

4   [INT. MIR ONE   ]   4

           Lovett and Bodine jerk awake at the landing.   *Deleted for*
                                                                  pacing
                                         ANATOLY
                         (heavy Russian accent)
                      We are here.

                                                                      CUT TO:

      EXT. / INT. MIR ONE AND TWO

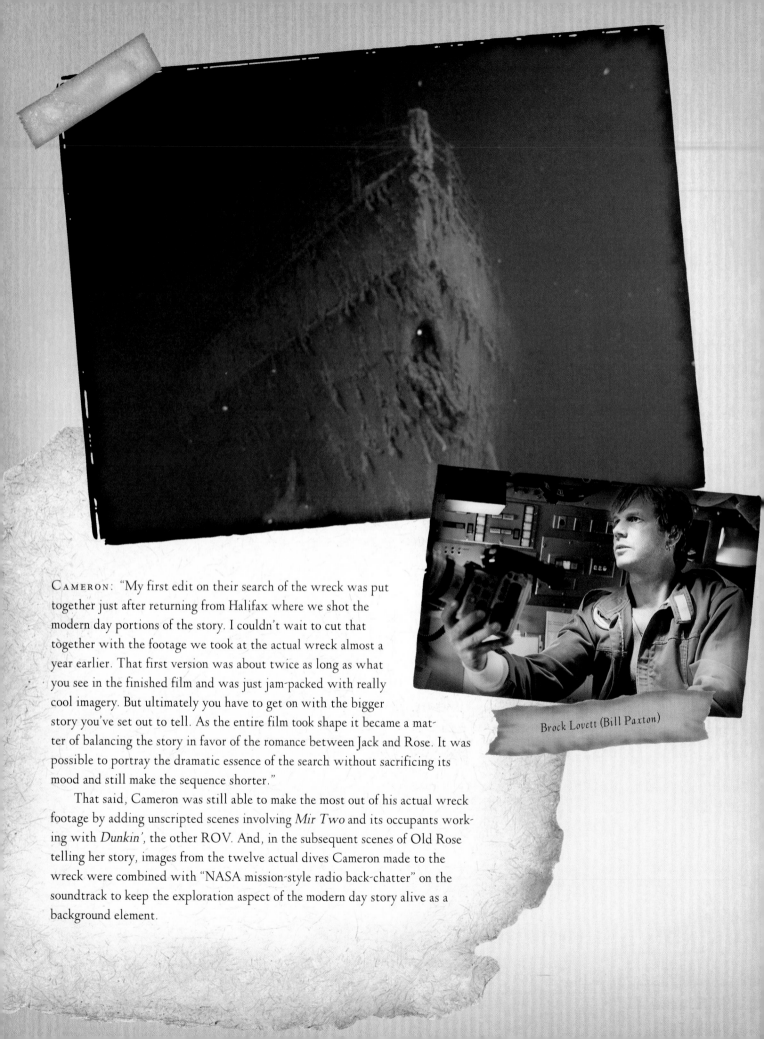

CAMERON: "My first edit on their search of the wreck was put together just after returning from Halifax where we shot the modern day portions of the story. I couldn't wait to cut that together with the footage we took at the actual wreck almost a year earlier. That first version was about twice as long as what you see in the finished film and was just jam-packed with really cool imagery. But ultimately you have to get on with the bigger story you've set out to tell. As the entire film took shape it became a matter of balancing the story in favor of the romance between Jack and Rose. It was possible to portray the dramatic essence of the search without sacrificing its mood and still make the sequence shorter."

That said, Cameron was still able to make the most out of his actual wreck footage by adding unscripted scenes involving *Mir Two* and its occupants working with *Dunkin'*, the other ROV. And, in the subsequent scenes of Old Rose telling her story, images from the twelve actual dives Cameron made to the wreck were combined with "NASA mission-style radio back-chatter" on the soundtrack to keep the exploration aspect of the modern day story alive as a background element.

Brock Lovett (Bill Paxton)

5   MINUTES LATER: THE TWO SUBS skim over the seafloor to the sound of sidescan   5
      sonar and the THRUM of big thrusters.

6   The featureless gray clay of the bottom unrolls in the lights of the subs. Bodine is   6
      watching the sidescan sonar display, where the outline of a huge pointed object
      is visible. Anatoly lies prone, driving the sub, his face pressed to the center port.

> BODINE
> Come left a little. She's right in front of us, eighteen
> meters. Fifteen. Thirteen... you should see it.

> ANATOLY
> Do you see it? I don't see it... there!

Out of the darkness, like a ghostly apparition, the bow of a ship appears. Its
knife-edge prow is coming straight at us, seeming to plow the bottom sediment like
ocean waves. It towers above the seafloor, standing just as it landed 84 years ago.

THE TITANIC. Or what is left of her. Mir One goes up and over the bow railing,
intact except for an overgrowth of "rusticles" draping it like mutated Spanish
moss.

TIGHT ON THE EYEPIECE MONITOR of a video camcorder. Brock Lovett's face fills
the BLACK AND WHITE FRAME.

> LOVETT
> It still gets me every time.

The image pans to the front viewport, looking over Anatoly's shoulder, to the bow
railing visible in the lights beyond. Anatoly turns.

> ANATOLY
> Is just your guilt because of stealing from the dead.

CUT WIDER, to show that Brock is operating the camera himself, turning it in his
hand so it points at his own face.

> BROCK
> Thanks, Tolya. Work with me, here.

Brock resumes his serious, pensive gaze out the front port, with the camera aimed
at himself at arm's length.

> BROCK
> It still gets me every time... to see the sad ruin of the
> great ship sitting here, where she landed at 2:30 in the
> morning, April 15, 1912, after her long fall from the world
> above.

Anatoly rolls his eyes and mutters in Russian. Bodine chuckles and watches the
sonar.

> BODINE
> You are so full of shit, boss.

Deleted in post for pacing

Cameron often used his non-linear editing system in the same way a writer uses a word processor, cutting and pasting images and dialogue from one place to another to help reinforce a concept or emotion crucial to a latter part of the story. Here, Cameron mixed in the sounds of *Titanic's* orchestra with the chaotic sounds of First Officer Murdoch calling for women and children from Scene 208. These sounds are an echo from the past as *Mir Two* settles onto the present-day remains of the Boat Deck. With subtle touches like this one our attention as an audience is being focused backward in time.

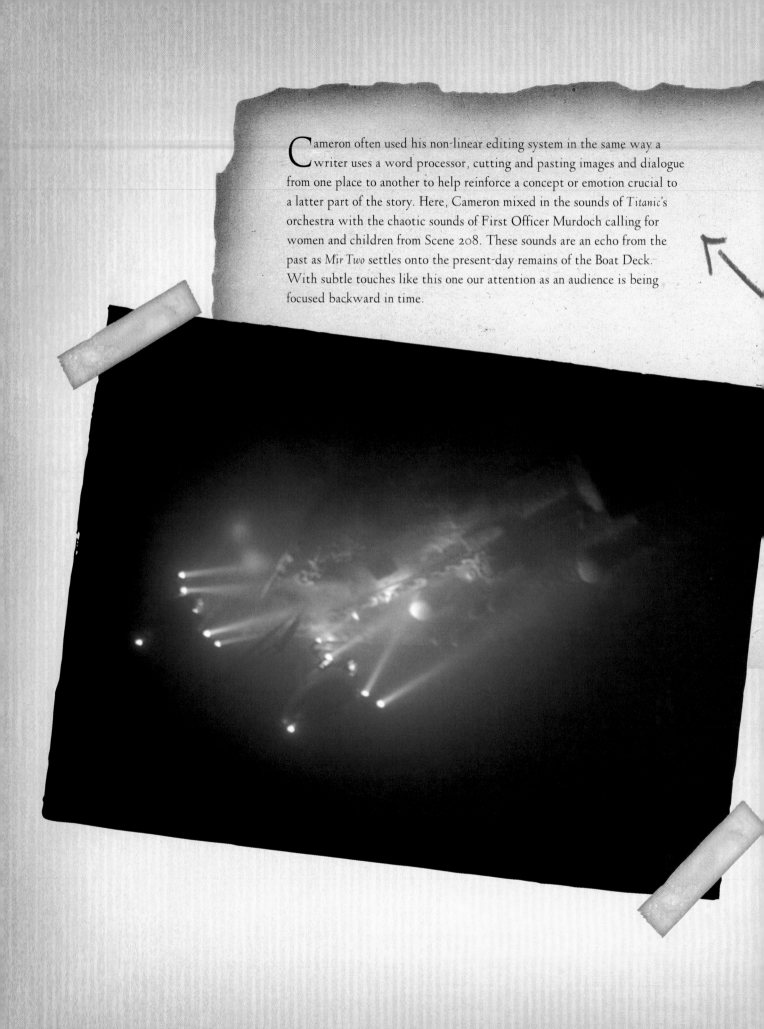

7   Mir Two drives aft down the starboard side, past the huge anchor while Mir One   7
     passes over the seemingly endless forecastle deck, with its massive anchor chains
     still laid out in two neat rows, its bronze windlass caps gleaming. The 22 foot
     long subs are like white bugs next to the enormous wreck.

> LOVETT (V.O.)
> Dive nine. Here we are again on the deck of Titanic...
> two and a half miles down. The pressure is three tons
> per square inch, enough to crush us like a freight train
> going over an ant if our hull fails. These windows are
> nine inches thick and if they go, it's sayonara in two
> microseconds.

8   Mir Two lands on the boat deck, next to the ruins of the Officer's Quarters.   8
     Mir One lands on the roof of the deck house nearby,

> LOVETT
> Right. Let's go to work.

Bodine slips on a pair of 3-D electronic goggles, and grabs the joystick controls
of the ROV.

9   OUTSIDE THE SUB, the ROV, a small orange and black robot called SNOOP DOG, lifts   9
     from its cradle and flies forward.

> BODINE (V.O.)
> Walkin' the dog.

SNOOP DOG drives itself away from the sub, paying out its umbilical behind it like
a robot yo-yo. Its twin stereo-video cameras swivel like insect eyes. The ROV
descends through an open shaft that once was the beautiful First Class Grand
Staircase.

Snoop Dog goes down several decks, then moves laterally into the First Class
Reception Room.

SNOOP'S VIDEO POV, moving through the cavernous interior. The remains of the ornate
handcarved woodwork which gave the ship its elegance move through the floodlights,
the lines blurred by slow dissolution and descending rusticle formations.
Stalactites of rust hang down so that at times it looks like a natural grotto, then
the scene shifts and the lines of a ghostly undersea mansion can be seen again.

MONTAGE STYLE, as Snoop passes ghostly images of Titanic's opulence:

10   A grand piano in amazingly good shape, crashed on its side against a wall. The keys   10
     gleam black and white in the lights.

11   A chandelier, still hanging from the ceiling by its wire... glinting as Snoop   11
     moves around it.

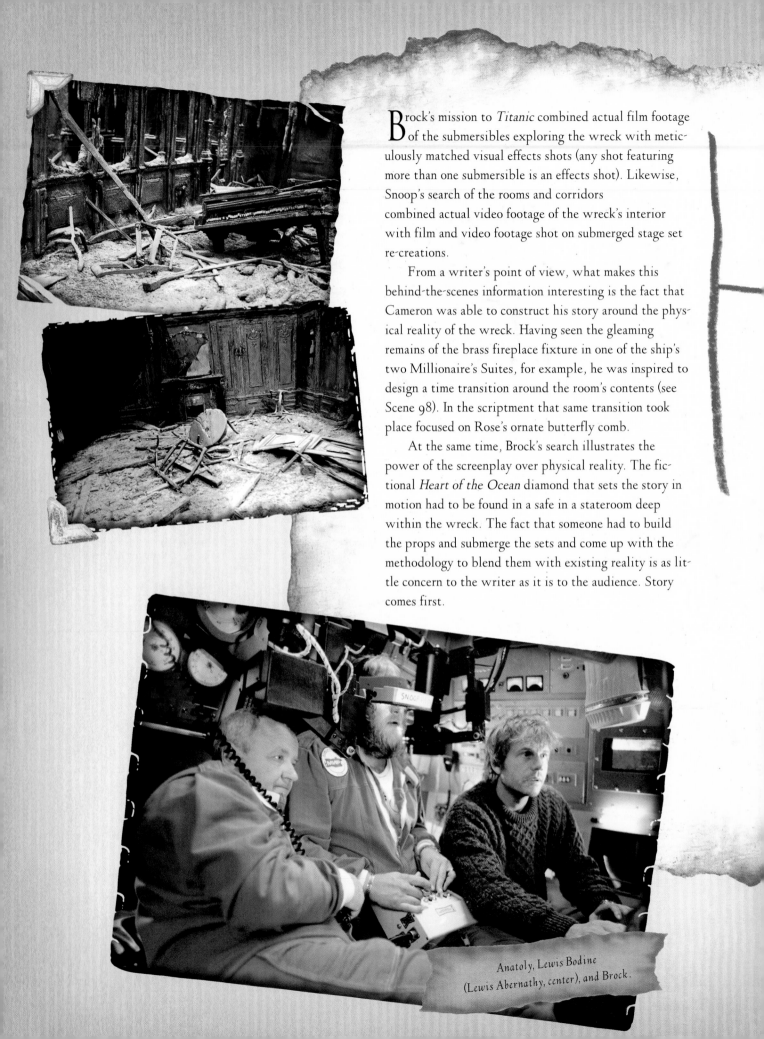

Brock's mission to *Titanic* combined actual film footage of the submersibles exploring the wreck with meticulously matched visual effects shots (any shot featuring more than one submersible is an effects shot). Likewise, Snoop's search of the rooms and corridors combined actual video footage of the wreck's interior with film and video footage shot on submerged stage set re-creations.

From a writer's point of view, what makes this behind-the-scenes information interesting is the fact that Cameron was able to construct his story around the physical reality of the wreck. Having seen the gleaming remains of the brass fireplace fixture in one of the ship's two Millionaire's Suites, for example, he was inspired to design a time transition around the room's contents (see Scene 98). In the scriptment that same transition took place focused on Rose's ornate butterfly comb.

At the same time, Brock's search illustrates the power of the screenplay over physical reality. The fictional *Heart of the Ocean* diamond that sets the story in motion had to be found in a safe in a stateroom deep within the wreck. The fact that someone had to build the props and submerge the sets and come up with the methodology to blend them with existing reality is as little concern to the writer as it is to the audience. Story comes first.

Anatoly, Lewis Bodine (Lewis Abernathy, center), and Brock.

12 Its lights play across the floor, revealing a champagne bottle, then some WHITE STAR   12
    LINE china... a woman's high-top "granny shoe". Then something eerie: what looks
    like a child's skull resolves into the porcelain head of a doll.

    Snoop enters a corridor which is much better preserved. Here and there a door still
    hangs on its rusted hinges. An ornate piece of molding, a wall sconce... hint at
    the grandeur of the past.

13 THE ROV turns and goes through a black doorway, entering room B-52, the sitting   13
    room of a "promenade suite", one of the most luxurious staterooms on Titanic.

                              BODINE
            I'm in the sitting room. Heading for bedroom B-54.

                              LOVETT
            Stay off the floor. Don't stir it up like you did yesterday.

                              BODINE
            I'm tryin' boss.

    Glinting in the lights are the brass fixtures of the near-perfectly preserved fire-
    place. An albino Galathea crab crawls over it. Nearby are the remains of a divan
    and a writing desk. The Dog crosses the ruins of the once elegant room toward
    another DOOR. It squeezes through the doorframe, scraping rust and wood chunks
    loose on both sides. It moves out of a cloud of rust and keeps on going.

                              BODINE
            I'm crossing the bedroom.

    The remains of a pillared canopy bed. Broken chairs, a dresser. Through the col-
    lapsed wall of the bathroom, the porcelain commode and bathtub look almost new,
    gleaming in the dark.

                              LOVETT
            Okay, I want to see what's under that wardrobe door.

    SEVERAL ANGLES as the ROV deploys its MANIPULATOR ARMS and starts moving debris
    aside. A lamp is lifted, its ceramic colors as bright as they were in 1912.

                              LOVETT
            Easy, Lewis. Take it slow.

    Lewis grips a wardrobe door, lying at an angle in a corner, and pulls it with
    Snoop's gripper. It moves reluctantly in a cloud of silt. Under it is a dark
    object. The silt clears and Snoop's cameras show them what was under the door...

                              BODINE
            Ooohh daddy-oh, are you seein' what I'm seein'?

    CLOSE ON LOVETT, watching his monitors. By his expression it is like he is seeing
    the Holy Grail.

                                                                    (CONTINUED)

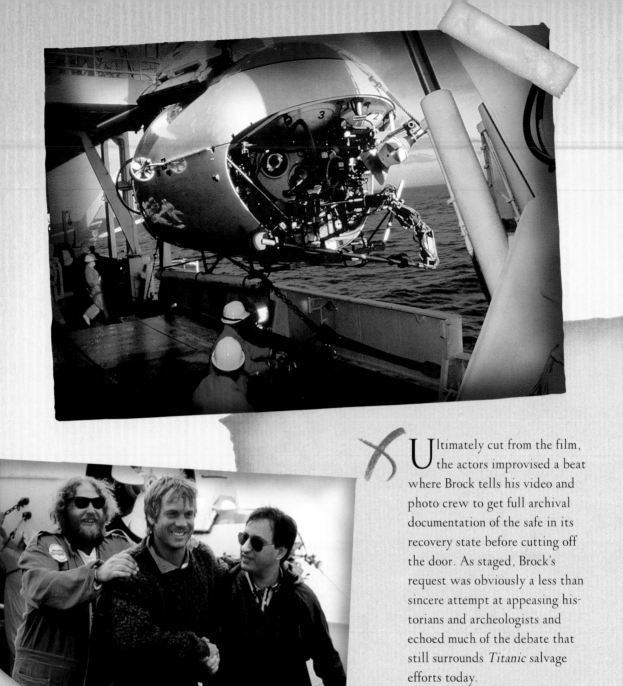

Ultimately cut from the film, the actors improvised a beat where Brock tells his video and photo crew to get full archival documentation of the safe in its recovery state before cutting off the door. As staged, Brock's request was obviously a less than sincere attempt at appeasing historians and archeologists and echoed much of the debate that still surrounds *Titanic* salvage efforts today.

> LOVETT
> Oh baby baby baby.
>   (grabs the mike)
> It's payday, boys.

ON THE SCREEN, in the glare of the lights, is the object of their quest: a small STEEL COMBINATION SAFE.

                                                                    CUT TO:

14   EXT. STERN DECK OF KELDYSH - DAY   14

THE SAFE, dripping wet in the afternoon sun, is lowered onto the deck of a ship by a winch cable.

We are on the Russian research vessel **AKADEMIK MISTISLAV KELDYSH**. A crowd has gathered, including most of the crew of KELDYSH, the sub crews, and a hand-wring-ing money guy named BOBBY BUELL who represents the limited partners. There is also a documentary video crew, hired by Lovett to cover his moment of glory.

Everyone crowds around the safe. In the background Mir Two is being lowered into its cradle on deck by a massive hydraulic arm. Mir One is already recovered with Lewis Bodine following Brock Lovett as he bounds over to the safe like a kid on Christmas morning.

> BODINE
> Who's the best? Say it.

> LOVETT
> You are, Lewis.
>   (to the video crew)
> You rolling?

Deleted

> CAMERAMAN
> Rolling.

Brock nods to his technicians, and they set about drilling the safe's hinges. During this operation, Brock amps the suspense, working the lens to fill the time.

> LOVETT
> Well, here it is, the moment of truth. Here's where we
> find out if the time, the sweat, the money spent to
> charter this ship and these subs, to come out here to
> the middle of the North Atlantic... were worth it. If
> what we think is in that safe... <u>is</u> in that safe... it
> will be.

Lovett grins wolfishly in anticipation of his greatest find yet. The door is pried loose. It clangs onto the deck. Lovett moves closer, peering into the safe's wet interior. A long moment, then... his face says it all.

> LOVETT
> Shit.

                                                            (CONTINUED)

Brock Lovett was originally written slightly older and gruffer. Several small changes to dialogue and performance made the character younger and less harsh.

Anatoly, Brock and Buell (Nicholas Cascone, far right).

                              BODINE
          You know, boss, this happened to Geraldo and his
          career never recovered.

                              LOVETT
                 (to the video cameraman)
          Get that outta my face.

Changed to "Turn the camera off."   CUT TO:

15   INT. LAB DECK, PRESERVATION ROOM - DAY   15

Technicians are carefully removing some papers from the safe and placing them in a tray of
water to separate them safely. Nearby, other artifacts from the staterooms are
being washed and preserved.

Buell is on the satellite phone with the INVESTORS. Lovett is yelling at the video crew

                              LOVETT
          You send out what I tell you when I tell you. I'm
          signing your paychecks, not 60 minutes. Now get set
          up for the uplink.

Buell covers the phone and turns to Lovett.

Deleted in post for pacing and to soften character

                              BUELL
          The partners want to know how it's going?

                              LOVETT
          How it's going? It's going like a first date in prison,
          whattaya think?!

Lovett grabs the phone from Buell and goes instantly smooth.

                              LOVETT
          Hi, Dave? Barry? Look, it wasn't in the safe... no,
          look, don't worry about it, there're still plenty of
          places it could be... in the floor debris in the suite,
          in the mother's room, in the purser's safe on C
          deck...
                 (seeing something)
          Hang on a second.

A tech coaxes some letters in the water tray to one side with a tong... revealing a
pencil (conte crayon) drawing of a woman.

Brock looks closely at the drawing, which is in excellent shape, though its edges
have partially disintegrated. The woman is beautiful, and beautifully rendered. In
her late teens or early twenties, she is nude, though posed with a kind of casual
modesty. She is on an Empire divan, in a pool of light that seems to radiate outward from her eyes. Scrawled in the lower right corner is the date: April 14 1912.
And the initials JD.

The girl is not entirely nude. At her throat is a diamond necklace with one large stone
hanging in the center.

                                                              (CONTINUED)

Old Rose (Gloria Stuart)

CAMERON: "Bill Paxton's wife loaned me "I Shock Myself," the autobiography of Beatrice Wood, an artist living in Ojai, California, who was still producing works at the age of 102. The first chapter describes almost literally the character I was already writing for Old Rose. Beatrice was educated in Paris and New York. She ran away from a domineering mother at the age of seventeen to live in a cold water garret and become an artist. She became romantically involved with cubist painter, Marcel Duchamps. Later, she went to India and fell in love with the place, wearing only Indian-style dress and jewelery from then on. She became a ceramic artist in the late forties and eventually set up shop in Ojai. Beatrice was proof that the attributes of Rose's character that I thought might have been perceived as far-fetched were not. When I met her she was charming, creative and devastatingly funny. And her memory of her teenage years was extremely lucid. Of course, the film's Rose is only a refraction of Beatrice, combined with many fictional elements, including memories of my two grandmothers (one of whom was named Rose)."

CONTINUED:

Lovett grabs a reference photo from the clutter on the lab table. It is a period black-and-white photo of a diamond necklace on a black velvet jeweller's display stand. He holds it next to the drawing. It is clearly the same piece... a complex setting with a massive central stone which is almost heart-shaped.

                    LOVETT
          I'll be God damned.

                                                        CUT TO:

16   INSERT   16

A CNN NEWS STORY: a live satellite feed from the deck of the Keldysh, intercut with the CNN studio.

                    ANNOUNCER
          Treasure hunter Brock Lovett is best known for
          finding Spanish gold in sunken galleons in the
          Caribbean. Now he is using deep submergence
          technology to work two and a half miles down at
          another famous wreck... the Titanic. He is with us
          live via satellite from a Russian research ship in the
          middle of the Atlantic... hello Brock?

                    BROCK
          Yes, hi, Tracy. You know, Titanic is not just A
          shipwreck, Titanic is THE shipwreck. It's the Mount
          Everest of shipwrecks.

                                                        CUT TO:

17   INT. HOUSE / CERAMICS STUDIO   17

PULL BACK from the screen, showing the CNN report playing on a TV set in the living room of a small rustic house. It is full of ceramics, figurines, folk art, the walls crammed with drawings and paintings... things collected over a lifetime.

PANNING to show a glassed-in studio attached to the house. Outside it is a quiet morning in Ojai, California. In the studio, amid incredible clutter, an ANCIENT WOMAN is throwing a pot on a potter's wheel. The liquid red clay covers her hands... hands that are gnarled and age-spotted, but still surprisingly strong and supple. A woman in her early forties assists her.

                    BROCK (V.O.)
          I've planned this expedition for three years, and
          we're out here recovering some amazing things...
          things that will have enormous historical and educa-
          tional value.

Deleted for pacing

                                                        (CONTINUED)

The reporter's interaction with Brock was refined to better match the pacing as Old Rose becomes aware of the news story and to soften Brock's character. In post, Cameron also took advantage of the fact that the TV is off-camera to change some of the dialogue to address an issue raised by test audiences.

Producer Jon Landau: "We were surprised to learn that a sizable portion of our audience were unfamiliar with the stories about *Titanic*'s band. As a consequence, they found the scene where they play "Nearer My God to Thee" right before the ship sinks to be unbelievable. So Jim reverse engineered Brock's interview dialogue to contain a reference to the band. It's a subtle change, but no one seemed to have a problem with those scenes after that change was made."

CNN REPORTER (V.O.)
              But it's no secret that education is not your main
              purpose. You're a treasure hunter. So what is the
              treasure you're hunting?

                          BROCK (V.O.)
              I'd rather show you than tell you, and we think we're
              very close to doing just that.

The old woman's name is ROSE CALVERT. Her face is a wrinkled mass, her
body shapeless and shrunken under a one-piece African-print dress.

But her eyes are just as bright and alive as those of a young girl.

Rose gets up and walks into the living room, wiping pottery clay from her hands
with a rag. A Pomeranian dog gets up and comes in with her.

The younger woman, LIZZY CALVERT, rushes to help her.

                          ROSE
              Turn that up please, dear.

                          REPORTER (V.O.)
              Your expedition is at the center of a storm of
              controversy over salvage rights and even ethics. Many
              are calling you a grave robber.

TIGHT ON THE SCREEN.

                          BROCK
              Nobody called the recovery of the artifacts from King
              Tut's tomb grave robbing. I have museum-trained
              experts here, making sure this stuff is preserved and
              catalogued properly. Look at this drawing, which was
              found today...

The video camera pans off Brock to the drawing, in a tray of water. The image of
the woman with the necklace FILLS FRAME.

                          BROCK
              ...a piece of paper that's been underwater for 84
              years... and my team are able to preserve it intact.
              Should this have remained unseen at the bottom of the
              ocean for eternity, when we can see it and enjoy it
              now...?

ROSE is galvanized by this image. Her mouth hangs open in amazement.

                          ROSE
              I'll be God damned.

                                                          CUT TO:

CAMERON: "Finding a professional actress in her eighties was a challenge. A younger actress would have required too much of a makeup job. An older actress may have been too frail to function for the long hours of production. I also didn't want somebody who was well known like Katherine Hepburn, because everyone knows what Hepburn looked like when she was young, which wasn't like Kate Winslet. I was looking for a seasoned professional who could seem anonymous to modern audiences. Gloria was a contract player during the golden age of Hollywood when they would crank out a feature every couple of months. And even though she retired from acting in the thirties she never lost her touch or the intensity of that work ethic."

18   EXT. KELDYSH DECK - NIGHT   18

CUT TO KELDSYH. The Mir subs are being launched. Mir Two is already in the water, and Lovett is getting ready to climb into Mir One when Bobby Buell runs up to him.

                            BUELL
          There's a satellite call for you.

                           LOVETT
          Bobby, we're launching. See these submersibles
          here, going in the water? <u>Take a message</u>.

                            BUELL
          No, trust me, you <u>want</u> to take this call.

                                                   CUT TO:

19   INT. LAB DECK / KELDYSH - NIGHT   19

Buell hands Lovett the phone, punching down the blinking line. The call is from Rose and we see both ends of the conversation. She is in her kitchen with a mystified Lizzy.

                            BROCK
        This is Brock Lovett. What can I do for you, Mrs... ?

                            BUELL
          Rose Calvert.

                            BROCK
         ... Mrs. Calvert?

                            ROSE
        I was just wondering if you had found the "Heart of
        the Ocean" yet, Mr. Lovett.

Brock almost drops the phone. Bobby sees his shocked expression...

                            BUELL
        I told you you wanted to take the call.

                            LOVETT
         (to Rose)
        Alright. You have my attention, Rose. Can you tell
        me who the woman in the picture is?

                            ROSE
        Oh yes. The woman in the picture is me.

                                                   CUT TO:

Bodine's reference had no conscious connection with Twentieth Century Fox's still-in-production animated musical "Anastasia." During a videotaped reading, actor Lewis Abernathy amusingly said "Anesthesia." Cameron penciled the ad lib into the scene.

20   EXT. OCEAN - DAY   20

    SMASH CUT TO AN ENORMOUS SEA STALLION HELICOPTER thundering across
    the ocean. PAN 180 degrees as it roars past. There is no land at either horizon.
    The Keldysh is visible in the distance.

    CLOSE ON A WINDOW of the monster helicopter. Rose's face is visible, looking out
    calmly.

                                                           CUT TO:

21   EXT. KELDYSH - DAY   21

    Brock and Bodine are watching Mir 2 being swung over the side to start a
    dive.

                         BODINE
              She's a goddamned liar! A nutcase. Like that ...
              what's her name? That Anastasia babe.

                         BUELL
              They're inbound.

    Brock nods and the three of them head forward to meet the approaching
    helo.

                         BODINE
              She says she's Rose DeWitt Bukater, right? Rose
              DeWitt Bukater died on the Titanic. At the age of 17.
              If she'd've lived, she'd be over a hundred now.

                         LOVETT
              A hundred and one next month.

                         BODINE
              Okay, so she's a very old goddamned liar. I traced
              her as far back as the 20's... she was working as an
              actress in L.A. An actress. Her name was Rose Dawson.
              Then she married a guy named Calvert, moved to Cedar
              Rapids, had two kids. Now Calvert's dead, and from
              what I've heard Cedar Rapids is dead.

    The Sea Stallion approaches the ship, BG, forcing Brock to yell over the rotors.

                         LOVETT
              And everybody who knows about the diamond is
              supposed to be dead... or on this ship. But she knows
              about it. And I want to hear what she has to say. Got
              it?

                                                           CUT TO:

22   EXT. KELDYSH HELIPAD   22

IN A THUNDERING DOWNBLAST the helicopter's wheels bounce down on the
helipad.

Lovett, Buell and Bodine watch as the HELICOPTER CREW CHIEF hands out about ten
suitcases, and then Rose is lowered to the deck in a wheelchair by Keldysh crewmen.
Lizzy, ducking unnecessarily under the rotor, follows her out, carrying FREDDY the
Pomeranian. The crew chief hands a puzzled Keldysh crewmember a goldfish bowl with
several fish in it. Rose does not travel light.

HOLD ON the incongruous image of this little old lady, looking impossibly fragile
amongst all the high tech gear, grungy deck crew and gigantic equipment.

                              BODINE
          S'cuse me, I have to go check our supply of Depends.

Changed to "Doesn't exactly travel light, does she?"   CUT TO:

23   INT. ROSE'S STATEROOM / KELDYSH - DAY   23

Lizzy is unpacking Rose's things in the small utilitarian room. Rose is
placing a number of FRAMED PHOTOS on the bureau, arranging them carefully
next to the fishbowl. Brock and Bodine are in the doorway.

                              BROCK
          Is your stateroom alright?

                              ROSE
          Yes. Very nice. Have you met my granddaughter,
          Lizzy? She takes care of me.

                              LIZZY
          Yes. We met just a few minutes ago, grandma.
          Remember? Up on deck?

                              ROSE
          Oh, yes.

Brock glances at Bodine... oh oh. Bodine rolls his eyes. Rose finishes arranging her
photographs. We get a general glimpse of them: the usual snapshots... children and
grandchildren, her late husband.

                              ROSE
          There, that's nice. I have to have my pictures when I
          travel. And Freddy of course.
              (to the Pomeranian)
          Isn't that right, sweetie.

                              BROCK
          Would you like anything?

                                                        (CONTINUED)

Brock, Old Rose and her granddaughter Lizzy (Suzy Amis) discuss the "Heart of the Ocean."

CAMERON: "Gloria did not believe in changing dialogue. She was interested in interpreting what was on the page and creating the right inflections, gestures and pacing. The 'Hot number' line was one exception. Gloria took me aside and said, 'You know, this doesn't mean I was beautiful. A hot number suggested a girl who was promiscuous or appeared to be promiscuous.' I agreed that was inappropriate, and she suggested she say 'dish' instead. She played it to the hilt and got a laugh."

> ROSE
> I should like to see my drawing.

                                                            CUT TO:

24   INT. LAB DECK, PRESERVATION AREA   24

Rose looks at the drawing in its tray of water, confronting herself across a span of 84 years. Until they can figure out the best way to preserve it, they have to keep it immersed. It sways and ripples, almost as if alive.

TIGHT ON Rose's ancient eyes, gazing at the drawing.

25   FLASHCUT of a man's hand, holding a conte crayon, deftly creating a shoulder and the   25
shape of her hair with two efficient lines.

26   THE WOMAN'S FACE IN THE DRAWING, dancing under the water.   26

27   A FLASHCUT of a man's eyes, just visible over the top of a sketching pad. They look   27
up suddenly, right into the LENS. Soft eyes, but fearlessly direct.

28   Rose smiles, remembering. Brock has the reference photo of the necklace in his hand.   28

> BROCK
> Louis the Sixteenth wore a fabulous stone, called the
> Blue Diamond of the Crown, which disappeared in
> 1792, about the time Louis lost everything from the
> neck up. The theory goes that the crown diamond was
> chopped too... recut into a heart-like shape... and it
> became Le Coeur de la Mer. The Heart of the Ocean.
> Today it would be worth more than the Hope
> Diamond.

> ROSE
> It was a dreadful, heavy thing.
>   (she points at the drawing)
> I only wore it this once.

> LIZZY
> You actually believe this is you, grandma?

> ROSE
> It is me, dear. Wasn't I a hot number?

> BROCK
> I tracked it down through insurance records...
> an old claim that was settled under terms of absolute
> secrecy.
> Do you know who the claimant was, Rose?

> ROSE
> Someone named Hockley, I should imagine.

                                                    (CONTINUED)

The deletion of this exchange between Brock and Old Rose was the first casualty of Cameron's decision to remove an entire sub-plot from the motion picture. As originally scripted and shot, Brock and his team discover that Old Rose has had the *Heart of the Ocean* the entire time (See Scene 189 and Cameron's interview, page ix). Having heard Old Rose's story, Brock's character was to experience a complete epiphany, giving up his quest for material wealth in favor of the simple spiritual treasures Rose so valued. To make this work, several scenes and dialogue exchanges were written to place Brock and Old Rose at opposite ends of that spectrum. When the ending was changed these scenes no longer served a dramatic purpose.

>   BROCK
>   Nathan Hockley, right. Pittsburgh steel tycoon. For
>   a diamond necklace his son Caledon Hockley bought in
>   France for his fiancee... you... a week before he
>   sailed on Titanic. And the claim was filed right after
>   the sinking. So the diamond had to've gone down with
>   the ship.
>   (to Lizzy)
>   See the date?

>   LIZZY
>   April 14, 1912.

>   BODINE
>   If your grandma is who she says she is, she was
>   wearing the diamond the day Titanic sank.

>   BROCK
>   (to Rose)
>   And that makes you my new best friend. I will
>   happily compensate you for anything you can tell us
>   that will lead to its recovery.

>   ROSE
>   I don't want your money, Mr. Lovett. I know how
>   hard it is for people who care greatly for money to
>   give some away.

>   BODINE
>   (skeptical)
>   You don't want anything?

>   ROSE
>   (indicating the drawing)
>   You may give me this, if anything I tell you is
>   of value.

>   BROCK
>   Deal.
>   (crossing the room)
>   Over here are a few things we've recovered from your
>   staterooms.

Deleted

Laid out on a worktable are fifty or so objects, from mundane to valuable. Rose, shrunken in her chair, can barely see over the table top. With a trembling hand she lifts a tortoise shell hand mirror, inlaid with mother of pearl. She caresses it wonderingly.

>   ROSE
>   This was mine. How extraordinary! It looks the same
>   as the last time I saw it.

She turns the mirror over and looks at her ancient face in the cracked glass.

>   ROSE
>   The reflection has changed a bit.

                                                         (CONTINUED)

The script contains many references to the concepts of metamorphosis and emergence, equating Rose's emotional transformation to that of a caterpillar becoming a butterfly. The butterfly comb was chosen to visualize that concept.

Deleted for pacing

She spies something else, a silver and moonstone art-nouveau brooch.

                              ROSE
                    My mother's brooch. She wanted to go back for it.
                    Caused quite a fuss.

Rose picks up an ornate art-nouveau HAIR COMB. A jade butterfly takes flight on the
ebony handle of the comb. She turns it slowly, remembering. We can see that Rose is
experiencing a rush of images and emotions that have lain dormant for eight decades as
she handles the butterfly comb.

                              BROCK
                    Are you ready to go back to Titanic?

                                                                    CUT TO:

29   INT. IMAGING SHACK / KELDYSH   29

It is a darkened room lined with TV monitors. IMAGES OF THE WRECK fill the
screens, fed from Mir One and Two, and the two ROVs, Snoop Dog and DUNCAN.

                              BODINE
                    Live from 12,000 feet.

ROSE stares raptly at the screens. She is enthralled by one in particular, an image of
the bow railing. It obviously means something to her. Brock is studying her reactions carefully.

                              BODINE
                    The bow's stuck in the bottom like an axe, from the
                    impact. Here... I can run a simulation we worked up
                    on this monitor over here.

Lizzy turns the chair so Rose can see the screen of Bodine's computer. As he is calling
up the file, he keeps talking.

                              BODINE
                    We've put together the world's largest database on the
                    Titanic. Okay, here...

                              BROCK
                    Rose might not want to see this, Lewis.

                              ROSE
                    No, no. It's fine. I'm curious.

Deleted in post for pacing

Bodine starts a COMPUTER ANIMATED GRAPHIC on the screen, which parallels
his rapid-fire narration.

                              BODINE
                    She hits the berg on the starboard side and it sort of
                    bumps along... punching holes like a morse code... <u>dit</u>
                    <u>dit dit</u>, down the side. Now she's flooding in the
                              (MORE)

                                                                    (CONTINUED)

The sinking simulation was a convenient way for Cameron to set up the mechanics of the sinking in the first act so he would not have to interrupt the action at its peak to account for the bizarre motions of the ship.

CAMERON: "You will not find Bodine's description of how the ship sank in any history book. That was my best guess based on years of research; reading every eyewitness account and trying to cross-reference that with the state of the ship on the bottom. People who have written about the *Titanic* are journalists, historians or oceanographers. Not one has been an engineer or has had to re-create the sinking physically. I fully acknowledge that my interpretation is just a theory, one I have reached through an intense process of mechanical forensics."

Rose's specific flash-memories of the sinking were altered. As she looks at an ROV view of the wrecked doors leading to the Reception Area on D-deck, there is a quick dissolve to those same doors swinging open in 1912 to reveal well-dressed passengers. This was done to make the memory visually splendid rather than terrifying, emphasizing the romance and creating an emotional resonance with the contrast.

                              BODINE (cont'd)
          forward compartments... and the water spills over the
          tops of the bulkheads, going aft. As her bow is going
          down, her stern is coming up... slow at first... and
          then faster and faster until it's lifting all that
          weight, maybe 20 or 30 thousand tons... out of the
          water and the hull can't deal... so SKRTTT!!
               (making a sound in time with the animation)
          ... it splits! Right down to the keel, which acts like
          a big hinge. Now the bow swings down and the stern
          falls back level... but the weight of the bow pulls
          the stern up vertical, and then the bow section
          detaches, heading for the bottom. The stern bobs like
          a cork, floods and goes under about 2:20 a.m. Two hours
          and forty minutes after the collision.

The animation then follows the bow section as it sinks. Rose watches this clinical
dissection of the disaster without emotion.

                              BODINE
          The bow pulls out of its dive and planes away, almost
          a half a mile, before it hits the bottom going maybe
          12 miles an hour. KABOOM!

The bow impacts, digging deeply into the bottom. The animation now follows the
stern.

                              BODINE
          The stern implodes as it sinks, from the pressure, and
          rips apart from the force of the current as it falls,
          landing like a big pile of junk.
               (indicating the simulation)
          Cool huh?

Deleted in post

                              ROSE
          Thank you for that fine forensic analysis, Mr. Bodine.
          Of course the experience of it was somewhat less
          clinical.

                              BROCK
          Will you share it with us?

Her eyes go back to the screens, showing the sad ruins far below them.

A VIEW from one of the subs TRACKING SLOWLY over the boat deck. Rose recognizes one of the Wellin davits, still in place. She hears ghostly waltz music. The
faint and echoing sound of an officer's voice, English accented, calling "Women and
children only".

30   FLASH CUTS of screaming faces in a running crowd. Pandemonium and terror. People   30
       crying, praying, kneeling on the deck. Just impressions... flashes in the dark.

31   Rose looks at another monitor. SNOOP DOG moving down a rusted, debris-filled   31
       corridor. Rose watches the endless row of doorways sliding past, like dark mouths.

The addition of dialogue not referenced in the script between Bert Cartmell and his daughter Cora ("Daddy, it's a ship") was an inside reference to a running joke between Cameron and members of the crew. Executive Producer Rae Sanchini: "He probably corrected people seven or eight times a day. Whenever they would refer to *Titanic* as a boat he would say, '*Titanic* is not a boat. It is a ship.' In some small way I think it reflected his reverence."

32   IMAGE OF A CHILD, three years old, standing ankle deep in water in the middle   32
      of an endless corridor. The child is lost and alone, crying.

33   Rose is shaken by the flood of memories and emotions. Her eyes well up and she   33
      puts her head down, sobbing quietly.

                              LIZZY
                    (taking the wheelchair)
                  I'm taking her to rest.

                              ROSE
            No!

      Her voice is surprisingly strong. The sweet little old lady is gone, replaced by a
      woman with eyes of steel. Lovett signals everyone to stay quiet.

                              LOVETT
                  Tell us, Rose.

      She looks from screen to screen, the images of the ruined ship.

                              ROSE
                  It's been 84 years...

                              BROCK
                  Just tell us what you can—

                              ROSE
                    (holds up her hand for silence)
                  It's been 84 years... and I can still smell the fresh
                  paint. The china had never been used. The sheets had
                  never been slept in.

      He switches on the minirecorder and sets it near her.

                              ROSE
                  Titanic was called the Ship of Dreams. And it was. It
                  really was...

      As the underwater camera rises past the rusted bow rail, WE DISSOLVE/ MATCH
      MOVE to that same railing in 1912...

                                                          MATCH DISSOLVE:

34   EXT. SOUTHAMPTON DOCK - DAY   34

      SHOT CONTINUES IN A GLORIOUS REVEAL as the gleaming white superstructure of
      Titanic rises mountainously beyond the rail, and above that the buff-colored funnels
      stand against the sky like the pillars of a great temple. Crewmen move across the deck,
      dwarfed by the awesome scale of the steamer.

                                                          (CONTINUED)

Rosé DeWitt Bukater (Kate Winslet)

Southampton, England, April 10, 1912. It is almost noon on sailing day. A crowd of hundreds blackens the pier next to Titanic like ants on a jelly sandwich.

IN FG a gorgeous burgundy RENAULT TOURING CAR swings into frame, hanging from a loading crane. It is lowered toward HATCH #2.

On the pier horsedrawn vehicles, motorcars and lorries move slowly through the dense throng. The atmosphere is one of excitement and general giddiness. People embrace in tearful farewells, or wave and shout bon voyage wishes to friends and relatives on the decks above.

A white RENAULT, leading a silver-gray DAIMLER-BENZ, pushes through the crowd leaving a wake in the press of people. Around the handsome cars people are streaming to board the ship, jostling with hustling seamen and stokers, porters, and barking WHITE STAR LINE officials.

The Renault stops and the LIVERIED DRIVER scurries to open the door for a YOUNG WOMAN dressed in a stunning white and purple outfit, with an enormous feathered hat. She is 17 years old and beautiful, regal of bearing, with piercing eyes.

It is the girl in the drawing. ROSE. She looks up at the ship, taking it in with cool appraisal.

>   ROSE
>   I don't see what all the fuss is about. It doesn't
>   look any bigger than the Mauretania.

A PERSONAL VALET opens the door on the other side of the car for CALEDON HOCKLEY, the 30 year old heir to the elder Hockley's fortune. "Cal" is handsome, arrogant and rich beyond meaning.

>   CAL
>   You can be blase about some things, Rose, but not
>   about Titanic. It's over a *hundred feet* longer than
>   Mauretania, and far more luxurious. It has squash
>   courts, a Parisian cafe... even Turkish baths.

Deleted for Pacing

Cal turns and gives his hand to Rose's mother, RUTH DEWITT BUKATER, who descends from the touring car behind him. Ruth is a 40ish society empress, from one of the most prominent Philadelphia families. She is a widow, and rules her household with an iron will.

>   CAL
>   Your daughter is much too hard to impress, Ruth.
>   (indicating a puddle)
>   Mind your step.

>   RUTH
>   (gazing at the leviathan)
>   So this is the ship they say is unsinkable.

>   CAL
>   It *is* unsinkable. God himself couldn't sink this ship.

>   (CONTINUED)

Cal speaks with the pride of a host providing a special experience.

This entire entourage of rich Americans is impeccably turned out, a quintessential example of the Edwardian upper class, complete with servants. Cal's VALET, SPICER LOVEJOY, is tall and impassive, dour as an undertaker. Behind him emerge TWO MAIDS, personal servants to Ruth and Rose.

A WHITE STAR LINE PORTER scurries toward them, harried by last minute loading.

> PORTER
> Sir, you'll have to check your baggage through the
> main terminal, round that way—

Cal nonchalantly hands the man a fiver. The porter's eyes dilate. *Five pounds was a monster tip in those days.*

> CAL
> I put my faith in you, good sir.
>   (curtly, indicating Lovejoy)
> See my man.

> PORTER
> Yes, sir. My pleasure, sir.

Cal never tires of the effect of money on the unwashed masses.

> LOVEJOY
>   (to the porter)
> These trunks here, and 12 more in the Daimler. We'll
> have all this lot up in the rooms.

The White Star man looks stricken when he sees the enormous pile of steamer trunks and suitcases loading down the second car, including wooden crates and a steel safe. He whistles frantically for some cargo-handlers nearby who come running.

Cal breezes on, leaving the minions to scramble. He quickly checks his pocket watch.

> CAL
> We'd better hurry. This way, ladies.

He indicates the way toward the first class gangway. They move into the crowd. TRUDY BOLT, Rose's maid, hustles behind them, laden with bags of her mistress's most recent purchases... things too delicate for the baggage handlers.

Cal leads, weaving between vehicles and handcarts, hurrying passengers (mostly second class and steerage) and well-wishers. Most of the first class passengers are avoiding the smelly press of the dockside crowd by using an elevated boarding bridge, twenty feet above.

They pass a line of steerage passengers in their coarse wool and tweeds, queued up inside movable barriers like cattle in a chute. A HEALTH OFFICER examines their heads one by one, checking scalp and eyelashes for lice.

(CONTINUED)

The dialogue where Cal exclaims "I've pulled every string I could to book us on the grandest ship in history" did not make it into the final edit of the film. (It did, however, receive prominent use in the first theatrical trailer.)

Cameron: "All of the information from that dialogue between Cal, Rose and Ruth proved to be non-essential, just as clearly conveyed by gestures, context and other dialogue."

They pass a well-dressed young man cranking the handle of a wooden Biograph "cinematograph" camera mounted on a tripod. DANIEL MARVIN (whose father founded the Biograph Film Studio) is filming his young bride in front of the Titanic. MARY MARVIN stands stiffly and smiles, self conscious.

                         DANIEL
              Look up at the ship, darling, that's it. You're
              amazed! You can't believe how big it is! Like a
              mountain.
              That's great.

Mary Marvin, without an acting fiber in her body, does a bad Clara Bow pantomime of awe, hands raised.

Cal is jostled by two yelling steerage boys who shove past him. And he is bumped again a second later by the boys' father.

                         CAL   *Deleted in post*
              Steady!!   *for Pacing*

                         MAN
              Sorry squire!

The Cockney father pushes on, after his kids, shouting.

                         CAL
              Steerage swine. Apparently missed his annual bath.

                         RUTH
              Honestly, Cal, if you weren't forever booking
              everything at the last instant, we could have gone
              through the terminal instead of running along the dock
              like some squalid immigrant family.

                         CAL
              All part of my charm, Ruth. At any rate, it was my
              darling fiancee's beauty rituals which made us late.

                         ROSE
              You told me to change.

                         CAL
              I couldn't let you wear black on sailing day, sweet-
              pea. It's bad luck.

                         ROSE
              I felt like black.

Cal guides them out of the path of a horse-drawn wagon loaded down with two tons of OXFORD MARMALADE, in wooden cases, for Titanic's Victualling Department.

                         CAL
              Here I've pulled every string I could to book us on
              the grandest ship in history, in her most luxurious
                         (MORE)

                                                        (CONTINUED)

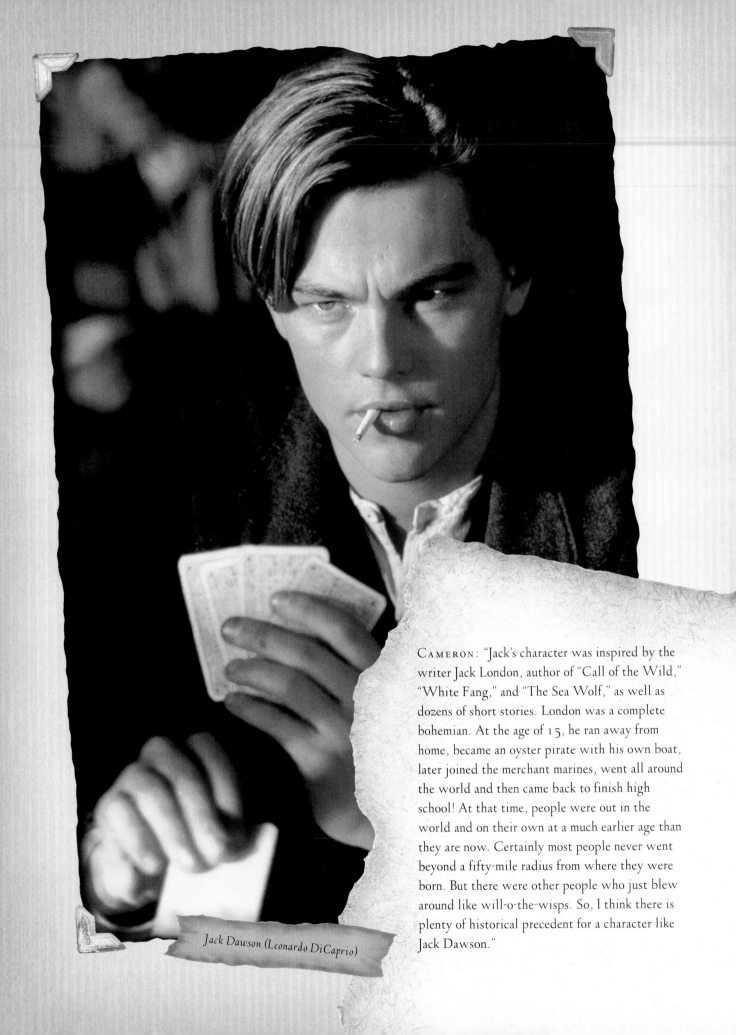

Jack Dawson (Leonardo DiCaprio)

CAMERON: "Jack's character was inspired by the writer Jack London, author of "Call of the Wild," "White Fang," and "The Sea Wolf," as well as dozens of short stories. London was a complete bohemian. At the age of 15, he ran away from home, became an oyster pirate with his own boat, later joined the merchant marines, went all around the world and then came back to finish high school! At that time, people were out in the world and on their own at a much earlier age than they are now. Certainly most people never went beyond a fifty-mile radius from where they were born. But there were other people who just blew around like will-o-the-wisps. So, I think there is plenty of historical precedent for a character like Jack Dawson."

                              CAL (cont'd)
          suites... and you act as if you're going to your
          execution.

Rose looks up as the hull of Titanic looms over them... a great iron wall, Bible black
and severe. Cal motions her forward, and she enters the gangway to the D Deck doors with
a sense of overwhelming dread.

                            OLD ROSE (V.O.)
          *It was the ship of dreams... to everyone else. To me it
          was a slave ship, taking me back to America in chains.*

CLOSE ON CAL'S HAND IN SLOW-MOTION as it closes possessively over Rose's
arm. He escorts her up the gangway and the black hull of Titanic swallows
them.

                            OLD ROSE (V.O.)
          *Outwardly I was everything a well brought up girl
          should be. Inside, I was screaming.*

35   CUT TO a SCREAMING BLAST from the mighty triple steam horns on Titanic's funnels,   35
      bellowing their departure warning.

                                                                      CUT TO:

36   EXT. SOUTHAMPTON DOCKS/ TITANIC - DAY   36

      A VIEW OF TITANIC from several blocks away, towering above the terminal build-
      ings like the skyline of a city. The steamer's whistle echoes across Southampton.

      PULL BACK, revealing that we were looking through a window, and back further to
      show the smoky inside of a pub. It is crowded with dockworkers and ship's crew.

      Just inside the window, a poker game is in progress. FOUR MEN, in working class
      clothes, play a very serious hand.

      JACK DAWSON and FABRIZIO DE ROSSI, both about 20, exchange a glance as the
      other two players argue in Swedish. Jack is American, a lanky drifter with his hair a little
      long for the standards of the times. He is also unshaven, and his clothes are rumpled
      from sleeping in them. He is an artist, and has adopted the bohemian style of the art
      scene in Paris. He is also very self-possessed and sure-footed for 20, having lived on
      his own since 15.

      The TWO SWEDES continue their sullen argument, in Swedish.

                               OLAF
                        (subtitled)
                   *You stupid fishhead. I can't believe you bet our
                   tickets.*

                               SVEN
                        (subtitled)
                   *You lost our money. I'm just trying to get it back.
                   Now shutup and take a card.*

                                                              (CONTINUED)

CAMERON: "The funny thing about scene 36 is that I'm not very familiar with the game of poker. The crew and the actors all sat around with me and figured out where the actors should sit, what order they dealt the cards and so on. Making Jack the dealer made him seem more in control and was more active for the hero."

Fabrizio De Rossi (Danny Nucci)

                                    JACK
                    (jaunty)
               Hit me again, Sven.

Jack takes the card and slips it into his hand.

ECU JACK'S EYES. They betray nothing.

CLOSE ON FABRIZIO licking his lips nervously as he refuses a card.

ECU STACK in the middle of the table. Bills and coins from four countries. This has been going on for a while. Sitting on top of the money are two 3RD CLASS TICKETS for RMS TITANIC.

The Titanic's whistle blows again. Final warning.

                                    JACK
               The moment of truth boys. Somebody's life's about to
               change.

Fabrizio puts his cards down. So do the Swedes. Jack holds his close.

                                    JACK
               Let's see... Fabrizio's got "niente." Olaf, you've got
               squat. Sven, uh oh... two pair... mmm.
                    (turns to his friend)
               Sorry Fabrizio.

                                 FABRIZIO
               What sorry? What you got? You lose my money??
               Ma va fa'n culo testa di cazzo—

                                    JACK
               Sorry, you're not gonna see your mama again for a
               long time...

He slaps a full house down on the table.

                                    JACK
                    (grinning)
               'Cause you're goin' to America!! Full house boys!

                                 FABRIZIO
               Porca Madonna!! YEEAAAAA!!!   Changed to "Dio Mio, Grazie!"

The table explodes into shouting in several languages. Jack rakes in the money and the tickets.

                                    JACK
                    (to the Swedes)
               Sorry boys. Three of a kind and a pair. I'm high and
               you're dry and...
                                 (MORE)
                                                            (CONTINUED)

Deleted

Deleted ↑

CONTINUED: (2)

                                    JACK (cont'd)
                         (to Fabrizio)
                    ... we're going to—

                         FABRIZIO/JACK
               L'AMERICA!!!

Olaf balls up one huge farmer's fist. We think he's going to clobber Jack, but he swings
round and punches Sven, who flops backward onto the floor and sits there, looking
depressed. Olaf forgets about Jack and Fabrizio, who are dancing around, and goes into
a rapid harangue of his stupid cousin.

Jack kisses the tickets, then jumps on Fabrizio's back and rides him around the pub.
It's like they won the lottery.

Cut   JACK
               Goin' home... to the land o' the free and the home of
               real hot-dogs! On the TITANIC!! We're ridin' in
               high style now! We're practically goddamned royalty,
               ragazzo mio!!

                         FABRIZIO   *Moved to*
               You see? Is my destinio!! Like I told you. I go to   *scene 37*
               l'America!! To be a millionaire!!
                    (to pubkeeper)
               Capito?? I go to America!!

                         PUBKEEPER
               No, mate. *Titanic* go to America. In five minutes.

                         JACK
               Shit!! Come on, Fabri!
                    (grabing their stuff)
               Come on!!
                    (to all, grinning)
               It's been grand.

They run for the door.   *Deleted in*
                                       post for pacing

                         PUBKEEPER
               'Course I'm sure if they knew it was you lot comin',
               they'd be pleased to wait!

                                                                   CUT TO:

EXT. TERMINAL - TITANIC

Jack and Fabrizio, carrying everything they own in the world in the kit bags on
their shoulders, sprint toward the pier. They tear through milling crowds next to the
terminal. Shouts go up behind them as they jostle slow-moving gentlemen. They dodge
piles of luggage, and weave through groups of people. They burst out onto the pier
and Jack comes to a dead stop... staring at the vast wall of the ship's hull, towering
seven stories above the wharf and over an eighth of a mile long. The Titanic is
monstrous.

                                                                   (CONTINUED)

CAMERON: "I had scripted more to the ship leaving Southampton, but I trimmed it down because it took away from what I call the "Ode to the ship" sequence later [starting with Scene 48]. Every film before mine has the ship leaving from Cherbourg, France. In fact it sailed from Southampton, traveled to Cherbourg and Queenstown, Ireland before starting across the Atlantic. At both Cherbourg and Queenstown, the passengers were loaded onto the ship from tender boats while *Titanic* waited off-shore in the harbor. For dramatic purposes, I wanted to show the ship leaving from a pier with waving crowds. So I separated the ship leaving Southampton and departing for the open sea by three or four short scenes."

Fabrizio runs back and grabs Jack, and they sprint toward the third class gangway aft, at E deck. They reach the bottom of the ramp just as SIXTH OFFICER MOODY detaches it at the top. It starts to swing down from the gangway doors.

                          JACK
              Wait!! We're passengers!

Flushed and panting, he waves the tickets.

                          MOODY
              Have you been through the inspection queue?

                          JACK
                (lying cheerfully)
              Of course! Anyway, we don't have lice, we're
              Americans.
                (glances at Fabrizio)
              Both of us.

                          MOODY
                (testy)
              Right, come aboard.

Moody has QUARTERMASTER ROWE reattach the gangway. Jack and Fabrizio come aboard. Moody glances at the tickets, then passes Jack and Fabrizio through to Rowe. Rowe looks at the names on the tickets to enter them in the passenger list.

                          ROWE   *Deleted in post*
              Gundersen. And...
                (reading Fabrizio's)
              Gundersen.

He hands the tickets back, eyeing Fabrizio's Mediterranean looks suspiciously.

                          JACK
                (grabbing Fabrizio's arm)
              Come on, Sven.

Jack and Fabrizio whoop with victory as they run down the white-painted corridor... grinning from ear to ear.

                          JACK
              We are the luckiest sons of bitches in the world!

                                                              CUT TO:

38   EXT. TITANIC AND DOCK - DAY   38

The mooring lines, as big around as a man's arm, are dropped into the water. A cheer goes up on the pier as SEVEN TUGS pull the Titanic away from the quay.

                                                              CUT TO:

39   EXT. AFT WELL DECK/ POOP DECK - DAY

JACK AND FABRIZIO burst through a door onto the aft well deck. TRACKING
WITH THEM as they run across the deck and up the steel stairs to the poop deck. They
get to the rail and Jack starts to yell and wave to the crowd on the dock.

                              FABRIZIO
                    You know somebody?

                                JACK
                    Of course not. That's not the point.
                        (to the crowd)
                    Goodbye! Goodbye!! I'll miss you!

Grinning, Fabrizio joins in, adding his voice to the swell of voices, feeling the exhilara-
tion of the moment.

                              FABRIZIO
                    Goodbye! I will never forget you!!

                                                            CUT TO:

40   EXT. SOUTHAMPTON DOCK - DAY   40

The crowd of cheering well-wishers waves heartily as a black wall of metal moves
past them. Impossibly tiny figures wave back from the ship's rails. Titanic gathers
speed.

                                                            CUT TO:

41   EXT. RIVER TEST - DAY   41

IN A LONG LENS SHOT the prow of Titanic FILLS FRAME behind the lead tug,
which is dwarfed. The bow wave spreads before the mighty plow of the liner's hull as
it moves down the River Test toward the English Channel.

                                                            CUT TO:

42   INT. THIRD CLASS BERTHING/ G-DECK FORWARD - DAY   42

Jack and Fabrizio walk down a narrow corridor with doors lining both sides like a college dorm. Total confusion as people argue over luggage in several languages, or wander
in confusion in the labyrinth. They pass emigrants studying the signs over the doors,
and looking up the words in phrase books.

They find their berth. It is a modest cubicle, painted enamel white, with four
bunks. Exposed pipes overhead. The other two guys are already there. OLAUS and
BJORN GUNDERSEN.

Jack throws his kit on one open bunk, while Fabrizio takes the other.

                                                            (CONTINUED)

To reveal character, Cameron wrote in Picasso for Rose (who admires his courage to try new things), Monet for Jack (who likes his visual truth), and Degas because he almost exclusively painted joyful dancers, indicative of the way Rose wants to feel (See Scene 71). The Degas is always present in the room when Rose has confrontations with Cal or her mother.

Caledon Hockley (Billy Zane)

42   CONTINUED: 42

                                     BJORN
                    (in Swedish/ subtitled)
                Where is Sven?

                                                                    CUT TO:

43   INT. SUITE B-52-56 - DAY   43

By contrast, the so-called "Millionaire Suite" is in the Empire style, and comprises two
bedrooms, a bath, WC, wardrobe room, and a large sitting room. In addition there is a
private 50 foot promenade deck outside.

A room service waiter pours champagne into a tulip glass of orange juice and hands
the Bucks Fizz to Rose. She is looking through her new paintings. There is a Monet of
water lilies, a Degas of dancers, and a few abstract works. They are all unknown
paintings... lost works.

Cal is out on the covered deck, which has potted trees and vines on trellises,
talking through the doorway to Rose in the sitting room.

                                     CAL
                Those mud puddles were certainly a waste of money.

ad libbed: "Finger Paintings"

                                     ROSE
                    (looking at a cubist portrait)
                You're wrong. They're fascinating. Like in a
                dream.... there's truth without logic. What's his name
                again... ?
                    (reading off the canvas)
                Picasso.

                                     CAL
                    (coming into the sitting room)
                He'll never amount to a thing, trust me. At least they
                were cheap.

A porter wheels Cal's private safe (which we recognize) into the room on a
handtruck.

                                     CAL
                Put that in the wardrobe.

44   IN THE BEDROOM Rose enters with the large Degas of the dancers. She sets it on the   44
      dresser, near the canopy bed. Trudy is already in there, hanging up some of Rose's
      clothes.

                                     TRUDY
                It smells so brand new. Like they built it all just
                for us. I mean... just to think that tonight, when I
                crawl between the sheets, I'll be the first—

Cal appears in the doorway of the bedroom.

                                                                    (CONTINUED)

scene deleted in post

                                                                          25

CAMERON: "Audiences need reinforcement of what I call the force field of ideas. The story beats must be maintained, continuously stressed and escalated. The first place to achieve this is in the script, making sure that the beats are there and that they work. Then, during production, the actors and the director create another level to these beats, through gesture, reaction or ad lib, such as when Cal calls Rose 'Sweatpea' and sort of 'snaps his fingers' with the tone of his voice to get her to follow him to dinner. These little moments may, in the context of editing, be all you need to replace a lot of dialogue. In this case, it was the whole scene."

Sacrificed, perhaps, was a moment of softness between Cal and Rose improvised on set by Billy Zane and Kate Winslet. Contrary to the scene description, the actors ended the scene with Rose giving a perfunctory peck on the cheek to Cal, who then comments that he too likes the Degas painting.

CAMERON: "Molly Brown was a reference point for Rose to demonstrate that the things Rose wanted for herself were possible to achieve. I also gave Molly a connection to Jack in how she takes him under her wing and eases him into Rose's world. All of which is very consistent with what she might have done."

44   CONTINUED: 44

                                    CAL
                      (looking at Rose)
                And when <u>I</u> crawl between the sheets tonight, I'll
                <u>still</u> be the first.

                                    TRUDY
                      (blushing at the innuendo)
                S'cuse me, Miss.

        She edges around Cal and makes a quick exit. Cal comes up behind Rose and
        puts his hands on her shoulders. An act of possession, not intimacy.

                                    CAL
                The first and only. Forever.

        Rose's expression shows how bleak a prospect this is for her, now.

                                                                    CUT TO:

45   EXT. CHERBOURG HARBOR, FRANCE - LATE DUSK   45

        Titanic stands silhouetted against a purple post-sunset sky. She is lit up like a float-
        ing palace, and her thousand portholes reflect in the calm harbor waters. The 150 foot
        tender Nomadic lies-to alongside, looking like a rowboat. The lights of Cherbourg
        harbor complete the postcard image.

                                                                    CUT TO:

46   INT. FIRST CLASS RECEPTION/ D-DECK   46

        Entering the first class reception room from the tender are a number of prominent
        passengers. A BROAD-SHOULDERED WOMAN in an enormous feathered hat comes
        up the gangway, carrying a suitcase in each hand, a spindly porter running to catch
        up with her to take the bags.

                                    WOMAN
                Well, I wasn't about to wait all day for you, sonny.
                Take 'em the rest of the way if you think you can
                manage.

                                    OLD ROSE (V.O.)
                At Cherbourg a woman came aboard named Margaret
                Brown, but we all called her Molly. History would
                call her the Unsinkable Molly Brown. Her husband
                had struck gold someplace out west, and she was
                what mother called "new money".

        At 45, MOLLY BROWN is a tough talking straightshooter who dresses in the finery
        of her genteel peers but will never be one of them.

                                                                    (CONTINUED)

*Captain Smith (Bernard Hill)
and the Deck Officers of the Titanic.*

The "Ode to the ship" sequence was altered only slightly in the finished film. Changes included altering the order of some shots, while adding and deleting others. As the audience had not yet been introduced to Master Shipbuilder Thomas Andrews, Cameron chose to remove his presence from the montage. The most pronounced change, however, was the addition of Jack's by-now signature line, "I'm King of the World!" which was improvised by Cameron while filming the scene because he felt Jack needed a line to clarify the joy of the moment and to punctuate the climax of the montage.

[NOTE: It is Cameron's own voice yelling Chief Bell's "All ahead full!" dialogue in the engine room.]

                          OLD ROSE (V.O.)
              By the next afternoon we had made our final stop
              and we were steaming west from the coast of Ireland,
              with nothing out ahead of us but ocean...

                                                          CUT TO:

47   EXT. BOW - DAY   47

      The ship glows with the warm creamy light of late afternoon. Jack and Fabrizio stand
      right at the bow gripping the curved railing so familiar from images of the wreck. Jack
      leans over, looking down fifty feet to where the prow cuts the surface like a knife,
      sending up two glassy sheets of water.

                                                          CUT TO:

48   INT. / EXT. TITANIC - SERIES OF SCENES - DAY   48

      ON THE BRIDGE, CAPTAIN SMITH turns from the binnacle to FIRST OFFICER
      WILLIAM MURDOCH.

                          CAPTAIN SMITH
              Take her to sea Mister Murdoch. Let's stretch her
              legs.

      Murdoch moves the engine telegraph lever to ALL AHEAD FULL.

49   **NOW BEGINS** a kind of musical/visual setpiece... an ode to the great ship. The music   49
      is rhythmic, surging forward, with a soaring melody that addresses the majesty and
      optimism of the ship of dreams.

      IN THE ENGINE ROOM the telegraph clangs and moves to "All Ahead Full".

                          CHIEF ENGINEER BELL
              All ahead full!

      On the catwalk THOMAS ANDREWS, the shipbuilder, watches carefully as the engi-
      neers and greasers scramble to adjust valves. Towering above them are the twin
      RECIPROCATING engines, four stories tall, their ten-foot-long connecting rods
      surging up and down with the turning of the massive crankshafts. The engines thun-
      der like the footfalls of marching giants.

50   IN THE BOILER ROOMS the STOKERS chant a song as they hurl coal into the roaring   50
      furnaces. The "black gang" are covered with sweat and coal dust, their muscles
      working like part of the machinery as they toil in the hellish glow.

51   UNDERWATER the enormous bronze screws chop through the water, hurling the steamer   51
      forward and churning up a vortex of foam that lingers for miles behind the juggernaut
      ship. Smoke pours from the funnels as—

52   The riven water flares higher at the bow as the ship's speed builds. THE   52
      CAMERA SWEEPS UP the prow to find Jack, the wind streaming through his hair
      and -

53   Captain Smith steps out of the enclosed bridge onto the wing. He stands with his hands   53
          on the rail, looking every bit the storybook picture of a Captain... a great patriarch of
          the sea.

                                  FIRST OFFICER MURDOCH   *Deleted in post*
                        Twenty one knots, sir!

                        [SMITH   ]
                        [She's got a bone in her teeth now, eh, Mr. Murdoch.]

          Smith accepts a cup of tea from FIFTH OFFICER LOWE. He contentedly watches
          the white V of water hurled outward from the bows like an expression of his own
          personal power. They are invulnerable, towering over the sea.

          AT THE BOW Jack and Fabrizio lean far over, looking down.

54   In the glassy bow-wave two dolphins appear, under the water, running fast just in front   54
          of the steel blade of the prow. They do it for the sheer joy and exultation of motion.
          Jack watches the dolphins and grins. They breach, jumping clear of the water and
          then dive back, crisscrossing in front of the bow, dancing ahead of the juggernaut.

          FABRIZIO looks forward across the Atlantic, staring into the sunsparkles.

                                  FABRIZIO
                        I can see the Statue of Liberty already.
                            (grinning at Jack)
                        Very small...of course.

          THE CAMERA ARCS around them, until they are framed against the sea.

          NOW WE PULL BACK, across the forecastle deck. Rising, as we continue back, and
          the ship rolls endlessly forward underneath. Over the bridge wing, along the boat
          deck until her funnels come INTO FRAME beside us and march past like the pillars of
          heaven, one by one. We pull back and up, until we are looking down the funnels, and
          the people strolling on the decks and standing at the rail become antlike.

          And still we pull back until the great lady is seen whole, in a gorgeous aerial portrait,
          black and severe in her majesty.

                                  ISMAY (V.O.)
                        She is the largest moving object ever made by the hand
                        of man in all history...

                                                                          CUT TO:

55   INT. PALM COURT RESTAURANT - DAY   55

          CLOSE ON J. BRUCE ISMAY, Managing Director of White Star Line.

                                  ISMAY
                        ...and our master shipbuilder, Mr. Andrews here,
                        designed her from the keel plates up.

                                                                    (CONTINUED)

Molly Brown (Kathy Bates)

He indicates a handsome 39 year old Irish gentleman to his right, THOMAS
ANDREWS, of Harland and Wolf Shipbuilders.

WIDER, showing the group assembled for lunch the next day. Ismay seated with Cal,
Rose, Ruth, Molly Brown and Thomas Andrews in the Palm Court, a beautiful sunny
spot enclosed by high arched windows.

                          ANDREWS
             (disliking the attention)
        Well, I may have knocked her together, but the idea
        was Mr. Ismay's. He envisioned a steamer so grand
        in scale, and so luxurious in its appointments, that
        its supremacy would never be challenged. And here
        she is...
             (he slaps the table)
        ...willed into solid reality.

                          MOLLY
        Why're ships always bein' called "she"? Is it because
        men think half the women around have big sterns and
        should be weighed in tonnage?
             (they all laugh)
        Just another example of the men settin' the rules
        their way.

Deleted in post

The waiter arrives to take orders. Rose lights a cigarette.

                          RUTH
        You know I don't like that, Rose.

                          CAL
        She knows.

Cal takes the cigarette from her and stubs it out.

                          CAL

             (to the waiter)
        We'll both have the lamb. Rare, with a little
        mint sauce.
             (to Rose, after the waiter moves on)
        You like lamb, don't you, sweetpea?

Molly is watching the dynamic between Rose, Cal and Ruth.

                          MOLLY
        So, you gonna cut her meat for her too, there, Cal?
             (turning to Ismay)
        Hey, who came up with the name Titanic? You Bruce?

                                                      (CONTINUED)

J. Bruce Ismay (Jonathan Hyde)

In the film, Ismay's line "Freud? Who is he? Is he a passenger?" was an ad lib by actor Jonathan Hyde.

Jack sketches Cora and Bert Cartmell
(Alexandre Owens and Rocky Taylor)

Tommy Ryan (Jason Barry)

Cameron wrote the character of Tommy Ryan to be "a voice for the Irish emigrants."

While not referenced in the script or the film, the dogs being walked on the Poop Deck are historically accurate down to their breeds. The Airedale was intended to represent "Kitty" the dog owned by Colonel John Jacob Astor. The little French Bulldog was intended to represent a prize-winning show dog with the improbable name of "Gamin de Pycombe," and originally played a larger part in the film (See Scene 266).

                              ISMAY
          Yes, actually. I wanted to convey sheer size. And
          size means stability, luxury... and safety—

                              ROSE
          Do you know of Dr. Freud? His ideas about the male
          preoccupation with <u>size</u> might be of particular inter-
          est to you, Mr. Ismay.

Andrews chokes on his breadstick, suppressing laughter.

                              RUTH
          My God, Rose, what's gotten into—

                              ROSE
          Excuse me.

She stalks away.

                              RUTH
               (mortified)
          I do apologize.

                              MOLLY
          She's a pistol, Cal. You sure you can handle her?

                              CAL
               (tense but feigning unconcern)
          Well, I may have to start minding what she reads from
          now on.

                                                      CUT TO:

56   EXT. POOP DECK/ AFTER DECKS - DAY   56

Jack sits on a bench in the sun. Titanic's wake spreads out behind him to the horizon.
He has his knees pulled up, supporting a leather bound sketching pad, his only valuable possession. With conte crayon he draws rapidly, using sure strokes. An emigrant
from Manchester named CARTMELL has his 3 year old daughter CORA standing on the
lower rung of the rail. She is leaned back against his beer barrel of a stomach,
watching the seagulls.

THE SKETCH captures them perfectly, with a great sense of the humanity of the
moment. Jack is good. Really good. Fabrizio looks over Jack's shoulder. He nods
appreciatively.

TOMMY RYAN, a scowling young Irish emigrant, watches as a crewmember
comes by, walking three small dogs around the deck. One of them, a BLACK
FRENCH BULLDOG, is among the ugliest creatures on the planet.

                              TOMMY
          That's typical. First class dogs come down here to
          take a shit.

                                                   (CONTINUED)

Jack looks up from his sketch.

> JACK
> That's so we know where we rank in the scheme
> of things.

> TOMMY
> Like we could forget.

Jack glances across the well deck. At the aft railing of B deck promenade stands ROSE,
in a long yellow dress and white gloves.

CLOSE ON JACK, unable to take his eyes off of her. They are across from each
other, about 60 feet apart, with the well deck like a valley between them. She on her
promontory, he on his much lower one. She stares down at the water.

He watches her unpin her elaborate hat and take it off. She looks at the frilly absurd
thing, then tosses it over the rail. It sails far down to the water and is carried away,
astern. A spot of yellow in the vast ocean. He is *riveted* by her. She looks like a figure
in a romantic novel, sad and isolated.

Fabrizio taps Tommy and they both look at Jack gazing at Rose. Fabrizio and Tommy
grin at each other.

Rose turns suddenly and looks right at Jack. He is caught staring, but he doesn't
look away. She does, but then looks back. Their eyes meet across the space of the well
deck, across the gulf between worlds.

Jack sees a man (Cal) come up behind her and take her arm. She jerks her arm away.
They argue in pantomime. She storms away, and he goes after her, disappearing along
the A-deck promenade. Jack stares after her.

> TOMMY
> Forget it, boyo. You'd as like have angels fly out o'
> yer arse as get next to the likes o' her.

                                                                    CUT TO:

57   INT. FIRST CLASS DINING SALOON - NIGHT   57

SLOWLY PUSHING IN ON ROSE as she sits, flanked by people in heated conversation. Cal and Ruth are laughing together, while on the other side LADY DUFF-
GORDON is holding forth animatedly. We don't hear what they are saying. Rose is staring
at her plate, barely listening to the inconsequential babble around her.

> OLD ROSE
> *I saw my whole life as if I'd already lived it... an*
> *endless parade of parties and cotillions, yachts and*
> *polo matches... always the same narrow people, the*
> *same mindless chatter. I felt like I was standing at a*
> *great precipice, with no one to pull me back, no one*
> *who cared ... or even noticed.*

                                                              (CONTINUED)

CAMERON: "I removed this section, which starts with Rose poking herself with the crab fork because it struck me as more intriguing to cut to Rose running to the railing, and not know precisely why she's there. That way, we're seeing her the way Jack sees her."

It is in the deleted Scene 59 that Rose throws her hand mirror and cracks it. This scene would have recalled Old Rose admiring the hand mirror in the present. As constructed, we automatically assume the cracks to have come from some impact suffered during the sinking.

57   CONTINUED: (2)   57

ANGLE BENEATH TABLE showing Rose's hand, holding a tiny fork from her crab salad. She pokes the crab-fork into the skin of her arm, harder and harder until it draws blood.

                                                            CUT TO:

58   INT. CORRIDOR/ B DECK - NIGHT   58

Rose walks along the corridor. A steward coming the other way greets her, and she nods with a slight smile. She is perfectly composed.

                                                            CUT TO:

59   INT. ROSE'S BEDROOM - NIGHT   59

She enters the room. Stands in the middle, staring at her reflection in the large vanity mirror. Just stands there, then—

With a primal, anguished cry she claws at her throat, ripping off her pearl necklace, which explodes across the room. In a frenzy she tears at herself, her clothes, her hair... then attacks the room. She flings everything off the dresser and it flies clattering against the wall. She hurls a handmirror against the vanity, cracking it.

                                                            CUT TO:

60   EXT. A DECK PROMENADE, AFT - NIGHT   60

Rose runs along the B deck promenade. She is dishevelled, her hair flying. She is crying, her cheeks streaked with tears. But also angry, furious! Shaking with emotions she doesn't understand... hatred, self-hatred, desperation. A strolling couple watch her pass. Shocked at the emotional display in public.

                                                            CUT TO:

61   EXT. POOP DECK - NIGHT   61

Jack is kicked back on one of the benches gazing at the stars blazing gloriously overhead. Thinking artist thoughts and smoking a cigarette.

Hearing something, he turns as Rose runs up the stairs from the well deck. They are the only two on the stern deck, except for QUARTERMASTER ROWE, twenty feet above them on the docking bridge catwalk. She doesn't see Jack in the shadows, and runs right past him.

TRACKING WITH ROSE as she runs across the deserted fantail. Her breath hitches in an occasional sob, which she suppresses. Rose slams against the base of the stern flagpole and clings there, panting. She stares out at the black water.

Then starts to climb over the railing. She has to hitch her long dress way up, and climbing is clumsy. Moving methodically she turns her body and gets her heels on the white-painted gunwale, her back to the railing, facing out toward blackness. 60 feet below her, the massive propellers are churning the Atlantic into white foam, and a ghostly wake trails off toward the horizon.

                                                            (CONTINUED)

CAMERON: "As a writer, I don't think Rose would really jump. But then this guy comes up and starts to 'talk her down' and she ends up in that awkward situation where she almost feels like she has to go through with it just to prove she was right. The scene is economical because the situation cuts through all of the personal boundaries and connects Jack and Rose immediately at the heart level. They have a bond. There can be no secrets. And then you have the great irony near the end of the movie in that they end up at the very same flagpole where they first met. There were too many great dramatic symmetries not to stage it that way."

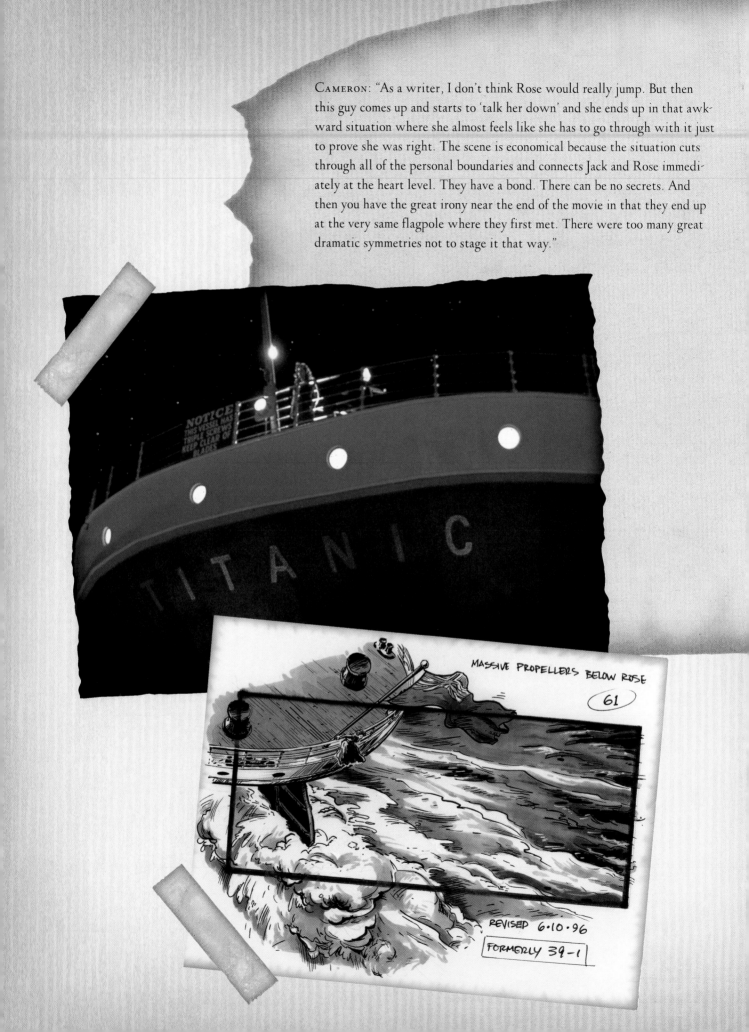

MASSIVE PROPELLERS BELOW ROSE

61

REVISED 6·10·96

FORMERLY 39-1

IN A LOW ANGLE, we see Rose standing like a figurehead in reverse. Below her are the huge letters of the name "TITANIC".

She leans out, her arms straightening... looking down hypnotized, into the vortex below her. Her dress and hair are lifted by the wind of the ship's movement. The only sound, above the rush of water below, is the flutter and snap of the big Union Jack right above her.

                    JACK
          Don't do it.

She whips her head around at the sound of his voice. It takes a second for her eyes to focus.

                    ROSE
          Stay back! Don't come any closer!

Jack sees the tear tracks on her cheeks in the faint glow from the stern running lights.

                    JACK
          Take my hand. I'll pull you back in.

                    ROSE
          No! Stay where you are. I mean it. I'll let go.

                    JACK
          No you won't.

                    ROSE
          What do you mean no I won't? Don't presume to tell
          me what I will and will not do. You don't know me.

                    JACK
          You would have done it already. Now come on, take
          my hand.

Rose is confused now. She can't see him very well through the tears, so she wipes them with one hand, almost losing her balance.

                    ROSE
          You're distracting me. Go away.

                    JACK
          I can't. I'm involved now. If you let go I have to
          jump in after you.

                    ROSE
          Don't be absurd. You'll be killed.

He takes off his jacket.

                    JACK
          I'm a good swimmer.

                                                      (CONTINUED)

                                                              33

He starts unlacing his left shoe.

                         ROSE
          The fall alone would kill you.

                         JACK
          It would hurt. I'm not saying it wouldn't. To be
          honest I'm a lot more concerned about the water being
          so cold.

She looks down. The reality factor of what she is doing is sinking in.

                         ROSE
          How cold?

                         JACK
             (taking off his left shoe)
          Freezing. Maybe a couple degrees over.

He starts unlacing his right shoe.

                         JACK
          Ever been to Wisconsin?

                         ROSE
             (perplexed)
          No.

                         JACK
          Well they have some of the coldest winters around,
          and I grew up there, near Chippewa Falls. Once
          when I was a kid me and my father were ice-fishing
          out on Lake Wissota... ice-fishing's where you chop a
          hole in the—

                         ROSE
          I know what ice fishing is!

                         JACK
          Sorry. Just... you look like kind of an indoor girl.
          Anyway, I went through some thin ice and I'm tellin'
          ya, water *that* cold... like that right down there...
          it hits you like a thousand knives stabbing all over
          your body. You can't breath, you can't think... least
          not about anything but the pain.
             (takes off his other shoe)
          Which is why I'm not looking forward to jumping in
          after you. But like I said, I don't see a choice.
             (smiling)
          I guess I'm kinda hoping you'll come back over the
          rail and get me off the hook here.

                                                  (CONTINUED)

                              ROSE
               You're crazy.

                              JACK
               That's what everybody says. But with all due respect,
               I'm not the one hanging off the back of a ship.

He slides one step closer, like moving up on a spooked horse.

                              JACK
               Come on. You don't want to do this. Give me your
               hand.

Rose stares at this madman for a long time. She looks at his eyes and they somehow
suddenly seem to fill her universe.

                              ROSE
               Alright.

She unfastens one hand from the rail and reaches it around toward him. He reaches out
to take it, firmly.

                              JACK
               I'm Jack Dawson.

                              ROSE
                  (voice quavering)
               Pleased to meet you, Mr. Dawson.

Rose starts to turn. Now that she has decided to live, the height is terrifying. She is
overcome by vertigo as she shifts her footing, turning to face the ship. As she starts
to climb, her dress gets in the way, and one foot slips off the edge of the deck.

She plunges, letting out a piercing SHRIEK. Jack, gripping her hand, is jerked
toward the rail. Rose barely grabs a lower rail with her free hand.

QUARTERMASTER ROWE, up on the docking bridge hears the scream and heads for the
ladder.

                              ROSE
               HELP! HELP!!

                              JACK
               I've got you. I won't let go.

Jack holds her hand with all his strength, bracing himself on the railing with his
other hand. Rose tries to get some kind of a foothold on the smooth hull. Jack tries to
lift her bodily over the railing. She can't get any footing in her dress and evening
shoes, and she slips back. Rose SCREAMS again.

Jack, awkwardly clutching Rose by whatever he can get a grip on as she flails, gets her
over the railing. They fall together onto the deck in a tangled heap, spinning in such a
way that Jack winds up slightly on top of her.

                                                              (CONTINUED)

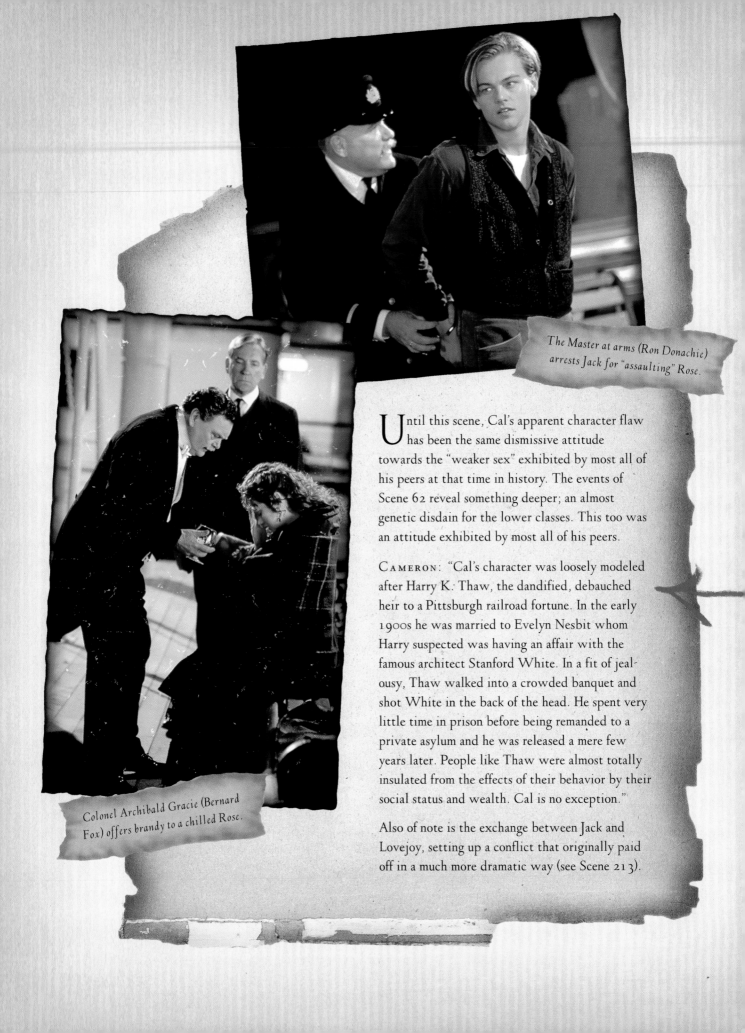

The Master at arms (Ron Donachie) arrests Jack for "assaulting" Rose.

Colonel Archibald Gracie (Bernard Fox) offers brandy to a chilled Rose.

Until this scene, Cal's apparent character flaw has been the same dismissive attitude towards the "weaker sex" exhibited by most all of his peers at that time in history. The events of Scene 62 reveal something deeper; an almost genetic disdain for the lower classes. This too was an attitude exhibited by most all of his peers.

CAMERON: "Cal's character was loosely modeled after Harry K. Thaw, the dandified, debauched heir to a Pittsburgh railroad fortune. In the early 1900s he was married to Evelyn Nesbit whom Harry suspected was having an affair with the famous architect Stanford White. In a fit of jealousy, Thaw walked into a crowded banquet and shot White in the back of the head. He spent very little time in prison before being remanded to a private asylum and he was released a mere few years later. People like Thaw were almost totally insulated from the effects of their behavior by their social status and wealth. Cal is no exception."

Also of note is the exchange between Jack and Lovejoy, setting up a conflict that originally paid off in a much more dramatic way (see Scene 213).

Rowe slides down the ladder from the docking bridge like it's a fire drill and sprints across the fantail.

                              ROWE
          Here, what's all this?!

Rowe runs up and pulls Jack off of Rose, revealing her dishevelled and sobbing on the deck. Her dress is torn, and the hem is pushed up above her knees, showing one ripped stocking . He looks at Jack, the shaggy steerage man with his jacket off, and the first class lady clearly in distress, and starts drawing conclusions. Two seamen chug across the deck to join them.

                              ROWE
               (to Jack)
          Here you, stand back! Don't move an inch!
               (to the seamen)
          Fetch the Master at Arms.

                                                          CUT TO:

62   EXT. POOP DECK - NIGHT   62

A few minutes later. Jack is being detained by the burly MASTER AT ARMS, the closest thing to a cop on board. He is handcuffing Jack. Cal is right in front of Jack, and furious. He has obviously just rushed out here with Lovejoy and another man, and none of them have coats over their black tie evening dress. The other man is COLONEL ARCHIBALD GRACIE, a mustachioed blowhard who still has his brandy snifter. He offers it to Rose, who is hunched over crying on a bench nearby, but she waves it away. Cal is more concerned with Jack. He grabs him by the lapels.

                              CAL
          What made you think you could put your hands on
          my fiancee?! Look at me, you filth! What did you think
          you were doing?!

                              ROSE
          Cal, stop! It was an accident.

                              CAL
          An accident?!

                              ROSE
          It was... stupid really. I was leaning over and I
          slipped.

Rose looks at Jack, getting eye contact.

                              ROSE
          I was leaning *way* over, to see the... ah... pro-
          pellers. And I slipped and I would have gone over-
          board... and Mr. Dawson here saved me and he almost
          went over himself.

                                                        (CONTINUED)

                              CAL
            You wanted to see the propellers?

                            GRACIE
                (shaking his head)
            Women and machinery do not mix.

                        MASTER AT ARMS
                (to Jack)
            Was that the way of it?

Rose is begging him with her eyes not to say what really happened.

                             JACK
            Uh huh. That was pretty much it.

He looks at Rose a moment longer. Now they have a secret together.

                        COLONEL GRACIE
            Well! The boy's a hero then. Good for you son, well
            done!
                (to Cal)
            So it's all's well and back to our brandy, eh?

Jack is uncuffed. Cal gets Rose to her feet and moving.

                              CAL
                (rubbing her arms)
            Let's get you in. You're freezing.

Cal is leaving without a second thought for Jack.

                            GRACIE
                (low)
            Ah... perhaps a little something for the boy?

                              CAL
            Oh, right. Mr. Lovejoy. A twenty should do it.

                             ROSE
            Is that the going rate for saving the woman you love?

                              CAL
            Rose is displeased. Mmm... what to do?

Cal turns back to Jack. He appraises him condescendingly... a steerage ruffian,
unwashed and ill-mannered.

                              CAL
            I know.
                (to Jack)
            Perhaps you could join us for dinner tomorrow, to
            regale our group with your heroic tale?

                                                          (CONTINUED)

Cal's personal valet, Spicer Lovejoy
(David Warner).

                              JACK
               (looking straight at Rose)
          Sure. Count me in.

                              CAL
          Good. Settled then.

Cal turns to go, putting a protective arm around Rose. He leans close to Gracie as
they walk away.

                              CAL
          This should be amusing.

                              JACK
               (as Lovejoy passes)
          Can I bum a cigarette?

Lovejoy smoothly draws a silver cigarette case from his jacket and snaps it open. Jack
takes a cigarette, then another, popping it behind his ear for later. Lovejoy lights
Jack's cigarette.

                              LOVEJOY
          You'll want to tie those.
               (Jack looks at his shoes)
          Interesting that the young lady slipped so mighty all
          of a sudden and you still had time to take off your
          jacket and shoes. Mmmm?

Lovejoy's expression is bland, but the eyes are cold. He turns away to join his
group.

                                                              CUT TO:

63   INT. ROSE'S BEDROOM - NIGHT   63

As she undresses for bed Rose sees Cal standing in her doorway, reflected in the
cracked mirror of her vanity. He comes toward her.

                              CAL
               (unexpectedly tender)
          I know you've been melancholy, and I don't pretend
          to know why.

From behind his back he hands her a large black velvet jewel case. She takes it,
numbly.

                              CAL
          I intended to save this till the engagement gala next
          week. But I thought tonight, perhaps a reminder of
          my feeling for you...

Rose slowly opens the box. Inside is the necklace... "HEART OF THE OCEAN" in all
its glory. It is huge... a malevolent blue stone glittering with an infinity of scalpel-
like inner reflections.

                                                              (CONTINUED)

The morph transi-
tion between
Scene 63 and 64 was
revised during produc-
tion to focus on Rose's
hands, saving the
"eye-morph" for the
more romantic Scene
100 when Jack
sketches Rose.

                              ROSE
          My God... Cal. Is it a—

                              CAL
          Diamond. Yes it is. 56 carats.

He takes the necklace and during the following places it around her
throat. He turns her to the mirror, standing behind her.

                              CAL
          It was once worn by Louis the Sixteenth. They call it
          Le Coeur de la Mer, the—

                              ROSE
          The Heart of the Ocean. Cal, it's... it's
          overwhelming.

He gazes at the image of the two of them in the mirror.

                              CAL
          It's for royalty. And we are royalty.

His fingers caress her neck and throat. He seems himself to be disarmed by
Rose's elegance and beauty. His emotion is, for the first time, unguarded.

                              CAL
          There's nothing I couldn't give you. There's nothing
          I'd deny you if you would not deny me. Open your
          heart to me, Rose.

CAMERA begins to TRACK IN ON ROSE. Closer and closer, during the following:

                              OLD ROSE (V.O.)
          Of course his gift was only to reflect light back onto
          himself, to illuminate the greatness that was Caledon
          Hockley. It was a cold stone... a heart of ice.

Finally, when Rose's eyes FILL FRAME, we MORPH SLOWLY to her eyes as they
are now... transforming through 84 years of life...

                                                            TRANSITION

64   INT. KELDYSH IMAGING SHACK   64

Without a cut the wrinkled, weathered landscape of age has appeared around her eyes.
But the eyes themselves are the same.

                              OLD ROSE
          After all these years, I can still feel it closing
          around my throat like a dog collar.

THE CAMERA PULLS BACK to show her whole face.

                                                            (CONTINUED)

*Delete through
scene 68*

CAMERON: "Scenes 64 through 67 were all shot and edited and worked beautifully by themselves. The morph transition from Rose's young hand holding the diamond to Old Rose's withered hand in the present was great. And the morph back
to the past went from a shot of the real wreck to the 1912 re-creation. But after the
decision to eliminate Brock Lovett's epiphany [See notes regarding Scene 28] these
scenes became a 'closed loop.' They led from A to B to C to D and then back to A
without any substantial changes to the characters or plot. They had to be cut."

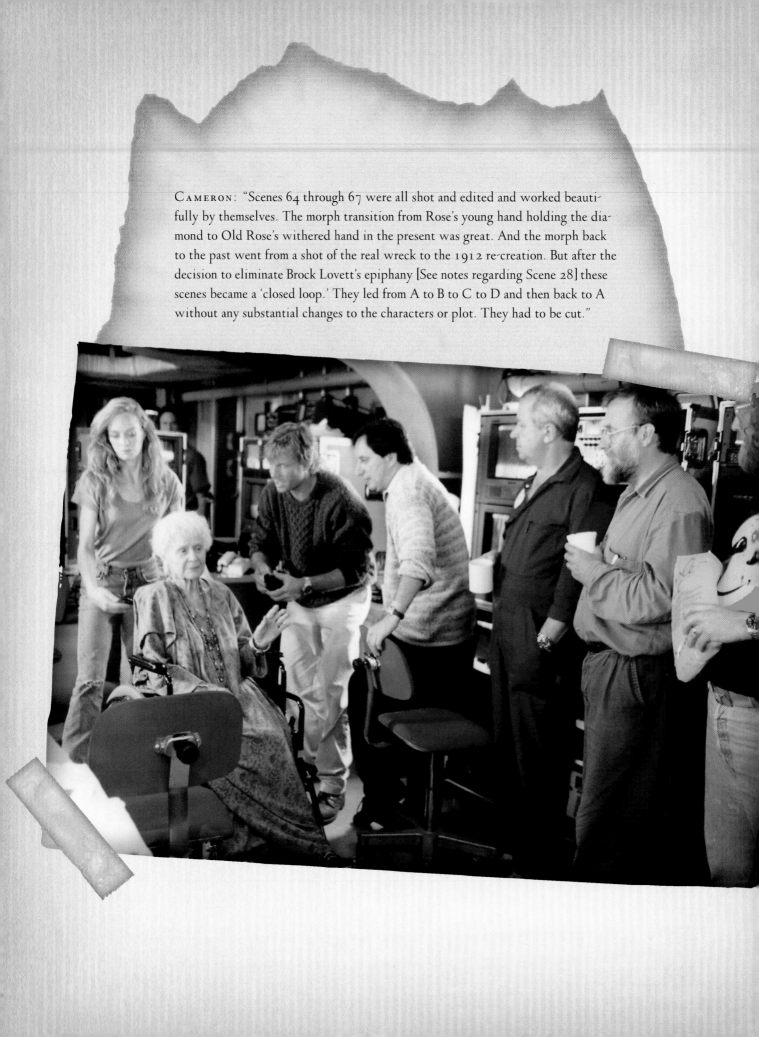

Deleted

                                        ROSE
                    I can still feel its weight. If you could have felt it,
                    not just seen it...

                                        LOVETT
                    Well, that's the general idea, my dear.

                                        BODINE
                    So let me get this right. You were gonna kill yourself
                    by jumping off the Titanic?
                            (he guffaws)
                    That's great!

                                        LOVETT
                            (warningly)
                    Lewis...

But Rose laughs with Bodine.

                                        BODINE
                            (still laughing)
                    All you had to do was wait two days!

Lovett, standing out of Rose's sightline, checks his watch. Hours have passed.
This process is taking too long.

                                        LOVETT
                    Rose, tell us more about the diamond. What did
                    Hockley do with it after that?

                                        ROSE
                    I'm afraid I'm feeling a little tired, Mr. Lovett.

Lizzy picks up the cue and starts to wheel her out.

                                        LOVETT
                    Wait! Can you give us something to go on, here.
                    Like who had access to the safe. What about this
                    Lovejoy guy? The valet. Did he have the
                    combination?

                                        LIZZY

                    That's enough.

Lizzy takes her out. Rose's old hand reappears at the doorway in a frail wave goodbye.

                                                            CUT TO:

65   EXT. LAUNCH AREA/KELDYSH DECK - NIGHT   65

As the big hydraulic jib swings one of the Mir subs out over the water. Lovett walks as he talks with Bobby Buell, the partners' rep. They weave among deck cranes, launch crew, sub maintenance guys.

                         BUELL
          The partners are pissed.

                         BROCK
          Bobby, buy me time. I need time.

                         BUELL
          We're running thirty thousand a day, and we're six
          days over. I'm telling you what they're telling me.
          The hand is on the plug. It's starting to pull.

                         BROCK
          Well you tell *the* hand I need another two days!
          Bobby, Bobby, Bobby... we're close! I smell it. I
          smell ice. She had the diamond on... now we just
          have to find out where it wound up. I just gotta work
          her a bit more. Okay?

Brock turns and sees Lizzy standing behind him. She has overheard the last part of his dialogue with Buell. He goes to her and hustles her away from Buell, toward a quiet spot on the deck.

                         BROCK
          Hey, Lizzy. I need to talk to you for a second.

                         LIZZY
          Don't you mean *work me*?

                         BROCK
          Look, I'm running out of time. I need your help.

                         LIZZY
          I'm not going to help you browbeat my hundred and
          one year old grandmother. I came down here to tell
          you to back off.

                         BROCK
              (with undisguised desperation)
          Lizzy... you gotta understand something. I've bet it
          all to find the Heart of the Ocean. I've got all my
          dough tied up in this thing. My wife even divorced me
          over this hunt. I need what's locked inside your
          grandma's memory.
              (he holds out his hand)
          You see this? Right here?

She looks at his hand, palm up. Empty. Cupped, as if around an imaginary shape.

                                                         (CONTINUED)

67 SNOOP DOG's P.O.V. ALTERNATION ANGLE FORMERLY 46-1

MATCH DISSOLVE FROM WRECK TO 1912 TITANIC B DECK

TRACKING

67 CONT. 46-1 CONT'D

ROSE ENTERS

TRACKING CONT'D

REVISED 5/6•0

65 CONTINUED: 65

                              LIZZY
          What?

                              BROCK
          That's the shape my hand's gonna be when I hold that
          thing. You understand? I'm not leaving here without
          it.

                              LIZZY
          Look, Brock, she's going to do this her way, in her
          own time. Don't forget, she contacted you. She's out
          here for her own reasons, God knows what they are.

                              LOVETT
          Maybe she wants to make peace with the past.

                              LIZZY
          What past? She has never once, not once, ever said a
          word about being on the Titanic until two days ago.

                              LOVETT
          Then we're all meeting your grandmother for the first
          time.

                              LIZZY
             (looks at him hard)
          You think she was really there?

                              LOVETT
          Oh, yeah. Yeah, I'm a believer. She was there.

                                                          CUT TO:

66 INT. IMAGING SHACK   66

Bodine starts the tape recorder. Rose is gazing at the screen, seeing THE LIVE FEED
FROM THE WRECK— SNOOP DOG is moving along the starboard side of the hull,
heading aft. The rectangular windows of A deck (forward) march past on the
right.

                              ROSE
          The next day, Saturday, I remember thinking how the
          sunlight felt.

                                                       DISSOLVE TO:

67 EXT. B DECK TITANIC - DAY   67

MATCH DISSOLVE from the rusting hulk to the gleaming new Titanic in 1912, passing
the end of the enclosed promenade just as Rose walks into the sunlight right in front of
us. She is stunningly dressed and walking with purpose.

                              OLD ROSE (V.O.)
          As if I hadn't felt the sun in years.

                                                       (CONTINUED)

CAMERON: "Ultimately, I felt like I only had time for one romance. I didn't think the audience would be willing to invest their emotional energy into following another couple. Fabrizio and Helga were to represent the hundreds of other lives intersecting, new relationships starting, that were ended abruptly and tragically by the sinking. I did miss showing that."

Deleted

CONTINUED:

IT IS SATURDAY APRIL 13, 1912. Rose unlatches the gate to go down into third class. The steerage men on the deck stop what they're doing and stare at her.

CUT TO:

INT. THIRD CLASS GENERAL ROOM

The social center of steerage life. It is stark by comparison to the opulence of first class, but is a loud, boisterous place. There are mothers with babies, kids running between the benches yelling in several languages and being scolded in several more. There are old women yelling, men playing chess, girls doing needlepoint and reading dime novels. There is even an upright piano and Tommy Ryan is noodling around on it.

Deleted

Three boys, shrieking and shouting, are scrambling around chasing a rat under the benches, trying to whomp it with a shoe and causing general havoc. Jack is playing with 5 year old CORA CARTMELL, drawing funny faces together in his sketchbook.

Fabrizio is struggling to get a conversation going with an attractive Norwegian girl, HELGA DAHL, sitting with her family at a table across the room.

                    FABRIZIO
          No Italian? Some little English?

                    HELGA
          No, no. Norwegian. Only.

Helga's eye is caught by something. Fabrizio looks, does a take ... and Jack, curious, follows their gaze to see ...

Rose, coming toward them. The activity in the room stops... a hush falls. Rose feels suddenly self-conscious as the steerage passengers stare openly at this princess, some with resentment, others with awe. She spots Jack and gives a little smile, walking straight to him. He rises to meet her, smiling.

                    ROSE
          Hello Jack.

Fabrizio and Tommy are floored. It's like the slipper fitting Cinderella.

                    JACK
          Hello again.

                    ROSE
          Could I speak to you in private?

                    JACK
          Uh, yes. Of course. After you.

He motions her ahead and follows. Jack glances over his shoulder, one eyebrow raised, as he walks out with her leaving a stunned silence.

CUT TO:

Having Jack rescue Rose may have been economical dramatically [See Scene 61], but Cameron realized it did not come without a price.

CAMERON: "Now you have to dig yourself out of a hole. For these two people to become romantically involved Jack has to get past her emotional confusion and Rose has to decide to stay with this uncouth steerage passenger when everything she's been taught is telling her to leave. They both have to move through these broad character arcs that usually take three or four scenes at least and complete them in only one."

The rewrite of Scene 69 came out of long discussions between Cameron, Winslet and DiCaprio during preproduction.

CAMERON: "We locked ourselves in the screening room at Lightstorm, which we were using as a rehearsal hall. We knew this scene was the pivot, the quintessence of Kate and Leo's on-screen relationship, so we worked on it for days.

I had Leo and Kate improvise the scene in their own words, but still in character, as if it were taking place present day. I video and audio taped the sessions. The night before we shot the actual scene, I played all the tapes back, made notes combining the best of all versions, then pounded out the scene. The actors had only a few hours to learn almost seven pages of dialogue. Considering these parameters, that this scene is a 10.0 in difficulty, I think it is 98% successful." (See page apx 9 for the rewritten Scene 69.)

scene rewritten

EXT. BOAT DECK - DAY

Jack and Rose walk side by side. They pass people reading and talking in steamer chairs, some of whom glance curiously at the mismatched couple. He feels out of place in his rough clothes. They are both awkward, for different reasons.

                          JACK
          So, you got a name by the way?

                          ROSE
          Rose. Rose DeWitt Bukater.

                          JACK
          That's quite a moniker. I may hafta get you to write
          that down.

Moved to scene 61

There is an awkward pause.

                          ROSE
          Mr. Dawson, I—

                          JACK
          Jack.

                          ROSE
          Jack... I feel like such an idiot. It took me all
          morning to get up the nerve to face you.

                          JACK
          Well, here you are.

                          ROSE
          Here I am. I... I want to thank you for what you did.
          Not just for... for pulling me back. But for your dis-
          cretion.

                          JACK
          You're welcome. Rose.

                          ROSE
          Look, I know what you must be thinking! Poor little
          rich girl. What does she know about misery?

                          JACK
          That's not what I was thinking. What I was thinking
          was... what could have happened to hurt this girl so
          much she thought she had no way out.

                          ROSE
          I don't... it wasn't just <u>one</u> thing. It was
          <u>everything</u>. It was <u>them</u>, it was their whole world. And
          I was trapped in it, like an insect in amber.
              (in a rush)
                          (MORE)

                                                        (CONTINUED)

Scene rewritten

> ROSE (cont'd)
> I just had to get away... just run and run and run...
> and then I was at the back rail and there was no more
> ship... even the <u>Titanic</u> wasn't big enough. Not
> enough to get away from <u>them</u>. And before I'd really
> thought about it, I was over the rail. I was so furi-
> ous. I'll show them. They'll sure be sorry!

> JACK
> Uh huh. They'll be sorry. `Course you'll be dead.

> ROSE
>   (she lowers her head)
> Oh God, I am such an utter fool.

> JACK
> That penguin last night, is he one of <u>them</u>?

> ROSE
> Penguin? Oh, Cal! He <u>is</u> them.

> JACK
> Is he your boyfriend?

> ROSE
> Worse I'm afraid.

She shows him her engagement ring. A sizable diamond.

> JACK
> Gawd look at that thing! You would have gone
> straight to the bottom.

They laugh together. A passing steward scowls at Jack, who is clearly not a first
class passenger, but Rose just glares him away.

> JACK
> So you feel like you're stuck on a train you can't get
> off 'cause you're marryin' this fella.

> ROSE
> Yes, exactly!

> JACK
> So don't marry him.

> ROSE
> If only it were that simple.

> JACK
> It is that simple.

> ROSE
> Oh, Jack... please don't judge me until you've seen
> my world.

(CONTINUED)

Scene rewritten

>   JACK
>   Well, I guess I will tonight.

Looking for another topic, any other topic, she indicates his sketchbook.

>   ROSE
>   What's this?

>   JACK
>   Just some sketches.

>   ROSE
>   May I?

The question is rhetorical because she has already grabbed the book. She sits on a deck chair and opens the sketchbook. ON JACK'S sketches... each one an expressive little bit of humanity: an old woman's hands, a sleeping man, a father and daughter at the rail. The faces are luminous and alive. His book is a celebration of the human condition.

>   ROSE
>   Jack, these are quite good! Really, they are.

>   JACK
>   Well, they didn't think too much of 'em in Paree.

Some loose sketches fall out and are taken by the wind. Jack scrambles after them... catching two, but the rest are gone, over the rail.

>   ROSE
>   Oh no! Oh, I'm so sorry. Truly!

>   JACK
>   Don't worry about it. Plenty more where they came
>   from.

He snaps his wrist, shaking his drawing hand in a flourish.

>   JACK
>   I just seem to spew 'em out. Besides, they're not
>   worth a damn anyway.

For emphasis he throws away the two he caught. They sail off.

>   ROSE
>   (laughing)
>   You're deranged!

She goes back to the book, turning a page.

>   ROSE
>   Well, well...

>   (CONTINUED)

scene rewritten

She has come upon a series of nudes. Rose is transfixed by the languid beauty he has
created. His nudes are soulful, real, with expressive hands and eyes. They feel more
like portraits than studies of the human form... almost uncomfortably intimate. Rose
blushes, raising the book as some strollers go by.

                    ROSE
          (trying to be very adult)
     And these were drawn from life?

                    JACK
     Yup. That's one of the great things about Paris. Lots
     of girls willing to take their clothes off.

She studies one drawing in particular, the girl posed half in sunlight, half in shadow.
Her hands lie at her chin, one furled and one open like a flower, languid and graceful.
The drawing is like an Alfred Steiglitz print of Georgia O'Keefe.

                    ROSE
     You liked this woman. You used her several times.

                    JACK
     She had beautiful hands.

                    ROSE
          (smiling)
     I think you must have had a love affair with her...

                    JACK
          (laughing)
     No, no! Just with her hands.

                    ROSE
          (looking up from the drawings)
     You have a gift, Jack. You do. You see people.

                    JACK
     I see you.

There it is. That piercing gaze again.

                    ROSE
     And...?

                    JACK
     You wouldn'ta jumped.

CUT TO:

70   INT. RECEPTION ROOM / D-DECK - DAY   70

Ruth is having tea with NOEL LUCY MARTHA DYER-EDWARDES, the COUNT-
ESS OF ROTHES, a 35ish English blue-blood with patrician features. Ruth
sees someone coming across the room and lowers her voice.

                                                          (CONTINUED)

In combining fiction with history, Cameron was concerned about showing events to which Rose could not have been a witness. The conversation between Captain Smith and J. Bruce Ismay is a perfect example. To Cameron's way of thinking, however, Old Rose has had decades to read the historical accounts of the sinking and incorporate the relevant information into her personal experience. It is a common technique in first-person narrative.

                              RUTH
          Oh no, that vulgar Brown woman is coming this way.
          Get up, quickly, before she sits with us.

Molly Brown walks up, greeting them cheerfully as they are rising.

                              MOLLY
          Hello girls, I was hoping I'd catch you at tea.

                              RUTH
          We're *awfully sorry* you missed it. The Countess and
          I are just off to take the air on the boat deck.

                              MOLLY
          That sounds great. Let's go. I need to catch up on the
          gossip.

Ruth grits her teeth as the three of them head for the Grand Staircase to go
up. TRACKING WITH THEM, as they cross the room, the SHOT HANDS OFF to
Bruce Ismay and Captain Smith at another table.

                              ISMAY
          So you've not lit the last four boilers then?

                              SMITH
          No, but we're making excellent time.

                              ISMAY
               (impatiently)
          Captain, the press knows the size of Titanic, let them
          marvel at her speed too. We must give them some-
          thing new to print. And the maiden voyage of
          Titanic must make headlines!

                              SMITH
          I prefer not to push the engines until they've been
          properly run in.

                              ISMAY
          Of course I leave it to your good offices to decide
          what's best, but what a glorious end to your last
          crossing if we get into New York Tuesday night and
          surprise them all.
               (Ismay slaps his hand on the table)
          Retire with a bang, eh, E.J.?

A beat. Then Smith nods, stiffly.

                                                              CUT TO:

The first half of Scene 71 was shot and ended with Rose striking a melodramatic silent movie pose for an anonymous "cinematograph enthusiast." In addition to the information we gain about Rose's character present in the text, additional dialogue was improvised in which Jack explained how his art was similar to the "Ash Can" school, a loosely affiliated group of artists who found their inspiration amidst the faces and venues of everyday life. (The movement never achieved the same level of celebrity as the post-impressionists.)

In losing the scene, Cameron lost one of the connections between Rose's desires for her life and the photographs next to Old Rose's bed representing their achievement. He was confident the audience would make the connection based on other scenes, such as the desire to ride horses at Santa Monica Beach mentioned in Scene 72 (which is the last photograph we see in the film before panning to Old Rose in bed). He also lost the A-side set-up of a private joke shared by Jack and Rose concerning caviar. (The B-side remains in the first-class dinner sequence, Scene 78, and plays unquestioned.)

Why did Cameron decide to cut the scene, other than for reasons of pacing? Cameron: "Watching the edited scene, I just began to get this twinge that the moment you hear a character talking about their dreams and aspirations you know they're going to die, like the guy in the war movie who can't wait to show you the snapshot of his wife and little girl. You just know he's a goner. I did miss the silent movie-style montage because that could have been fun for the characters and for the audience. But the studio was requesting cuts and the Marvins became sacrificial lambs."

71   EXT. A DECK PROMENADE - DAY   71

Rose and Jack stroll aft, past people lounging on deck chairs in the slanting late-after-
noon light. Stewards scurry to serve tea or hot cocoa.

                           ROSE
                   (girlish and excited)
               You know, my dream has always been to just chuck it
               all and become an artist... living in a garret, poor
               but free!

                           JACK
                   (laughing)
               You wouldn't last two days. There's no hot water,
               and hardly *ever* any caviar.

                           ROSE
                   (angry in a flash)
               Listen, buster... I hate caviar! And I'm tired of peo-
               ple dismissing my dreams with a chuckle and a pat on
               the head.

                           JACK
               I'm sorry. Really... I am.

                           ROSE
               Well, alright. There's something in me, Jack. I feel
               it. I don't know what it is, whether I should be an
               artist, or, I don't know... a dancer. Like Isadora
               Duncan... a wild pagan spirit...

She leaps forward, lands deftly and whirls like a dervish. Then she sees something
ahead and her face lights up.

                           ROSE
               ...or a <u>moving picture actress!</u>

She takes his hand and runs, pulling him along the deck toward—

DANIEL AND MARY MARVIN. Daniel is cranking the big wooden movie camera as
she poses stiffly at the rail.

                           MARVIN
               You're sad. Sad, sad, sad. You've left your lover on
               the shore. You may never see him again. Try to be
               sadder, darling.

SUDDENLY Rose shoots into the shot and strikes a theatrical pose at the rail next to
Mary. Mary bursts out laughing. Rose pulls Jack into the picture and makes him pose.

Marvin grins and starts yelling and gesturing. We see this in CUTS, with music
and no dialogue.

                                                            (CONTINUED)

scenes with Marvins not shot

71 CONTINUED:

Deleted - never shot

SERIES OF CUTS:

Rose posing tragically at the rail, the back of her hand to her forehead.

Jack on a deck chair, pretending to be a Pasha, the two girls pantomiming fanning him like slave girls.

Jack, on his knees, pleading with his hands clasped while Rose, standing, turns her head in bored disdain.

Rose cranking the camera, while Daniel and Jack have a western shoot-out. Jack wins and leers into the lens, twirling an air mustache like Snidely Whiplash.

                                                              CUT TO:

72   EXT. A DECK PROMENADE / AFT - SUNSET   72

Painted with orange light, Jack and Rose lean on the A-deck rail aft, shoulder to shoulder. The ship's lights come on.

It is a magical moment... perfect.

                          ROSE
        So then what, Mr. Wandering Jack?

                          JACK
        Well, then logging got to be too much like work, so I
        went down to Los Angeles to the pier in Santa Monica.
        That's a swell place, they even have a rollercoaster.
        I sketched portraits there for ten cents a piece.

                          ROSE
        A whole ten cents?!

                          JACK
            (not getting it)
        Yeah, it was great money... I could make a dollar a
        day, sometimes. But only in summer. When it got
        cold, I decided to go to Paris and see what the real
        artists were doing.

                          ROSE
            (looks at the dusk sky)
        Why can't I be like you, Jack? Just head out for the
        horizon whenever I feel like it.
            (turning to him)
        Say we'll go there, sometime... to that pier... even
        if we only ever just talk about it.

                          JACK
        Alright, we're going. We'll drink cheap beer and go
        on the rollercoaster until we throw up and we'll ride
                          (MORE)

                                                              (CONTINUED)

CAMERON: "The studio, the other producers and even the actors all thought the spitting scene vulgar, not in keeping with the *Titanic* legend. But I feel that's what's great about it. People are going to this movie expecting a certain creaky formality that they've always seen associated with historical dramas. Then here comes this scene which turns that on its head. On an emotional level, it is the exact moment that Rose steps into Jack's world. Also, Rose is very educated and mature for 17, and Jack is a very street smart 20. When they start spitting over the side, they both become kids again. I told Kate that I felt we needed the scene so the audience could see her as a girl. By the time we got to rehearsals, Kate and Leo were happy with the scene. Audiences seem to respond to it, too, and that's very satisfying to me as a writer."

                              JACK (cont'd)
          horses on the beach... right in the surf... but you
          have to ride like a cowboy, none of that side-saddle
          stuff.

                              ROSE
          You mean one leg on each side? Scandalous! Can you
          show me?

                              JACK

          Sure. If you like.

                              ROSE
              (smiling at him)
          I think I would.
              (she looks at the horizon)
          And teach me to spit too. Like a man. Why should
          only men be able to spit. It's unfair.

                              JACK
          They didn't teach you that in finishing school? Here,
          it's easy. Watch closely.

He spits. It arcs out over the water.

                              JACK
          Your turn.

Rose screws up her mouth and spits. A pathetic little bit of foamy spittle which
mostly runs down her chin before falling off into the water.

                              JACK
          Nope, that was pitiful. Here, like this... you hawk it
          down... HHHNNNK!... then roll it on your tongue,
          up to the front, like thith, then a big breath and
          PLOOOW!! You see the range on that thing?

She goes through the steps. Hawks it down, etc. He coaches her through it (ad lib)
while doing the steps himself. She lets fly. So does he. Two comets of gob fly out over
the water.

                              JACK
          That was great!

Rose turns to him, her face alight. Suddenly she blanches. He sees her expression
and turns.

RUTH, the Countess of Rothes, and Molly Brown have been watching them
hawking lugees. Rose becomes instantly composed.

                              ROSE
          Mother, may I introduce Jack Dawson.

                              RUTH
          Charmed, I'm sure.

                                                              (CONTINUED)

Jack has a little spit running down his chin. He doesn't know it. Molly Brown
is grinning. As Rose proceeds with the introductions, we hear...

                    OLD ROSE (V.O.)
          The others were gracious and curious about the man
          who'd saved my life. But my mother looked at him
          like an insect. A dangerous insect which must be
          squashed quickly.

                    MOLLY
          Well, Jack, it sounds like you're a good man to have
          around in a sticky spot—

They all jump as a BUGLER sounds the meal call right behind them.

                    MOLLY
          Why do they insist on announcing dinner like a damn
          cavalry charge?

                    ROSE
          Shall we go dress, mother?
             (over her shoulder)
          See you at dinner, Jack.

                    RUTH
             (as they walk away)
          Rose, look at you... out in the sun with no hat.
          Honestly!

The Countess exits with Ruth and Rose, leaving Jack and Molly alone on
deck.

                    MOLLY
          Son, do you have the slightest comprehension of what
          you're doing?

                    JACK
          Not really.

                    MOLLY
          Well, you're about to go into the snakepit. I hope
          you're ready. What are you planning to wear?

Jack looks down at his clothes. Back up at her. He hadn't thought about
that.

                    MOLLY
          I figured.

                                                                  CUT TO:

73   INT. MOLLY BROWN'S STATEROOM   73

Men's suits and jackets and formal wear are strewn all over the place. Molly is having a fine time. Jack is dressed, except for his jacket, and Molly is tying his bow
tie.

                                                            (CONTINUED)

In the film, Molly refers to her son rather than her husband because, by 1912, she and her husband were already separated.

In the "scriptment" Rose originally purchases Jack's formal wear for him at a small men's store on board. Not only did this scenario lack the fairytale surprise for Rose of seeing Jack appear perfectly dressed like a male version of Cinderella, but it also indebted Jack to Rose in a way that might impede the relationship. History provided an elegant solution. Historian Don Lynch: "The barber shop on *Titanic* sold many things, but nothing like Jack would have needed, because first-class passengers were expected to bring adequate dining attire with them for the journey." It was Lynch who suggested that Molly Brown might have been carrying clothes back from Europe for her family.

                              MOLLY
            Don't feel bad about it. My husband still can't tie
            one of these damn things after 20 years. There you go.

She picks up a jacket off the bed and hands it to him. Jack goes into the bathroom to put
it on. Molly starts picking up the stuff off the bed.

                              MOLLY
            I gotta buy everything in three sizes 'cause I never
            know how much he's been eating while I'm away.

She turns and sees him, though we don't.

                              MOLLY
            My, my, my... you shine up like a new penny.

                                                                    CUT TO:

74   EXT. BOAT DECK/ FIRST CLASS ENTRANCE - DUSK   74

A purple sky, shot with orange, in the west. Drifting strains of classical music.
We TRACK WITH JACK along the deck. By Edwardian standards he looks badass.
Dashing in his borrowed white-tie outfit, right down to his pearl studs.

A steward bows and smartly opens the door to the First Class Entrance.

                              STEWARD
            Good evening, sir.

Jack plays the role smoothly. Nods with just the right degree of disdain.

                                                                    CUT TO:

75   INT. UPPER LANDING/GRAND STAIRCASE AND A-DECK   75

Jack steps in and his breath is taken away by the splendor spread out before him.
Overhead is the enormous glass dome, with a crystal chandelier at its center.
Sweeping down six stories is the First Class Grand Staircase, the epitome of the
opulent naval architecture of the time.

And the people: the women in their floor length dresses, elaborate hairstyles and abun-
dant jewelry... the gentlemen in evening dress, standing with one hand at the small of
the back, talking quietly.

Jack descends to A deck. Several men nod a perfunctory greeting. He nods back,
keeping it simple. He feels like a spy.

Cal comes down the stairs, with Ruth on his arm, covered in jewelry. They both walk
right past Jack, neither one recognizing him. Cal nods at him, one gent to another. But
Jack barely has time to be amused. Because just behind Cal and Ruth on the stairs is
Rose, a vision in red and black, her low-cut dress showing off her neck and shoulders,
her arms sheathed in white gloves that come well above the elbow. Jack is hypnotized by her beauty.

                                                                    (CONTINUED)

In the movie, after Cal tells Jack that he "could almost pass for a gentleman," Jack responds with the line, "Almost." Cameron: "As we rehearsed the scene it seemed stronger to give Jack the last word. He may be in Cal's territory but he's still playing by his own rules."

In addition to reasons of pacing, Cameron felt that DiCaprio had nailed the "nose up" concept visually in the previous scene and deleted the line here. A minor rearrangement of beats created a better flow to the scene.

CLOSE ON ROSE, as she approaches Jack. He imitates the gentlemen's stance, hand behind his back. She extends her gloved hand and he takes it, kissing the backs of her fingers. Rose flushes, beaming noticeably. She can't take her eyes off him.

                        JACK
          I saw that in a nickelodeon once, and I always wanted
          to do it.

                        ROSE
          Cal, surely you remember Mr. Dawson.

                        CAL
             (caught off guard)
          Dawson! I didn't recognize you.
             (studies him)
          Amazing! You could almost pass for a gentleman.

                                                      CUT TO:

76   INT. D-DECK RECEPTION ROOM   76

CUT TO THE RECEPTION ROOM ON D DECK, as the party descends to dinner. They encounter Molly Brown, looking good in a beaded dress, in her own busty broad-shouldered way. Molly grins when she sees Jack. As they are going into the dining saloon she walks next to him, speaking low:

                        MOLLY
          Ain't nothin' to it, is there, Jack?

                        JACK
          Yeah, you just dress like a pallbearer and keep your
          nose up.

                        MOLLY
          Remember, the only thing they respect is money, so
          just act like you've got a lot of it and you're in the
          club.

As they enter the swirling throng, Rose leans close to him, pointing out several notables.

                        ROSE
          There's the Countess Rothes. And that's John Jacob
          Astor... the richest man on the ship. His little wifey
          there, Madeleine, is my age and in a delicate condition.
          See how she's trying to hide it. Quite the scandal.
             (nodding toward a couple)
          And over there, that's Sir Cosmo and Lucile, Lady
          Duff-Gordon. She designs naughty lingerie, among
          her many talents. Very popular with the royals.

Cal becomes engrossed in a conversation with Cosmo Duff-Gordon and Colonel Gracie, while Ruth, the Countess and Lucile discuss fashion. Rose pivots Jack smoothly, to show him another couple, dressed impeccably.

                                                      (CONTINUED)

In the film, Jack's "Chippewa Falls Dawsons, actually" line gets a nice laugh, but it was also intended to have a payoff of its own in a deleted confrontation with Lovejoy (See Scene 213). Cameron cut Madeleine's line about being spoken for because Eric Braeden's reaction as John Jacob Astor put a nice comic button on the scene.

ROSE
And that's Benjamin Guggenheim and his mistress,
Madame Aubert. *Mrs.* Guggenheim is at home with
the children, of course.

Cal, meanwhile, is accepting the praise of his male counterparts, who are
looking at Rose like a prize show horse.

SIR COSMO
Hockley, she is splendid.

CAL
Thank you.

Deleted in post for pacing

GRACIE
Cal's a lucky man. I know him well, and it can <u>only</u>
be luck.

Ruth steps over, hearing the last. She takes Cal's arm, somewhat
coquettishly.

RUTH
How can you say that Colonel? Caledon Hockley is a
great catch.

The entourage strolls toward the dining saloon, where they run into the
Astors going through the ornate double doors.

ROSE
J.J., Madeleine, I'd like you to meet Jack Dawson.

ASTOR
(shaking his hand)
Good to meet you Jack. Are you of the Boston
Dawsons?

JACK
No, the Chippewa Falls Dawsons, actually.

J.J. nods as if he's heard of them, then looks puzzled. Madeleine Astor appraises Jack
and whispers girlishly to Rose:

MADELEINE
It's a pity we're both spoken for, isn't it?

CUT TO:

77   INT. DINING SALOON   77

Like a ballroom at the palace, alive and lit by a constellation of chandeliers, full of elegantly dressed people and beautiful music from BANDLEADER WALLACE HARTLEY'S
small orchestra. As Rose and Jack enter and move across the room to their table, Cal
and Ruth beside them, we hear...

(CONTINUED)

changed to "heir to a railroad fortune."

John Jacob Astor (Eric Braeden)

Benjamin Guggenheim (Michael Ensign) and his mistress Madame Aubert (Fannie Brett)

                              OLD ROSE (V.O.)
          He must have been nervous but he never faltered.
          They assumed he was one of them... a young captain
          of industry perhaps... new money, obviously, but
          still a member of the club. Mother of course, could
          always be counted upon...

                                                         CUT TO:

78   INT. DINING SALOON   78

CLOSE ON RUTH.

                              RUTH
          Tell us of the accommodations in steerage, Mr.
          Dawson. I hear they're quite good on this ship.

WIDER: THE TABLE. Jack is seated opposite Rose, who is flanked by Cal and
Thomas Andrews. Also at the table are Molly Brown, Ismay, Colonel Gracie,
the Countess, Guggenheim, Madame Aubert, and the Astors.

                              JACK
          The best I've seen, m'am. Hardly any rats.

Rose motions surreptitiously for Jack to take his napkin off his plate.

                              CAL
          Mr. Dawson is joining us from third class. He was of
          some assistance to my fiancee last night.
              (to Jack, as if to a child)
          This is foie gras. It's goose liver.

We see whispers exchanged. Jack becomes the subject of furtive glances. Now they're
all feeling terribly liberal and dangerous.

                              GUGGENHEIM
              (low, to Madame Aubert)
          What is Hockley hoping to prove, bringing this...
          bohemian... up here?

                              WAITER
              (to Jack)
          How do you take your caviar, sir?   *Deleted in post*
                                                              for Pacing
                              CAL
              (answering for him)
          Just a soupcon of lemon...
              (to Jack, smiling)
           ... it improves the flavor with champagne.

                              JACK
              (to the waiter)
          No caviar for me, thanks.
                              (MORE)

                                                         (CONTINUED)

Jack's refusal of the caviar was originally a shared secret with Rose, a direct reference to dialogue from the eliminated Scene 71.

                              JACK (cont'd)
              (to Cal)
          Never did like it much.

He looks at Rose, pokerfaced, and she smiles.

                              RUTH
          And where exactly do you live, Mr. Dawson?

                              JACK
          Well, right now my address is the RMS Titanic. After
          that, I'm on God's good humor.

Salad is served. Jack reaches for the fish fork. Rose gives him a look and picks up
the salad fork, prompting him with her eyes. He changes forks.

                              RUTH
          You find that sort of rootless existence appealing, do
          you?

                              JACK
          Well... it's a big world, and I want to see it all before I
          go. My father was always talkin' about goin' to see
          the ocean. He died in the town he was born in, and
          never did see it. You can't wait around, because you
          never know what hand you're going to get dealt next.
          See, my folks died in a fire when I was fifteen, and
          I've been on the road since. Somethin' like that
          teaches you to take life as it comes at you.
          To make each day count.

Dialogue rewritten the night before shooting

Molly Brown raises her glass in a salute.

                              MOLLY
          Well said, Jack.

                         COLONEL GRACIE
              (raising his glass)
          Here, here.

Rose raises her glass, looking at Jack.

                              ROSE
          To making it count.

Ruth, annoyed that Jack has scored a point, presses him further.

                              RUTH
          How is it you have the means to travel, Mr. Dawson?

                              JACK
          I work my way from place to place. Tramp steamers
          and such. I won my ticket on Titanic here in a lucky
          hand at poker.
                              (MORE)

                                                            (CONTINUED)

The dinner scene as presented in the film eliminates some dialogue and juxtaposes beats to focus more on the verbal duel between Ruth and Jack, a process which included the addition of Jack's "life's a gift and I don't intend on wasting it" speech. Cameron added this dialogue the night before shooting.

                              JACK (cont'd)
                    (he glances at Rose)
               A very lucky hand.

                              GRACIE
               All life is a game of luck.

                               CAL
               A real man makes his own luck, Archie.

Rose notices that Thomas Andrews, sitting next to her, is writing in his note-
book, completely ignoring the conversation.

                              ROSE
               Mr. Andrews, what are you doing? I see you
               everywhere writing in this little book.
                    (grabs it and reads)
               Increase number of screws in hat hooks from 2 to 3.
               You built the biggest ship in the world and this
               preoccupies you?!

Andrews smiles sheepishly.

                              ISMAY
               He knows every rivet in her, don't you Thomas?

                              ANDREWS
               All three million of them.   Deleted
                                                             in post

                              ISMAY
               His blood and soul are in this ship. She may be mine
               on paper, but in the eyes of God she belongs to
               Thomas Andrews.

                              ROSE
               Your ship is a wonder, Mr. Andrews. Truly.

                              ANDREWS
               Thank you, Rose.

We see that Andrews has come under Rose's spell.

79   TIME TRANSITION: Dessert has been served and a waiter arrives with cigars   79
      in a humidor on a wheeled cart. The men start clipping ends and lighting.

                              ROSE
                    (low, to Jack)
               Next it'll be brandies in the Smoking Room.

                              GRACIE
                    (rising)
               Well, join me for a brandy, gentlemen?

                                                             (CONTINUED)

                             ROSE
          (low)
       Now they retreat into a cloud of smoke and
       congratulate each other on being masters of the
       universe.

                           GRACIE
       Joining us, Dawson? You don't want to stay out here
       with the women, do you?

Actually he *does*, but...

                           JACK
       No thanks. I'm heading back.

                           CAL
       Probably best. It'll be all business and politics,
       that sort of thing. Wouldn't interest you. Good of you
       to come.

Cal and the other gentlemen exit.

                           ROSE
       Jack, must you go?

                           JACK
       Time for my coach to turn back into a pumpkin.

[handwritten note: DiCaprio ad libbed the line, "Time for me to go row with the other slaves."]

He leans over to take her hand.

INSERT: We see him slip a tiny folded note into her palm.

Ruth, scowling, watches him walk away across the enormous room. Rose surreptitiously opens the note below table level. It reads: "Make it count. Meet me at the clock".

                                                   CUT TO:

80   INT. A-DECK FOYER - NIGHT   80

Rose crosses the A-Deck foyer, sighting Jack at the landing above. Overhead is the crystal dome. Jack has his back to her, studying the ornate clock with its carved figures of Honor and Glory. It softly strikes the hour.

MOVING WITH ROSE as she goes up the sweeping staircase toward him. He turns, sees her... smiles.

                           JACK
       Want to go to a real party?

                                                    CUT TO:

                                         (CONTINUED)

Titanic's ad hoc third class band (Gaelic Storm).

While it is not referenced in the screenplay, the "script-ment" indicated the brief humorous cutaway from the frenzied dancing below decks to the shockingly hushed and staid atmosphere of the first-class Smoking Room.

Crowded and alive with music, laughter and raucous carrying on. An ad hoc band is gathered near the upright piano, honking out lively stomping music on fiddle, accordion and tambourine. People of all ages are dancing, drinking beer and wine, smoking, laughing, even brawling.

Tommy hands Rose a pint of stout and she hoists it. Jack meanwhile dances with 5 year old Cora Cartmell, or tries to, with her standing on his feet. As the tune ends, Rose leans down to the little girl.

                         ROSE
            May I cut in, miss?

                         JACK
            You're still my best girl, Cora.

Cora scampers off. Rose and Jack face each other. She is trembling as he takes her right hand in his left. His other hand slides to the small of her back. It is an electrifying moment.

                         ROSE
            I don't know the steps.

                         JACK
            Just move with me. Don't think.

The music starts and they are off. A little awkward at first, she starts to get into it. She grins at Jack as she starts to get the rhythm of the steps.

                         ROSE
            Wait... stop!

She bends down, pulling off her high heeled shoes, and flings them to Tommy. Then she grabs Jack and they plunge back into the fray, dancing faster as the music speeds up.

                                                CUT TO:

82   INT. THIRD CLASS GENERAL ROOM   82

The scene is rowdy and rollicking. A table gets knocked over as a drunk crashes into it. And in the middle of it... Rose dancing with Jack in her stocking feet. The steps are fast and she shines with sweat. A space opens around them, and people watch them, clapping as the band plays faster and faster.

FABRIZIO AND HELGA. Dancing has obviated the need for a common language. He whirls her, then she responds by whirling him... Fabrizio's eyes go wide when he realizes she's stronger than he is.

The tune ends in a mad rush. Jack steps away from Rose with a flourish, allowing her to take a bow. Exhilarated and slightly tipsy, she does a graceful ballet *plié*, feet turned out perfectly. Everyone laughs and applauds. Rose is a hit with the steerage folks, who've never had a lady party with them.

                                                (CONTINUED)

They move to a table, flushed and sweaty. Rose grabs Fabrizio's cigarette and takes a big drag. She's feeling cocky. Fabrizio is grinning, holding hands with Helga.

                         JACK
        How you two doin'?

                       FABRIZIO
        I don't know what she's say, she don't know what I
        say, so we get along fine.

Deleted in editing

Tommy walks up with a pint for each of them. Rose chugs hers, showing off.

                         ROSE
        You think a first class girl can't drink?

Everybody else is dancing again, and Bjorn Gundersen crashes into Tommy, who sloshes his beer over Rose's dress. She laughs, not caring. But Tommy lunges, grabbing Bjorn and wheeling him around.

                        TOMMY
        You stupid bastard!!

Bjorn comes around, his fists coming up... and Jack leaps into the middle of it, pushing them apart.

                         JACK
        Boys, boys! Did I ever tell you the one about the
        Swede and the Irishman goin' to the whorehouse?

Tommy stands there, all piss and vinegar, chest puffed up. Then he grins and claps Bjorn on the shoulder.

                         ROSE
        So, you think you're big tough men? Let's see you do
        this.

In her stocking feet she assumes a ballet stance, arms raised, and goes up on point, taking her entire weight on the tips of her toes. The guys gape at her incredible muscle control. She comes back down, then her face screws up in pain. She grabs one foot, hopping around.

                         ROSE
        Oooowww! I haven't done that in years.

Jack catches her as she loses her balance, and everyone cracks up.

THE DOOR to the well deck is open a few inches as Lovejoy watches through the gap. He sees Jack holding Rose, both of them laughing.

LOVEJOY closes the door.

                                                       CUT TO:

Scene 83 was eliminated during post not only for pacing, but because Cameron liked the contrast of going from Rose feeling totally carefree at the party to Rose suffocating under the oppression of her probable future during breakfast with Cal.

One casualty of the scene's loss was the first occurrence of the song "Come Josephine in my Flying Machine," a popular tune which Jack later sings to Rose before they kiss at the bow (Scene 94) and which Rose sings to herself as she floats on the ice (Scene 274).

The stars blaze overhead, so bright and clear you can see the Milky Way. Rose and Jack walk along the row of lifeboats. Still giddy from the party, they are singing a popular song "Come Josephine in My Flying Machine".

>   JACK/ ROSE
> Come Josephine in my flying machine
> And it's up she goes! Up she goes!
> In the air she goes. Where? There she goes!

They fumble the words and break down laughing. They have reached the First Class Entrance, but don't go straight in, not wanting the evening to end. Through the doors the sound of the ship's orchestra wafts gently. Rose grabs a davit and leans back, staring at the cosmos.

>   ROSE
> Look. Isn't it magnificent? So grand and endless.

She goes to the rail and leans on it.

>   ROSE
> They're such small people, Jack... my crowd. They
> think they're giants on the earth, but they're not
> even dust in God's eye. They live inside this little
> tiny champagne bubble... and someday the bubble's
> going to burst.

He leans at the rail next to her, his hand just touching hers. It is the slightest contact imaginable, and all either one of them can feel is that square inch of skin where their hands are touching.

>   JACK
> You're not one of them. There's been a mistake.

>   ROSE
> A mistake?

>   JACK
> Uh huh. You got mailed to the wrong address.

>   ROSE
>   (laughing)
> I did, didn't I?
>   (pointing suddenly)
> Look! A shooting star.

>   JACK
> That was a long one. My father used to say that
> whenever you saw one, it was a soul going to heaven.

>   ROSE
> I like that. Aren't we supposed to wish on it?

>   (CONTINUED)

Deleted

CONTINUED:

Jack looks at her, and finds that they are suddenly very close together. It would be so easy to move another couple of inches, to kiss her. Rose seems to be thinking the same thing.

> JACK
> What would you wish for?

After a beat, Rose pulls back.

> ROSE
> Something I can't have.
> (she smiles sadly)
> Goodnight, Jack. And thank you.

She leaves the rail and hurries through the First Class Entrance

> JACK
> Rose!!

But the door bangs shut, and she is gone. Back to her world.

CUT TO:

84   INT. ROSE AND CAL'S SUITE / PRIVATE PROMENADE - DAY   84

SUNDAY APRIL 14, 1912. A bright clear day. Sunlight splashing across the promenade. Rose and Cal are having breakfast in silence. The tension is palpable. Trudy Bolt, in her maid's uniform, pours the coffee and goes inside.

> CAL
> I had hoped you would come to me last night.

> ROSE
> I was tired.

> CAL
> Yes. Your exertions below decks were no doubt exhausting.

> ROSE
> (stiffening)
> I see you had that undertaker of a manservant follow me.

> CAL
> You will never behave like that again! Do you understand?

> ROSE
> I'm not some foreman in your mills that you can command! I am your fiancee—

(CONTINUED)

The scene as written was for Rose to lace Ruth's corset but Cameron decided before shooting that the reverse situation would be more dramatically powerful.

CAMERON: "The corset sort of defines Ruth's generation. By 1912 younger women were more interested in the 'Empire' waist and its more flowing look and it would have been less likely that Rose wore a corset. And yet the best way to reveal character is by action, so the act of corseting Rose more strongly underlines Ruth's character and helps the audience viscerally feel how trapped Rose is."

Cal explodes, sweeping the breakfast china off the table with a crash. He moves to her in one shocking moment, glowering over her and gripping the sides of her chair, so she is trapped between his arms.

> CAL
> Yes! You are! And my wife... in practice, if not yet by law. So you will honor me, as a wife is required to honor her husband! I will not be made out a fool! Is this in any way unclear?

Rose shrinks into the chair. She sees Trudy, frozen, partway through the door bringing the orange juice. Cal follows Rose's glance and straightens up. He stalks past the maid, entering the stateroom.

> ROSE
> We... had a little accident. I'm sorry, Trudy.

CUT TO:

85   INT. RUTH'S SUITE - DAY   85

Rose is dressed for the day, and is in the middle of helping Ruth with her corset. The tight bindings do not inhibit Ruth's fury at all.

> RUTH
> You are not to see that boy again, do you understand me Rose? I forbid it!

Rose has her knee at the base of her mother's back and is pulling the corset strings with both hands.

> ROSE
> Oh, stop it, Mother. You'll give yourself a nosebleed.

Ruth pulls away from her, and crosses to the door, locking it. CLACK!

> RUTH
> (wheeling on her)
> Rose, this is not a game! Our situation is precarious. You know the money's gone!

> ROSE
> Of course I know it's gone. You remind me every day!

> RUTH
> Your father left us nothing but a legacy of bad debts hidden by a good name. And that name is the only card we have to play.

Rose turns her around and grabs the corset strings again. Ruth sucks in her waist and Rose pulls.

(CONTINUED)

> RUTH
>
> I don't understand you. It is a fine match with
> Hockley, and it will insure our survival.

> ROSE
>
> (hurt and lost)
> How can you put this on my shoulders?

Ruth turns to her, and we see what Rose sees—the naked fear in her
mother's eyes.

> RUTH
>
> Do you want to see me working as a seamstress? Is
> that what you want? Do you want to see our fine
> things sold at auction, our memories scattered to the
> winds? My God, Rose, how can you be so selfish?

> ROSE
>
> It's so unfair.

> RUTH
>
> Of course it's unfair! We're women. Our choices are
> never easy.

Rose pulls the corset tighter.

                                                              CUT TO:

86   INT. FIRST CLASS DINING SALOON   86

At the divine service, Captain Smith is leading a large group in the hymn "Almighty
Father Strong To Save." Rose and Ruth sing in the middle of the group.

Lovejoy stands well back, keeping an eye on Rose. He notices a commotion at the
entry doors. Jack has been halted there by two stewards. He is dressed in his
third class clothes, and stands there, hat in hand, looking out of place.

> STEWARD
>
> Look, you, you're not supposed to be in here.

> JACK
>
> I was just here last night... don't you remember?
> (seeing Lovejoy coming toward him)
> He'll tell you.

> LOVEJOY
>
> Mr. Hockley and Mrs. DeWitt Bukater continue to be
> most appreciative of your assistance. They asked me
> to give you this in gratitude—

He holds out two twenty dollar bills, which Jack refuses to take.

                                                              (CONTINUED)

                                    JACK
                I don't want money, I—

                                  LOVEJOY
                —and also to remind you that you hold a third class
                ticket and your presence here is no longer appropriate.

Jack spots Rose but she doesn't see him.

                                    JACK
                I just need to talk to Rose for a—

                                  LOVEJOY
                Gentlemen, please see that Mr. Dawson gets back
                where he belongs.
                     (giving the twenties to the stewards)
                And that he stays there.

                                  STEWARD
                Yes sir!
                     (to Jack)
                Come along you.

END ON ROSE, not seeing Jack hustled out.

                                    ROSE
                     (singing)
                *O hear us when we cry to thee for those in peril
                on the sea.*

                                                            CUT TO:

87   INT. GYMNASIUM - DAY   87

An Edwardian nautilus room. There are machines we recognize, and some we don't.
A woman pedals a stationary bicycle in a long dress, looking ridiculous. Thomas
Andrews is leading a small tour group, including Rose, Ruth and Cal. Cal is working
the oars of a stationary rowing machine with a well trained stroke.

                                    CAL
                Reminds me of my Harvard days.

T.W. McCAULEY, the gym instructor, is a bouncy little man in white flannels, eager
to show off his modern equipment, like his present-day counterpart on an "Abflex"
infomercial. He hits a switch and a machine with a saddle on it starts to undulate.
Rose puts her hand on it, curious.

                                  MCCAULEY
                The electric horse is very popular. We even have an
                electric camel.
                     (to Ruth)
                Care to try your hand at the rowing, m'am?

                                                        (CONTINUED)

Cut for Pacing

The tour of the gymnasium was shot but deleted in post for pacing. This eliminated Ruth's ironic line about rowing, which would have come back to haunt her during the lifeboat scenes as she struggles with the oars. Both sequences were cut.

87 CONTINUED: 87

                                RUTH
              Don't be absurd. I can't think of a skill I should
              likely <u>need less.</u>

                                ANDREWS
              The next stop on our tour will be the bridge. This
              way, please.

                                                          CUT TO:

88 EXT. AFT WELL DECK, B-DECK AND A-DECK - DAY   88

    Jack, walking with determination, is followed closely by Tommy and Fabrizio. He
    quickly climbs the steps to B-Deck and steps over the gate separating 3rd from 2nd
    class.

                                TOMMY
              She's a goddess amongst mortal men, there's no
              denyin'. But she's in another world, Jackie, forget
              her. She's closed the door.

    Jack moves furtively to the wall below the A-Deck promenade, aft.

                                JACK
              It was them, not her.
                   (glancing around the deck)
              Ready... go.

    Tommy shakes his head resignedly and puts his hands together, crouching down.
    Jack steps into Tommy's hands and gets boosted up to the next deck, where he
    scrambles nimbly over the railing, onto the First Class deck.

                                TOMMY
              He's not bein' logical, I tell ya.   *Deleted in post*

                                FABRIZIO
              Amore is'a not logical.

                                                          CUT TO:

89 EXT. A-DECK / AFT - DAY   89

    A man is playing with his son, who is spinning a top with a string. The man's overcoat
    and hat are sitting on a deck chair nearby. Jack emerges from behind one of the huge
    deck cranes and calmly picks up the coat and bowler hat. He walks away, slipping into
    the coat, and slicks his hair back with spit. Then puts the hat on at a jaunty angle. At
    a distance he could pass for a gentleman.

                                                          CUT TO:

90 INT. BRIDGE/ CHARTROOM - DAY   90

    HAROLD BRIDE, the 21 year old Junior Wireless Operator, hustles in and skirts
    around Andrews' tour group to hand a Marconigram to Captain Smith.

                                                          (CONTINUED)

                                    BRIDE
          Another ice warning, sir. This one from the "Baltic".

                                    SMITH
          Thank you, Sparks.

Smith glances at the message then nonchalantly puts it in his pocket. He
nods reassuringly to Rose and the group.

                                    SMITH
          Not to worry, it's quite normal for this time of year.
          In fact, we're speeding up. I've just ordered the last
          boilers lit.

Andrews scowls slightly before motioning the group toward the door. They exit just
as SECOND OFFICER CHARLES HERBERT LIGHTOLLER comes out of the chartroom,
stopping next to First Officer Murdoch.

                                    LIGHTOLLER
          Did we ever find those binoculars for the lookouts?

                                    FIRST OFFICER MURDOCH
          Haven't seen them since Southampton.

Moved to the tail of scene 119

                                                                          CUT TO:

91   EXT. BOAT DECK/ STARBOARD SIDE - DAY   91

Andrews leads the group back from the bridge along the boat deck.

                                    ROSE
          Mr. Andrews, I did the sum in my head, and with the
          number of lifeboats times the capacity you
          mentioned... forgive me, but it seems that there are
          not enough for everyone aboard.

                                    ANDREWS
          About half, actually. Rose, you miss nothing, do
          you? In fact, I put in these new type davits, which
          can take an extra row of boats here.
                  (he gestures along the deck)
          But it was thought... by some... that the deck would
          look too cluttered. So I was over-ruled.

                                    CAL
                  (slapping the side of a boat)
          Waste of deck space as it is, on an unsinkable ship!

                                    ANDREWS
          Sleep soundly, young Rose. I have built you a good
          ship, strong and true. She's all the lifeboat you
          need.

                                                              (CONTINUED)

Jack's line comparing Rose to a butterfly in a jar was deleted in post. As shot the line was slightly different: "Have you ever seen a butterfly in a jar? It beats its wings against the glass." The reference seemed too "on the nose" to Cameron, who decided that the butterfly theme associated with Rose's character would best be played out with visuals only.

As they are passing Boat 7, a gentleman turns from the rail and walks up behind the group. It is Jack. He taps Rose on the arm and she turns, gasping. He motions and she cuts away from the group toward a door which Jack holds open. They duck into the—

                                                                    CUT TO:

92   INT. GYMNASIUM - DAY   92

Jack closes the door behind her, and glances out through the ripple-glass window to the starboard rail, where the gym instructor is chatting up the woman who was riding the bike. Rose and Jack are alone in the room.

                              ROSE
                Jack, this is impossible. I can't see you.

He takes her by the shoulders.

                              JACK
                Rose, you're no picnic... you're a spoiled little brat
                even, but under that you're a strong, pure heart, and
                you're the most amazingly astounding girl I've ever
                known and—

                              ROSE
                Jack, I—

                              JACK
                No wait. Let me try to get this out. You're amazing...
                and I know I have nothing to offer you, Rose. I know
                that. But I'm involved now. You jump, I jump,
                remember? I can't turn away without knowin' you're
                goin' to be alright.

Rose feels the tears coming to her eyes. Jack is so open and real... not like anyone she has ever known.

                              ROSE
                You're making this very hard. I'll be fine. Really.

                              JACK
                I don't think so. They've got you in a glass jar like
                some butterfly, and you're goin' to die if you don't
                break out. Maybe not right away, 'cause you're
                strong. But sooner or later the fire in you is goin' to
                go out.

                              ROSE
                It's not up to you to save me, Jack.

                              JACK
                You're right. Only you can do that.

                                                            (CONTINUED)

Deleted
in post

                              ROSE
               I have to get back, they'll miss me. Please, Jack, for
               both our sakes, leave me alone.

Rose runs out onto the deck. Jack watches her go, through the rippled windows of
the gymnasium... like a figure underwater.

                                                                 CUT TO:

93   INT. FIRST CLASS LOUNGE - DAY   93

The most elegant room on the ship, done in Louis Quinze Versaille style. Rose sits
on a divan, with a group of other women arrayed around her. Ruth, the Countess
Rothes and Lady Duff-Gordon are taking tea. Rose is silent and still as a porcelain
figurine as the conversation washes around her.

                              RUTH
               Of course the invitations had to be sent back to the
               printers twice. And the bridesmaids dresses! Let me
               tell you what an odyssey that has been...

TRACKING SLOWLY IN on Rose as Ruth goes on.

REVERSE, ROSE'S POV: A tableau of MOTHER and DAUGHTER having tea. The four
year old girl, wearing white gloves, daintily picking up a cookie. The mother cor-
recting her on her posture, and the way she holds the teacup. The little girl trying
so hard to please, her expression serious. A glimpse of Rose at that age, and we see
the relentless conditioning... the path to becoming an Edwardian geisha.

ON ROSE. She calmly and deliberately turns her teacup over, spilling tea all over
her dress.

                              ROSE
               Oh, look what I've done.

                                                                 CUT TO:

94   EXT. TITANIC - DAY   94

TITANIC STEAMS TOWARD US, in the dusk light, as if lit by the embers of a giant
fire. As the ship looms, FILLING FRAME, we push in on the bow. Jack is there,
right at the apex of the bow railing, his favorite spot. He closes his eyes, letting
the chill wind clear his head.

Jack hears her voice, behind him...

                              ROSE
               Hello, Jack.

He turns and she is standing there.

                              ROSE
               I changed my mind.

                                                              (CONTINUED)

In the film, Cameron added dialogue to this scene. Jack asked Rose if she trusts him. She says yes. These words resonate again during *Titanic's* final death plunge in Scene 261.

He smiles at her, his eyes drinking her in. Her cheeks are red with the chill wind, and her eyes sparkle. Her hair blows wildly about her face.

>   ROSE
>   Fabrizio said you might be up—

>   JACK
>   Sssshh. Come here.

He puts his hands on her waist. As if he is going to kiss her.

>   JACK
>   Close your eyes.

She does, and he turns her to face forward, the way the ship is going. He presses her gently to the rail, standing right behind her. Then he takes her two hands and raises them until she is standing with her arms outstetched on each side. Rose is going along with him. When he lowers his hands, her arms stay up... like wings.

>   JACK
>   Okay. Open them.

Rose gasps. There is nothing in her field of vision but water. It's like there is no ship under them at all, just the two of them soaring. The Atlantic unrolls toward her, a hammered copper shield under a dusk sky. There is only the wind, and the hiss of the water 50 feet below.

>   ROSE
>   I'm flying!

She leans forward, arching her back. He puts his hands on her waist to steady her.

>   JACK
>   (singing softly)
>   Come Josephine in my flying machine...

Rose closes her eyes, feeling herself floating weightless far above the sea. She smiles dreamily, then leans back, gently pressing her back against his chest. He pushes forward slightly against her.

Slowly he raises his hands, arms outstretched, and they meet hers... fingertips gently touching. Then their fingers intertwine. Moving slowly, their fingers caress through and around each other like the bodies of two lovers.

Jack tips his face forward into her blowing hair, letting the scent of her wash over him, until his cheek is against her ear.

Rose turns her head until her lips are near his. She lowers her arms, turning further, until she finds his mouth with hers. He wraps his arms around her from behind, and they kiss like this with her head turned and tilted back, surrendering to him, to the emotion, to the inevitable. They kiss, slowly and tremulously, and then with building passion.

                                                            (CONTINUED)

Deleted to maintain mood

Jack and the ship seem to merge into one force of power and optimism, lifting her, buoying her forward on a magical journey, soaring onward into a night without fear.

95   IN THE CROW'S NEST, high above and behind them, lookout FREDERICK FLEET   95
nudges his mate, REGINALD LEE, pointing down at the figures in the bow.

>   FLEET
Wish I had those bleedin' binoculars.

96   JACK AND ROSE, embracing at the bow rail, DISSOLVE SLOWLY AWAY, leaving the   96
ruined bow of the WRECK—

                                               CUT TO:

97   INT. KELDYSH IMAGING SHACK   97

OLD ROSE blinks, seeming to come back to the present. She sees the wreck on the screen, the sad ghost ship deep in the abyss.

                        ROSE
That was the last time Titanic ever saw daylight.

Brock Lovett changes the tape in the minicassette recorder.

                        BROCK
So we're up to dusk on the night of the sinking. Six hours to go.

                        BODINE
Don't you love it? There's Smith, he's standing there with the iceberg warning in his fucking hand...
    (remembering Rose)
...excuse me... in his hand, and he's ordering more speed.

                        BROCK
26 years of experience working against him. He figures anything big enough to sink the ship they're going to see in time to turn. But the ship's too big, with too small a rudder... it can't corner worth shit. Everything he knows is wrong.

ROSE is ignoring this conversation. She has the art-nouveau comb with the jade butterfly on the handle in her hands, turning it slowly. She is watching a monitor, which shows the ruins of Suite B-52/56. PUSH IN until the image fills frame.

                                   TRANSITION:

98   INT. ROSE'S SUITE   98

... 1912. Like in a dream the beautiful woodwork and satin upholstery emerge from the rusted ruin. Jack is overwhelmed by the opulence of the room. He sets his sketchbook and drawing materials on the marble table.

                                    (CONTINUED)

> ROSE
> Will this light do? Don't artists need good light?

> JACK
> (bad French accent)
> Zat is true, I am not used to working in such 'orree-
> ble conditions.
> (seeing the paintings)
> Hey... Monet!

He crouches next to the paintings stacked against the wall.

> JACK
> Isn't he great... the use of color? [I saw him once...
> through a hole in his garden fence in Giverny.]

Deleted in post

She goes into the adjoining walk-in wardrobe closet. He sees her go to the safe and start working the combination. He's fascinated.

> ROSE
> Cal insists on lugging this thing everywhere.

> JACK
> Should I be expecting him anytime soon?

> ROSE
> Not as long as the cigars and brandy hold out.

CLUNK! She unlocks the safe. Glancing up, she meets his eyes in the mirror behind the safe. She opens it and removes the necklace, then holds it out to Jack who takes it nervously.

> JACK
> What is it? A sapphire?

> ROSE
> A diamond. A very rare diamond, called the Heart of
> the Ocean.

Jack gazes at wealth beyond his comprehension.

> ROSE
> I want you to draw me like your French girl.
> Wearing this.
> (she smiles at him)
> Wearing only this.

He looks up at her, surprised, and we

>   CUT TO:

99   ROSE'S BEDROOM. ON THE BUTTERFLY COMB as Rose draws it out of her hair.   99
      She shakes her head and her hair falls free around her shoulders.

Rose's kimono was designed for the film to support the butterfly theme.

Shot at the beginning of the production, this scene was the very first time Winslet and DiCaprio worked together on camera. Actors often hope that such intimate work will happen later in the schedule when they've had a chance to develop a rapport, but Cameron credits the performers for using their nervous energy effectively in the course of the scene. Cameron: "There's an accidental ad lib from Leo in the film. When Kate opened her kimono, Leo told her to 'get on the bed...er, couch.' I thought it was a perfect reaction for Jack to have."

IN THE SITTING ROOM Jack is laying out his pencils like surgical tools. His sketchbook is open and ready. He looks up as she comes into the room, wearing a silk kimono.

                         ROSE
          The last thing I need is another picture of me looking
          like a china doll. As a paying customer, I expect to
          get what I want.

She hands him a dime and steps back, parting the kimono. The blue stone lies on her creamy breast. Her heart is pounding as she slowly lowers the robe.

Jack looks so stricken, it is almost comical. The kimono drops to the floor (this is all in cuts, lyrical).

                         ROSE
          Tell me when it looks right to you.

She poses on the divan, settling like a cat into the position we remember from the drawing... almost.

                         JACK
          Uh... just bend your left leg a little and... and
          lower your head. Eyes to me. That's it.

Jack starts to sketch. He drops his pencil and she stifles a laugh.

                         ROSE
          I believe you are blushing, Mr. Big Artiste. I can't
          imagine Monsieur Monet blushing.

                         JACK
               (sweating)
          He does landscapes.

TIGHT ON JACK as his eyes come up to look at her over the top edge of his sketch-pad. We have seen this image of him before, in her memory. It is an image she will carry the rest of her life.

Despite his nervousness, he draws with sure strokes, and what emerges is the best thing he has ever done. Her pose is languid, her hands beautiful, and her eyes radiate her energy.

PUSH SLOWLY IN ON ROSE'S FACE...

                                                        TRANSITION:

101   INT. KELDYSH/ IMAGING SHACK   101

MATCH DISSOLVE/MORPH to Rose, 101 years old. Only her eyes are the same.

                         OLD ROSE
          My heart was pounding the whole time. It was the
          most erotic moment of my life... up till then at
          least.

                                                        (CONTINUED)

CUT TO REVERSE: A semicircle of listeners staring in rapt, frozen silence. The story of Jack and Rose has finally and completely grabbed them.

> BODINE
> What, uh... happened next?

> OLD ROSE
> (smiling)
> You mean, did we "do it"?

                                                                CUT TO:

102   INT. ROSE AND CAL'S SUITE - NIGHT   102

BACK TO 1912. Jack is signing the drawing. Rose, wearing her kimono again, is leaning on his shoulder, watching.

> OLD ROSE (V.O.)
> Sorry to disappoint you Mr. Bodine.

Rose gazes at the drawing. He has X-rayed her soul.

> ROSE
> Date it, Jack. I want to always remember this night.

He does: 4/14/1912. Rose meanwhile scribbles a note on a piece of Titanic stationary. We don't see what it says. She accepts the drawing from him, and crosses to the safe in the wardrobe.

She puts the diamond back in the safe, placing the drawing and the note on top of it. Closes the door with a CLUNK!

                                                                CUT TO:

103   INT. FIRST CLASS SMOKING ROOM - NIGHT   103

Lovejoy enters from the Palm Court through the revolving door and crosses the room toward Hockley. A fire is blazing in the marble fireplace, and the usual fatcats are playing cards, drinking and talking. Cal sees Lovejoy and detaches from his group, coming to him.

> LOVEJOY
> None of the stewards have seen her.

> CAL
> (low but forceful)
> This is ridiculous, Lovejoy. Find her.

                                                                CUT TO:

According to Lightoller's testimony, this conversation took place nearly word for word.

104   EXT. ATLANTIC - NIGHT   104

TITANIC glides across an unnatural sea, black and calm as a pool of oil. The ship's
lights are mirrored almost perfectly in the black water. The sky is brilliant with
stars. A meteor traces a bright line across the heavens.

105   ON THE BRIDGE, Captain Smith peers out at the blackness ahead of the ship.   105
QUARTERMASTER HITCHINS brings him a cup of hot tea with lemon. It steams in
the bitter cold of the open bridge. Second Officer Lightoller is next to him, staring out
at the sheet of black glass the Atlantic has become.

                        LIGHTOLLER
            I don't think I've _ever_ seen such a flat calm, in 24
            years at sea.

                        SMITH
            Yes, like a mill pond. Not a breath of wind.

                        LIGHTOLLER
            It'll make the bergs harder to see, with no breaking
            water at the base.

                        SMITH
            Mmmmm. Well, I'm off. Maintain speed and
            heading, Mr. Lightoller.

                        LIGHTOLLER
            Yes sir.

                        SMITH
            And wake me, of course, if anything becomes in the
            slightest degree doubtful.

                                                        CUT TO:

106   INT. ROSE AND CAL'S SUITE   106

Rose, fully dressed now, returns to the sitting room. They hear a key in the lock.
Rose takes Jack's hand and leads him silently through the bedrooms. Lovejoy enters by
the sitting room door.

                        LOVEJOY
            Miss Rose? Hello?

He hears a door opening and goes through Cal's room toward hers.

                                                        CUT TO:

107   INT. CORRIDOR OUTSIDE SUITE   107

Rose and Jack come out of her stateroom, closing the door. She leads him quickly along
the corridor toward the B deck foyer. They are halfway across the open space when the

                                            (CONTINUED)

ose's "gesture" was invented by the Romans over 2000 years ago. Called "digitus impudicus," the impudent finger, they used it to taunt their enemies. It is not an anachronism for her to use it in 1912.

sitting room door opens in the corridor and Lovejoy comes out. The valet sees Jack
with Rose and hustles after them.

                              ROSE
              Come on!

She and Jack break into a run, surprising the few ladies and gentlemen about. Rose
leads him past the stairs to the bank of elevators. They run into one, shocking the hell
out of the OPERATOR.

                              ROSE
              Take us down. Quickly, quickly!

The Operator scrambles to comply. Jack even helps him close the steel gate. Lovejoy
runs up as the lift starts to descend. He slams one hand on the bars of the gate. Rose
makes a very rude and unladylike gesture, and laughs as Lovejoy disappears above. The
Operator gapes at her.

                                                      CUT TO:

108   INT. E-DECK FOYER/ ELEVATORS   108

Lovejoy emerges from another lift and runs to the one Jack and Rose were in. The
Operator is just closing the gate to go back up. Lovejoy runs around the bank of elevators and scans the foyer... no Jack and Rose. He tries the stairs going down to F-Deck.

                                                      CUT TO:

109   INT. F-DECK CORRIDORS/ FAN ROOM   109

A functional space, with access to a number of machine spaces (fan rooms,
boiler uptakes). Jack and Rose are leaning against a wall, laughing.

                         JACK   *Revised/shortened*
              Pretty tough for a valet, this fella.   *for Pacing*

                         ROSE
              He's an ex-Pinkerton. Cal's father hired him to keep
              Cal out of trouble... to make sure he always got back
              to the hotel with his wallet and watch, after some
              crawl through the less reputable parts of town...

                         JACK
              Kinda like we're doin' right now— uh oh!

Lovejoy has spotted them from a cross-corridor nearby. He charges toward them.
Jack and Rose run around a corner into a blind alley. There is one door, marked
CREW ONLY, and Jack flings it open.

The scene of Jack kissing Rose in the boiler room was shot but deleted. Instead, Cameron decided to save that beat for Scene 114 in the #2 Cargo Hold where a deeper kiss would happen. Cameron: "Without that kiss you have better dynamic in the relationship. Jack initiates the first passionate kiss with Rose on the bow. Now, it's her turn. It shows that she's taking control of her destiny by investing in the relationship. I wanted that second, meaningful kiss to happen in the Renault where they end up making love for the first time."

110   They enter a roaring FAN ROOM, with no way out but a ladder going down. Jack   110
        latches the deadbolt on the door, and Lovejoy slams against it a moment later. Jack
        grins at Rose, pointing to the ladder.

                                JACK
                    After you, m'lady.

                                                                        CUT TO:

111   INT. BOILER ROOM FIVE AND SIX   111

        Jack and Rose come down the escape ladder and look around in amazement. It is like a
        vision of hell itself, with the roaring furnaces and black figures moving in the smoky
        glow. They run the length of the boiler room, dodging amazed stokers, and trimmers with
        their wheelbarrows of coal.

                                JACK
                    (shouting over the din)
                    Carry on! Don't mind us!

        They run through the open watertight door into BOILER ROOM SIX. Jack pulls
        her through the fiercely hot alley between two boilers and they wind up in the
        dark, out of sight of the working crew. Watching from the shadows, they see the
        stokers working in the hellish glow, shovelling coal into the insatiable maws of the
        furnaces. The whole place thunders with the roar of the fires.

                                                                        CUT TO:

112   INT. FIRST CLASS SMOKING ROOM   112

        Amid unparalleled luxury, Cal sits at a card game, sipping brandy.

                                COLONEL GRACIE
                    We're going like hell I tell you. I have fifty dollars
                    that says we make it into New York Tuesday night!

        Cal looks at his gold pocket watch, and scowls, not listening.

                    Deleted in post   CUT TO:

113   INT. BOILER ROOM SIX   113

        The furnaces roar, silhouetting the glistening stokers. JACK kisses Rose's face,
        tasting the sweat trickling down from her forehead. They kiss passionately in the
        steamy, pounding darkness.

                                                                        CUT TO:

114   INT. HOLD #2   114

        Jack and Rose enter and run laughing between the rows of stacked cargo. She
        hugs herself against the cold, after the dripping heat of the boiler room.

                                                                        (CONTINUED)

A poetic metaphor connecting the sparks of love with sparks of electricity was sacrificed when Cameron decided to cut a scene from history. The wireless exchange between the *Titanic* and the *Californian* is only one of many events that contributed to the liner's fate, and Cameron found himself looking for scenes to cut as he honed the film down to its final running length.

CAMERON: "We all know the ship sinks, so it becomes a matter of when you remind the audience of this inescapable fact and how it affects your main characters. I think cutting from Jack and Rose in an embrace to a wide shot of the *Titanic* isolated in the black heart of the ocean was a stronger statement."

They come upon William Carter's brand new RENAULT touring car, lashed down to a pallet. It looks like a royal coach from a fairy tale, its brass trim and headlamps nicely set off by its deep burgundy color.

Rose climbs into the plushly upholstered back seat, acting very royal. There are cut crystal bud vases on the walls back there, each containing a rose. Jack jumps into the driver's seat, enjoying the feel of the leather and wood.

> JACK
> Where to, Miss?

> ROSE
> To the stars.

ON JACK as her hands come out of the shadows and pull him over the seat into the back. He lands next to her, and his breath seems loud in the quiet darkness. He looks at her and she is smiling. It is the moment of truth.

> JACK
> Are you nervous?

changed on set to a simple 'No.'

> ROSE
> Au contraire, mon cher.

He strokes her face, cherishing her. She kisses his artist's fingers.

> ROSE
> Put your hands on me Jack.

He kisses her, and she slides down in the seat under his welcome weight.

> CUT TO:

115   INT. WIRELESS ROOM   115

A BRILLIANT ARC OF ELECTRICITY fills frame— the spark gap of the Marconi instrument as SENIOR WIRELESS OPERATOR JACK PHILLIPS (24) rapidly keys out a message. Junior Operator Bride looks through the huge stack of outgoing messages swamping them.

> BRIDE
> Look at this one, he wants his private train to meet
> him. La dee da.
> (slaps them down)
> We'll be up all bloody night on this lot.

Phillips starts to receive an incoming message from a nearby ship, the Leyland freighter CALIFORNIAN, which jams his outgoing signal. At such close range, the beeps are deafening.

> PHILLIPS
> Christ! It's that idiot on the Californian.

> (CONTINUED)

shot but deleted

Witreless shack on the Californian

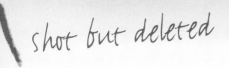

115   CONTINUED: 115

Cursing, Phillips furiously keys a rebuke.

                                                        CUT TO:

116   INT. / EXT. WIRELESS SHACK/ FREIGHTER *CALIFORNIAN*   *116*

Wireless Operator CYRIL EVANS pulls his earphone off his ear as the Titanic's
spark deafens him. He translates the message for THIRD OFFICER GROVES.

                          EVANS
            Stupid bastard. I try to warn him about the ice, and
            he says *"Keep out. Shut up. I'm working Cape Race."*

                          GROVES
            Now what's he sending?

                          EVANS
            "No seasickness. Poker business good. Al". Well
            that's it for me. I'm shutting down.

As Evans wearily switches off his generator, Groves goes out on deck. PAN OFF HIM
to reveal the ship is stopped fifty yards from the edge of a field of pack ice and
icebergs stretching as far as the eye can see.

                                                        CUT TO:

117   EXT. OCEAN/ TITANIC   117

ON TITANIC, steaming hellbent through the darkness, hurling up white water at
the bow. The bow comes straight at us, until the bow wave WIPES THE FRAME—

                                                        CUT TO

118   INT. HOLD #2   118

PUSHING IN on the rear window of the Renault, which is completely fogged up.
Rose's hand comes up and slams against the glass for a moment, making a handprint in
the veil of condensation.

INSIDE THE CAR, Jack's overcoat is like a blanket over them. It stirs and Rose pulls
it down. They are huddled under it, intertwined, still mostly clothed. Their faces are
flushed and they look at each other wonderingly. She puts her hand on his face, as if
making sure he is real.

                          ROSE
            You're trembling.

                          JACK
            It's okay. I'm alright.

He lays his cheek against her chest.

                                                  (CONTINUED)

                                                                       80

After Jack lays his head on Rose's chest the rest of the scene, including Old Rose's voice-over, was deleted in post to keep the suspense building.

The removal of Scene 115 left a time gap that needed to be filled before Cameron could cut back to the young lovers without events feeling too telescoped in time. In the final film, Scene 119, along with the beat about binoculars moved from Scene 90, worked perfectly.

> JACK
> I can feel your heart beating.

She hugs his head to her chest, and just holds on for dear life.

> OLD ROSE (V.O.)
> *Well, I wasn't the first teenage girl to get seduced*
> *in the backseat of a car, and certainly not the last,*
> *by several million. He had such fine hands, artists'*
> *hands, but strong too... roughened by work. I*
> *remember their touch even now.*

                                                                    CUT TO:

119   EXT. ATLANTIC/ TITANIC - NIGHT   119

The bow sweeps under us, and the CAMERA CLIMBS toward the foremast and the
tiny half-cylinder of the crow's nest, which grows as we push in on lookouts Fleet
and Lee. They are stamping their feet and swinging their arms, trying to keep warm
in the 22 knot freezing wind, which whips the vapor of their breath away behind.

> FLEET
> You can *smell* ice, you know, when it's near.

> LEE
> Bollocks.

> FLEET
> Well I can.

                                                                    CUT TO:

120   INT. BOILER ROOM SIX   120

Without hearing the words over the roar of the furnaces, we see stokers telling
TWO STEWARDS which way Rose and Jack went. The stewards move off toward the
forward holds.

                                                                    CUT TO:

121   INT. CAL AND ROSE'S SUITE   121

Cal stands at the open safe. He stares at the drawing of Rose and his face clenches
with fury. He reads the note again: "DARLING, NOW YOU CAN KEEP US
BOTH LOCKED IN YOUR SAFE, ROSE"

Lovejoy, standing behind him, looks over his shoulder at the drawing. Cal
crumples Rose's note, then takes the drawing in both hands as if to rip it in half. He
tenses to do it, then stops himself.

                                                                  (CONTINUED)

                              CAL
        I have a better idea.

                                                                          CUT TO:

122   INT. HOLD #2 - NIGHT   122

       The two stewards enter. They have electric torches and play the beams around the
       hold. They spot the Renault with its fogged up rear window and approach it slowly.

       FROM INSIDE we see the torch light up Rose's passionate handprint, still there on
       the fogged up glass. One steward whips open the door.

                            STEWARD
           Got yer!

       REVERSE: the back seat is empty.

                                                                          CUT TO:

123   EXT. FORWARD WELL DECK AND CROW'S NEST - NIGHT   123

       Rose and Jack, fully dressed, come through a crew door onto the deck. They can
       barely stand, they are laughing so hard.

       UP ABOVE THEM, IN THE CROW'S NEST, lookout Fleet hears the disturbance
       below and looks around and back down to the well deck, where he can see
       two figures embracing.

       Jack and Rose stand in each other's arms. Their breath clouds around them in the
       now freezing air, but they don't even feel the cold.

                              ROSE
           When this ship docks, I'm getting off with you.

                              JACK
           This is crazy.

                              ROSE
           I know. It doesn't make any sense. That's why I
           trust it.

       Jack pulls her to him and kisses her fiercely.

124   IN THE CROW'S NEST Fleet nudges Lee.   124

                             FLEET
           Cor... look at that, would ya.

                              LEE
           They're a bloody sight warmer than we are.

                                                                       (CONTINUED)

Cameron intended Jack and Rose's embrace to distract the lookouts and prevent them from seeing the iceberg in time, an ironic twist coming at the very moment Rose exercises her will to change her life.

FLEET
          Well if that's what it takes for us two to get warm,
          I'd rather not, if it's all the same.

They both have a good laugh at that one. It is Fleet whose expression falls first.
Glancing forward again, he does a double take. The color drains out of his face.

FLEET'S POV: a massive iceberg right in their path, 500 yards out.

                              FLEET
          Bugger me!!

Fleet reaches past Lee and rings the lookout bell three times, then grabs the telephone, calling the bridge. He waits precious seconds for it to be picked up, never taking his eyes off the black mass ahead.

                              FLEET
          Pick up, ya bastard.

                                                                CUT TO:

125   INT./ EXT. BRIDGE   125

Inside the enclosed wheelhouse, SIXTH OFFICER MOODY walks unhurriedly to
the telephone, picking it up.

                         FLEET (V.O.)
          Is someone there?

                                   MOODY   *This dialogue is from*
          Yes. What do you see?   *the inquiry transcripts*

                                   FLEET
          Iceberg right ahead!

                                   MOODY
          Thank you.
               (hangs up, calls to Murdoch)
          Iceberg right ahead!

Murdoch sees it and rushes to the engine room telegraph. While signaling "FULL
SPEED ASTERN" he yells to Quartermaster Hitchins, who is at the wheel.

                         MURDOCH
          Hard a' starboard.

                         MOODY
          (standing behind Hitchins)
          Hard a' starboard. The helm is hard over, sir.

CRASH SEQUENCE/ SERIES OF CUTS:

126   CHIEF ENGINEER BELL is just checking the soup he has warming on a steam manifold   126
when the engine telegraph clangs, then goes... incredibly... to FULL SPEED ASTERN.
He and the other ENGINEERS just stare at it a second, unbelieving. Then Bell reacts.

> BELL
> Full astern! FULL ASTERN!!

The engineers and greasers scramble like madmen to close steam valves and start brak-
ing the mighty propeller shafts, big as Sequoias, to a stop.

127   IN BOILER ROOM SIX, Leading Stoker FREDERICK BARRETT is standing with 2nd   127
Engineer JAMES HESKETH when the red warning light and "STOP" indicator come on.

> BARRETT
> Shut all dampers! Shut 'em!!

128   FROM THE BRIDGE Murdoch watches the berg growing... straight ahead. The bow   128
finally starts to come left (since the ship turns the reverse of the helm setting).

MURDOCH'S jaw clenches as the bow turns with agonizing slowness. He holds
his breath as the horrible physics play out.

129   IN THE CROW'S NEST Frederick Fleet braces himself.   129

130   THE BOW OF THE SHIP thunders right at CAMERA and—   130

KRUUUNCH!! The ship hits the berg on its starboard bow.

131   UNDERWATER we see the ice smashing in the steel hull plates. The iceberg bumps   131
and scrapes along the side of the ship. Rivets pop as the steel plate of the hull flexes
under the load.

132   IN #2 HOLD the two stewards stagger as the hull buckles in four feet with a sound like   132
THUNDER. Like a sledgehammer beating along outside the ship, the berg splits the hull
plates and the sea pours in, sweeping them off their feet. The icy water swirls around
the Renault as the men scramble for the stairs.

133   ON G-DECK forward Fabrizio is tossed in his bunk by the impact. He hears a sound   133
like the greatly amplified squeal of a skate on ice.

134   IN BOILER ROOM SIX Barrett and Hesketh stagger as they hear the ROLLING   134
THUNDER of the collision. They see the starboard side of the ship buckle in toward
them and are almost swept off their feet by a rush of water coming in about two feet
above the floor.

135   ON THE FORWARD WELL DECK Jack and Rose break their kiss and look up in   135
astonishment as the berg sails past, blocking out the sky like a mountain. Fragments
break off it and crash down onto the deck, and they have to jump back to avoid flying
chunks of ice.

Deleted for
Pacing

The scene with Molly asking for
ice survived many early cuts of
the film with opinion divided as to
whether or not it was too whimsical
for such a dramatically tense
sequence. Cameron studied audience
reaction to the scene very carefully
because he knew that a tension-
breaker is sometimes called for to
keep a story moving. Also, the scene
really appealed to his mischievous
sense of humor. Ultimately, the scene
was cut and the exchange between
the lookouts in Scene 152 drew
laughs from audience members ready
for a release.

136   ON THE BRIDGE Murdoch rings the watertight door alarm. He quickly throws   136
       the switch that closes them.

                              MURDOCH
                   Hard a' port!

       Judging the berg to be amidships, he is trying to clear the stern.

137   BARRETT AND HESKETH hear the DOOR ALARM and scramble through the swirling water   137
       to the watertight door between Boiler Rooms 6 and 5. The room is full of watervapor
       as the cold sea strikes the red hot furnaces. Barrett yells to the stokers
       scrambling through the door as it comes down like a slow guillotine.

                              BARRETT
                   Go Lads! Go! Go!

       He dives through into Boiler Room 5 just before the door rumbles down with a
       CLANG.

138   JACK AND ROSE rush to the starboard rail in time to see the berg moving aft down   138
       the side of the ship.

139   In his stateroom, surrounded by piles of plans while making notes in his ever-   139
       present book, Andrews looks up at the sound of a cut-crystal light fixture tinkling
       like a windchime.

       He feels the shudder run through the ship. And we see it in his face. Too much of
       his soul is in this great ship for him not to feel its mortal wound.

140   IN THE FIRST CLASS SMOKING ROOM Gracie watches his highball vibrating   140
       on the table.

141   IN THE PALM COURT, with its high arched windows, Molly Brown holds up her drink   141
       to a passing waiter.

                              MOLLY
                   Hey, can I get some ice here, please?

       Silently, a moving wall of ice fills the windows behind her. She doesn't see
       it. It disappears astern.

142   IN THE CROW'S NEST Fleet turns to Lee...   142

                              FLEET
                   Oy, mate... that was a close shave

                              LEE
                   Smell ice, can you? Bleedin' Christ!

                                                        CUT TO:

All of the dialogue from the Bridge was taken from transcripts of Hichens' testimony during the inquiries held after the disaster. No dramatic liberties were taken.

CLOSE ON MURDOCH. The alarm bells still clatter mindlessly, seeming to reflect his inner state. He is in shock, unable to get a grip on what just happened. *He just ran the biggest ship in history into an iceberg on its maiden voyage.*

> MURDOCH
> (stiffly, to Moody)
> Note the time. Enter it in the log.

Captain Smith rushes out of his cabin onto the bridge, tucking in his shirt.

> SMITH
> What was that, Mr. Murdoch?

> MURDOCH
> An iceberg, sir. I put her hard a' starboard and run the engines full astern, but it was too close. I tried to port around it, but she hit... and I —

> SMITH
> Close the emergency doors.

> MURDOCH
> The doors are closed.

Together they rush out onto the starboard wing, and Murdoch points. Smith looks into the darkness aft, then wheels around to FOURTH OFFICER BOXHALL.

> SMITH
> Find the Carpenter and get him to sound the ship.

>   CUT TO:

144 INT. G-DECK FORWARD 144

In steerage, Fabrizio comes out into the hall to see what's going on. He sees dozens of rats running toward him in the corridor, fleeing the flooding bow. Fabrizio jumps aside as the rats run by.

> FABRIZIO
> Ma— che cazzo!

145 IN HIS STATEROOM Tommy gets out of his top bunk in the dark and drops down to 145
the floor. SPLASH!!

> TOMMY
> Cor!! What in hell—?!

He snaps on the light. The floor is covered with 3 inches of freezing water, and more coming in. He pulls the door open, and steps out into the corridor, which is flooded. Fabrizio is running toward him, yelling something in Italian. Tommy and Fabrizio start pounding on doors, getting everybody up and out. The alarm spreads in several languages.

>   CUT TO:

As filmed, Scene 147 ended with Rose dropping a piece of ice down the back of Jack's shirt and Jack playfully threatening to throw her overboard. However the entire scene was cut during post for pacing.

146   INT. FIRST CLASS CORRIDOR/ A-DECK   146

A couple of people have come out into the corridor in robes and slippers. A
STEWARD hurries along, reassuring them.

                              WOMAN
          Why have the engines stopped? I felt a shudder?

                              STEWARD #1
          I shouldn't worry, m'am. We've likely thrown a
          propeller blade, that's the shudder you felt. May I
          bring you anything?

THOMAS ANDREWS brushes past them, walking fast and carrying an armload of
rolled up ship's plans.

                                                        CUT TO:

147   EXT. FORWARD WELL DECK   147

Jack and Rose are leaning over the starboard rail, looking at the hull of
the ship.

                              JACK
          Looks okay. I don't see anything.

                              ROSE
          Could it have damaged the ship?

                              JACK
          It didn't seem like much of a bump. I'm sure we're
          okay.

Behind them a couple of steerage guys are kicking the ice around the deck,
laughing.

                                                        CUT TO:

148   INT. STEERAGE FORWARD   148

Fabrizio and Tommy are in a crowd of steerage men clogging the corridors, heading
aft away from the flooding. Many of them have grabbed suitcases and duffel bags,
some of which are soaked.

                              TOMMY
          If this is the direction the rats were runnin', it's
          good enough for me.

                                                        CUT TO:

Bruce Ismay, dressed in pajamas under a topcoat, hurries down the corridor, headed for the bridge. An officious steward named BARNES comes along the other direction, getting the few concerned passengers back into their rooms.

>   STEWARD BARNES
>   There's no cause for alarm. Please, go back to your
>   rooms.

He is stopped in his tracks by Cal and Lovejoy.

>   STEWARD BARNES
>   Please, sir. There's no emergency—

>   CAL
>   Yes there is, I've been robbed. Now get the Master at
>   Arms. Now, you moron!

                                                            CUT TO:

150   INT. BRIDGE/ CHARTROOM   150

C.U. CAPTAIN SMITH studying the commutator.

He turns to Andrews, standing behind him.

>   SMITH
>   A five degree list in less than ten minutes.

SHIP'S CARPENTER JOHN HUTCHINSON enters behind him, out of breath and clearly unnerved.

>   HUTCHINSON
>   She's making water fast... in the forepeak tank and
>   the forward holds, and in boiler room six.

ISMAY enters, his movements quick with anger and frustration. Smith glances at him with annoyance.

>   ISMAY
>   Why have we stopped?

>   SMITH
>   We've struck ice.

>   ISMAY
>   Well, do you think the ship is seriously damaged?

>   SMITH
>   (glaring)
>   Excuse me.

                                                       (CONTINUED)

Deleted before shooting

In the film, Scene 152 ends after Rose says that they have to tell Ruth and Cal about the disaster. Cameron: "I took out the echo of Jack's line from Scene 61, "You jump I jump," because I wanted to save that beat for when Rose has her biggest epiphany and risks everything to stay with Jack on the ship [See Scene 211]."

Deleted before shooting

150   CONTINUED: 150

Smith pushes past him, with Andrews and Hutchinson in tow.

                                                                    CUT TO:

151   INT. BOILER ROOM 6   151

Stokers and firemen are struggling to draw the fires. They are working in waist deep
water churning around them as it flows into the boiler room, ice cold and swirling
with grease from the machinery. Cheif Engineer Bell comes partway down the ladder
and shouts.

                              BELL
                That's it, lads. Get the hell up!   *Deleted in post*

They scramble up the escape ladders

                                                                    CUT TO:

152   EXT. B-DECK FORWARD/ WELL DECK   152

The gentleman, now joined by another man, leans on the forward rail watching the
steerage men playing soccer with chunks of ice.

                            GENTLEMAN   *Deleted*
                I guess it's nothing serious. I'm going back to my   *in post*
                cabin to read.

A 20ish YALE MAN pops through the door wearing a topcoat over pajamas.

                             YALEY
                Say, did I miss the fun?

Rose and Jack come up the steps from the well deck, which are right next to the three
men. They stare as the couple climbs over the locked gate.

A moment later Captain Smith rounds the corner, followed by Andrews and Carpenter
Hutchinson. They have come down from the bridge by the outside stairs. The three
men, their faces grim, brush right past Jack and Rose. Andrews barely glances at
her.

                             SMITH
                Can you shore up?

                           HUTCHINSON
                Not unless the pumps get ahead.

The inspection party goes down the stairs to the well deck.

                             JACK
                   (low, to her)
                It's bad.

                             ROSE
                We have to tell Mother and Cal.

                                                              (CONTINUED)

In the film, just prior to Scene 153, an unscripted comic beat in Cal and Rose's Sitting Room shows the Master at Arms examining some of Jack's sketches as Cal and Ruth wait for Rose to return. When he comments on the drawings' quality, Cal blows up and tells him to photograph the room for evidence.

Cameron often shot brief moments not referenced in the script that took advantage of the resources at hand (in this case the cast required for Scene 154). The reasons for straying from the script vary, but they usually offered Cameron some kind of insurance. In this case, for example, he did not know he was going to cut Scenes 150 and 151, but he did know that there was a possibility he would have to lose scenes in order to reduce the running time of the final film. The added scene provides just enough of a beat to get Jack and Rose from the Well Deck to the Sitting Room in a reasonable period of time.

                              JACK
          Now it's worse.

                              ROSE
          Come with me, Jack. I jump, you jump... right?

                              JACK
          Right.

Jack follows Rose through the door inside the ship.

Deleted in post

                                                    CUT TO:

153   INT. B-DECK FOYER/ CORRIDOR   153

Jack and Rose cross the foyer, entering the corridor. Lovejoy is waiting for them in
the hall as they approach the room.

                            LOVEJOY
          We've been looking for you miss.

Lovejoy follows and, unseen, moves close behind Jack and smoothly *slips
the diamond necklace into the pocket of his overcoat.*

                                                    CUT TO:

154   INT. ROSE AND CAL'S SUITE   154

Cal and Ruth wait in the sitting room, along with the Master at Arms and two stewards (Steward #1 and Barnes). Silence as Rose and Jack enter. Ruth closes her robe
at her throat when she sees Jack.

                              ROSE
          Something serious has happened.

                              CAL
          That's right. Two things dear to me have disappeared
          this evening. Now that _one_ is back...
             (he looks from Rose to Jack)
          ... I have a pretty good idea where to find the other.
             (to Master at Arms)
          Search him.

The Master at Arms steps up to Jack.

                         MASTER AT ARMS
          Coat off, mate.

Lovejoy pulls at Jack's coat and Jack shakes his head in dismay, shrugging out of it.
The Master at Arms pats him down.

                              JACK
          This is horseshit.

                                                    (CONTINUED)

                              ROSE
          Cal, you can't be serious! We're in the middle of an
          emergency and you—

Steward Barnes pulls the Heart of the Ocean out of the pocket of Jack's
coat.

                         STEWARD BARNES
          Is this it?

Rose is stunned. Needless to say, so is Jack.

                              CAL
          That's it.

                         MASTER AT ARMS
          Right then. Now don't make a fuss.

He starts to handcuff Jack.

                              JACK
          Don't you believe it, Rose. Don't!

                              ROSE
             (uncertain)
          He couldn't have.

                              CAL
          Of course he could. Easy enough for a professional.
          He memorized the combination when you opened the
          safe.

FLASHBACK: *Rose at the safe, looking in the mirror and meeting Jack's eyes
as he stands behind her, watching.*

                              ROSE
          But I was with him the whole time.   *Deleted prior
                                                         to shooting*

                              CAL
             (just to her, low and cold)
          *Maybe he did it while you were putting your clothes
          back on.*

                              JACK
          They put it in my pocket!

                            LOVEJOY
             (holding Jack's coat)
          It's not even your pocket, son.
             (reading)
          "Property of A. L. Ryerson".

Lovejoy shows the coat to the Master at Arms. There is a label inside the collar with
the owner's name.

                                                            (CONTINUED)

CAMERON: "Ruth's last line in the scene as written was appropriate to the situation and her character, but I wanted to focus more on Jack's hope that Rose would believe in his innocence and not be swayed by the evidence to the contrary. The scene is about the faith that comes from love. Ending the moment with Jack pleading to Rose from the hallway helps motivate why later she comes back through a flooding ship for him.

MASTER AT ARMS
That was reported stolen today.

JACK
I was going to return it! Rose—

Rose feels utterly betrayed, hurt and confused. She shrinks away from him. He
starts shouting to her as Lovejoy and the Master at Arms drag him out into the
hall. She can't look him in the eye.

JACK
Rose, don't listen to them... I didn't do this! You
know I didn't! You know it!

She is devastated. Her mother lays a comforting hand on her shoulder as the tears well
up.

RUTH
Why do women believe men?

CUT TO:

155   INT. MAIL SORTING ROOM/ HOLD   155

Smith and Andrews come down the steps to the Mail Sorting Room and find the
clerks scrambling to pull mail from the racks. They are furiously hauling wet sacks
of mail up from the hold below.

Andrews climbs partway down the stairs to the hold, which is almost full. Sacks of
mail float everywhere. The lights are still on below the surface, casting an eerie
glow. The Renault is visible under the water, the brass glinting cheerfully. Andrews
looks down as the water covers his shoe, and scrambles back up the stairs.

CUT TO:

Deleted for Pacing

156   INT. BRIDGE/ CHARTROOM   156

Andrews unrolls a big drawing of the ship across the chartroom table. It is a
side elevation, showing all the watertight bulkheads. His hands are shaking.
Murdoch and Ismay hover behind Andrews and the Captain.

ISMAY
When can we get underway, do you think?

Smith glares at him and turns his attention to Andrews' drawing. The builder points to
it for emphasis as he talks.

ANDREWS
Water 14 feet above the keel in ten minutes... in the
forepeak... in all three holds... and in boiler room
six.

(CONTINUED)

Due to the film's running time an intermission was proposed. The portentous ending of Scene 156 seemed like a logical break point to create two separate "acts." Cameron was vehemently opposed to the concept.

CAMERON: "I don't believe in intermissions because I've worked hard as a filmmaker to capture an audience's hearts and minds. I don't want to let them leave the dramatic space I've created for ten minutes so they can get more popcorn or go to the restroom. If they need a break, let them pick their own time to run to the lobby. If I do my job as a story-teller then no one will want to take a break, even after three hours. I told people 'There will be an intermission in this movie over my dead body.'"

Ironically, it proved impractical to fit the entire movie onto a single videocassette, so people who watch the movie at home will experience an intermission, of sorts, after all.

                              SMITH
          That's right.

                              ANDREWS
          Five compartments. She can stay afloat with the first
          four compartments breached. But not five. Not five.
          As she goes down by the head the water will spill over
          the tops of the bulkheads... at E Deck... from one to
          the next... back and back. There's no stopping it.

                              SMITH
          The pumps—

                              ANDREWS
          The pumps buy you time... but minutes only. From
          this moment, no matter what we do, Titanic will
          founder.

                              ISMAY
          But this ship can't sink!

                              ANDREWS
          She is made of iron, sir. I assure you, she can. And
          she _will_. It is a mathematical certainty.

          Smith looks like he has been gutpunched.

                              SMITH
          How much time?

                              ANDREWS
          An hour, two at most.

          Ismay reels as his dream turns into his worst nightmare.

                              SMITH
          And how many aboard, Mr. Murdoch?

                              MURDOCH
          Two thousand two hundred souls aboard, sir.

          A long beat. Smith turns to face his employer.

                              SMITH
          I believe you may get your headlines, Mr. Ismay.

                                                           CUT TO:

157   EXT. BOAT DECK   157

          Andrews is striding along the boat deck, as seamen and officers scurry to
          uncover the boats. Steam is venting from pipes on the funnels overhead,
          and the din is horrendous. Speech is difficult adding to the crew's level
          of disorganization. Andrews sees some men fumbling with the mechanism of
          one of the Wellin davits and yells to them over the roar of steam.

                                                        (CONTINUED)

          Deleted
          before shooting

During post, Ruth's exit was cut so that the scene would begin already focused on the tension between Rose and Cal.

Deleted

> ANDREWS
> Turn to the right! Pull the falls taut before you
> unchock. Have you never had a boat drill?

> SEAMAN
> No sir! Not with these new davits, sir.

He looks around, disgusted as the crew fumble with the davits, and the tackle for the "falls"... the ropes which are used to lower the boats. A few passengers are coming out on deck, hesitantly in the noise and bitter cold.

CUT TO:

158   INT. ROSE AND CAL'S SUITE   158

From inside the sitting room they can hear knocking and voices in the corridor.

> RUTH   *Deleted*
> I had better go dress.

Ruth exits and Hockley crosses to Rose. He regards her coldly for a moment, then SLAPS her across the face.

> CAL
> It is a little slut, isn't it?

To Rose the blow is inconsequential compared to the blow her heart has been given. Cal grabs her shoulders roughly.

> CAL
> Look at me, you little—

There is a loud knock on the door and an urgent voice. The door opens and their steward puts his head in.

> STEWARD BARNES
> Sir, I've been told to ask you to please put on your
> lifebelt, and come up to the boat deck.

> CAL
> Get out. We're busy.

The steward persists, coming in to get the lifebelts down from the top of a dresser.

> STEWARD
> I'm sorry about the inconvenience, Mr. Hockley, but
> it's Captain's orders. Please dress warmly, it's quite
> cold tonight.
>   (he hands a lifebelt to Rose)
> Not to worry, miss, I'm sure it's just a precaution.

(CONTINUED)

"C.Q.D." refers to a radio distress code in use at the time. C.Q. meant to stop transmission and await information. D. indicated "distress." A new code had been adopted shortly before the *Titanic* disaster that replaced "C.Q.D." with "S.O.S." Contrary to popular belief, S.O.S. did not mean "Save Our Ship," or "Save Our Souls." The letters were simply chosen because they were the easiest to transmit and repeat. Even as Morse code recedes into the history books, the "dot dot dot, dash dash dash, dot dot dot" that spells S.O.S. still holds a place in popular culture.

While it was cut from the film for pacing, it is worth noting that it was Bride's little joke to Phillips about using the new distress call that made S.O.S. a household term. (Bride sold his story to *The New York Times*.) During the remaining hours, Phillips would broadcast both C.Q.D. and S.O.S.

                                    CAL
            This is ridiculous.

In the corridor outside the stewards are being so polite and obsequious they are con-
veying no sense of danger whatsoever. However, it's another story in...

                                                              CUT TO:

159   INT. STEERAGE BERTHING AFT   159

BLACKNESS. Then BANG! The door is thrown open and the light snapped on by
a steward. The Cartmell family rouses from a sound sleep.

                              STEWARD #2
            Everybody up. Let's go. Put your lifebelts on.

IN THE CORRIDOR outside, another steward is going from door to door along the
hall, pounding and yelling.

                              STEWARD #3
            Lifebelts on. Lifebelts on. Everybody up, come on.
            Lifebelts on...

People come out of the doors behind the steward, perplexed. In the foreground a
SYRIAN WOMAN asks her husband what was said. He shrugs.

                                                              CUT TO:

160   INT. WIRELESS ROOM   160

ON PHILLIPS, looking shocked.

                              PHILLIPS
            CQD, sir?

                              SMITH
            That's right. The distress call. CQD. Tell whoever
            responds that we are going down by the head and need
            immediate assistance.

Smith hurries out.

                              PHILLIPS   *Deleted in post*
            Blimey.

                              BRIDE
            Maybe you ought to try that new distress call...
            S.O.S.
                (grinning)
            It may be our only chance to use it.

Phillips laughs in spite of himself and starts sending history's first
S.O.S. Dit dit dit, da da da, dit dit dit... over and over.

                                                              (CONTINUED)

Prior to Scene 162, Cameron added a scene in which Andrews crosses through the first-class Lounge and sees the ship's orchestra playing "Alexander's Ragtime Band" (rather than just hearing them playing in the A-deck Foyer).

CAMERON: "Imagine what Andrews must have been feeling. He is in hell. He knows the ship is sinking and yet he's trapped at this surreal, catered party with live entertainment."

160   CONTINUED: 160

                                                              CUT TO:

161   EXT. BOAT DECK   161

Thomas Andrews looks around in amazement. The deck is empty except for the
crew fumbling with the davits. He yells over the roar of the steam to First Officer
Murdoch.

                          ANDREWS
              Where are the passengers?

                          MURDOCH
              They've all gone back inside. Too damn cold and
              noisy for them.

Andrews feels like he is in a bad dream. He looks at his pocketwatch and heads for
the foyer entrance.

                                                              CUT TO:

162   INT. A-DECK FOYER   162

A large number of First Class passengers have gathered near the staircase. They
are getting indignant about the confusion. Molly Brown snags a passing
YOUNG STEWARD.

                          MOLLY
              What's doing, sonny? You've got us all trussed up
              and now we're cooling our heels.

The YOUNG STEWARD backs away, actually stumbling on the stairs.

                          YOUNG STEWARD
              Sorry, mum. Let me go and find out.

The jumpy piano rhythm of "Alexander's Ragtime Band" comes out of the first
class lounge a few yards away. Band leader WALLACE HARTLEY has assembled
some of his men on Captain's orders, to allay panic.

Hockley's entourage comes up to the A-deck foyer. Cal is carrying the lifebelts, almost
as an afterthought. Rose is like a sleepwalker.

                          CAL
              It's just the God damned English doing everything by
              the book.

                          RUTH
              There's no need for language, Mr. Hockley.
                  (to Trudy)
              Go back and turn the heater on in my room, so it
              won't be too cold when we get back.

                                                              (CONTINUED)

*Turned into its own scene
and put before scene 162*

                                                                        96

Thomas Andrews enters, looking around the magnificent room, which he knows is doomed. Rose, standing nearby, sees his heartbroken expression. She walks over to him and Cal goes after her.

                              ROSE
          I saw the iceberg, Mr. Andrews. And I see it in your
          eyes. Please tell me the truth.

                              ANDREWS
          The ship will sink.

                              ROSE
          You're certain?

                              ANDREWS
          Yes. In an hour or so... all this... will be at the
          bottom of the Atlantic.

                              CAL
          My God.

Now it is Cal's turn to look stunned. The Titanic? Sinking?

                              ANDREWS
          Please tell only who you must, I don't want to be
          responsible for a panic. And get to a boat quickly.
          Don't wait. You remember what I told you about the
          boats?

                              ROSE
          Yes, I understand. Thank you.

Andrews goes off, moving among the passengers and urging them to put on their lifebelts and get to the boats.

                                                              CUT TO:

163   INT. MASTER AT ARMS OFFICE   163

Lovejoy and the Master at Arms are handcuffing Jack to a 4" WATER PIPE as a crewman rushes in anxiously and almost blurts to the Master at Arms ...

                              CREWMAN
          You're wanted by the Purser, sir. Urgently.

                              LOVEJOY
          Go on. I'll keep an eye on him.

Lovejoy pulls a pearl handled Colt .45 automatic from under his coat. The Master at Arms nods and tosses the handcuff key to Lovejoy, then exits with the crewman. Lovejoy flips the key in the air. Catches it.

                                                              CUT TO:

Junior Wireless Operator Bride (Craig Kelly) relays a message to Captain Smith.

Second Officer Lightoller (Jonny Phillips) confronts Captain Smith.

INT. BRIDGE

Junior Wireless Operator Bride is relaying a message to Captain Smith from the CUNARD LINER CARPATHIA.

                             BRIDE
           Carpathia says they're making 17 knots, full steam for
           them, sir.

                             SMITH
           And she's the only one who's responding?

                             BRIDE
           The only one close, sir. She says they can be here in
           four hours.

                             SMITH
           Four hours!

The enormity of it hits Smith like a sledgehammer blow.

                             SMITH
           Thank you, Bride.

He turns as Bride exits, and looks out onto the blackness.

                             SMITH
             (to himself)
           My God.

                                                  CUT TO:

165   EXT. BOAT DECK - NIGHT   165

Lightoller has his boats swung out. He is standing amidst a crowd of uncertain passengers in all states of dress and undress. One first class woman is barefoot. Others are in stockings. The maitre d' of the restaurant is in top hat and overcoat. Others are still in evening dress, while some are in bathrobes and kimonos. Women are wearing lifebelts over velvet gowns, then topping it with sable stoles. Some brought jewels, others books, even small dogs.

Lightoller sees Smith walking stiffly toward him and quickly goes to him. He yells into the Captain's ear, through cupped hands, over the roar of the steam...

                         LIGHTOLLER
          <u>Hadn't we better get the women and</u>
          <u>children into the boats sir?</u>

Smith just nods, a bit abstractly. The fire has gone out of him. Lightoller sees the awesome truth in Smith's face.

                                       (CONTINUED)

As discussed earlier, preview audiences had an unexpected adverse reaction to scenes involving the band. In addition to planting their story within the context of Brock Lovett's interview [See the notes for Scene 17], Cameron added dialogue in post for bandleader Wallace Hartley: "Alright, boys. Like the Captain said, nice and cheery so there's no panic." The addition of this dialogue (making it Captain's orders) explained the motivation for playing on deck. *Titanic* Historian Don Lynch: "In this day and age when we can push a button and hear practically any kind of music we want, it can be hard to appreciate what sort of impact live music could have on a crowd in 1912. That's one of the reasons Hartley's band is remembered with so much fondness."

In addition to pacing, Cameron cut the latter half of the scene in which Ruth wants to go back for her brooch for two reasons. First, he had already cut the beat where Old Rose talks about the brooch. Second, he wanted to keep Ruth blithely unaware of the disaster happening around her until Rose shocks Ruth to awareness in Scene 170.

LIGHTOLLER
> (to the men)
> <u>Right!</u> <u>Start the loading.</u> <u>Women and children!</u>

The appalling din of escaping steam abruptly cuts off, leaving a sudden unearthly silence in which Lightoller's voice echoes.

ON WALLACE HARTLEY raising his violin to play.

HARTLEY
> Number 26. Ready and—

The band has reassembled just outside the First Class Entrance, port side, near where Lightoller is calling for the boats to be loaded. They strike up a waltz, lively and elegant. The music wafts all over the ship.

LIGHTOLLER
> (indicating the boat)
> Ladies, this way.

No one moves. A couple of women look down the side of the ship. It's a long way to the water. With the steam cut off, and the music playing, the ship seems very safe and sound. Like a big rock in the middle of the ocean.

LIGHTOLLER
> Ladies, please. Step into the boat.

Finally one woman steps across the gap, into the boat, terrified of the drop to the water far below.

WOMAN IN CROWD
> You watch. They'll put us off in these silly little boats to freeze, and we'll all be back on board by breakfast.

CAL, ROSE AND RUTH come out of the doors near the band.

RUTH
> My brooch, I left my brooch. I must have it!

She turns back to go to her room but Cal takes her by the arm, refusing to let her go. The firmness of his hold surprises her.

CAL
> Stay here, Ruth.

Ruth sees his expression, and knows fear for the first time.

CUT TO:

166   INT. STEERAGE BERTHING AFT/ CORRIDORS AND STAIRWELL   166

It is chaos, with stewards pushing their way through narrow corridors clogged with people carrying suitcases, duffel bags, children. Some have lifebelts on, others don't.

(CONTINUED)

*S*cene 167 was
expanded in the
film to illustrate just
how precarious getting
into a lifeboat was and
why many women
were reluctant to leave
the ship.

> STEWARD #2
> (to Steward #3)
> I told the stupid sods no luggage. Aw, <u>bloody hell</u>!

He throws up his hands at the sight of a family, loaded down with cases and bags, completely blocking the corridor.

Fabrizio and Tommy push past the stewards, going the other way. They reach a huge crowd gathered at the bottom of the MAIN 3RD CLASS STAIRWELL. [Fabrizio spots Helga with the rest of the Dahl family, standing patiently with suitcases in hand. He reaches her and she grins, hugging him.]   *Deleted for Pacing*

Tommy pushes to where he can see what's holding up the group. There is a steel gate across the top of the stairs, with several stewards and seamen on the other side.

> STEWARD
> Stay calm, please. It's not time to go up to the boats yet.

Near Tommy, an IRISHWOMAN stands stoically with two small children and their battered luggage.

> LITTLE BOY
> What are we doing, mummy?

> WOMAN
> We're just waiting, dear. When they finish putting First Class people in the boats, they'll be startin' with us, and we'll want be all ready, won't we?

>   CUT TO:

167   EXT. STARBOARD SIDE   167

Boat 7 is less than half full, with 28 aboard a boat made for 65.

> FIRST OFFICER MURDOCH
> Lower away! By the left and right together, steady lads!

The boat lurches as the falls start to pay out through the pulley blocks. The women gasp. The boat descends, swaying and jerking, toward the water 60 feet below. The passengers are terrified.

>   CUT TO:

168   EXT. / INT. TITANIC HULL AND MASTER AT ARMS OFFICE   168

TRACKING along the rows of portholes angling down into the water. Under the surface, they glow green. Pushing in on one porthole which is half submerged. Inside we see Jack, looking apprehensively at the water rising up the glass.

>   (CONTINUED)

First distress rocket fired <u>here</u>

ovejoy's parting line to Jack was originally to be echoed in a confrontation with the valet in Scene 213.

INSIDE THE MASTER AT ARMS' OFFICE Jack sits chained to the waterpipe, next
to the porthole. Lovejoy sits on the edge of a desk. He puts a .45 bullet on the
desk and watches it roll across and fall off. He picks up the bullet.

> LOVEJOY
> You know... I believe this ship may sink.
>   (crosses to Jack)
> I've been asked to give you this small token of our
> appreciation...

He punches Jack hard in the stomach, knocking the wind out of him.

> LOVEJOY
> Compliments of Mr. Caledon Hockley.

Lovejoy flips the handcuff key in the air, catches it and puts it in his pocket. He
exits. Jack is left gasping, handcuffed to the pipe.

CUT TO:

169   EXT. BOAT DECK/ STARBOARD SIDE, FORWARD   169

At the stairwell rail on the bridge wing, Fourth Officer Boxhall and Quartermaster
Rowe light the first distress rocket. It shoots into the sky and EXPLODES with a
thunderclap over the ship, sending out white starbursts which light up the entire
deck as they fall.

WHIP PAN off the starbursts to Ismay. The Managing Director of White Star Line
is cracking. Already at the breaking point from his immense guilt, the rocket panics
him. He starts shouting at the officers struggling with the falls of BOAT 5.

> ISMAY
> There is no time to waste!
>   (yelling and waving his arms)
> Lower away! Lower away ! Lower away!

FIFTH OFFICER LOWE, a baby-faced 28, and the youngest officer, looks up from
the tangled falls at the madman.

> LOWE
> Get out of the way, you fool!

> ISMAY
> *Do you know who I am?*

Lowe, not having a clue nor caring, squares up to Ismay.

> LOWE
> You're a passenger. And I'm a ship's bloody officer.
> Now do what you're told!
>   (turning away)
> Steady men! Stand by the falls!

(CONTINUED)

*Deleted in post
for Pacing*

A distress rocket being fired
startles the passengers.

"It's a pity . . . ." line taken from
Scene 209 to clarify Cal's smug-
ness at Jack's jeopardy, and cement
Rose's decision to go find Jack.

CONTINUED:

                              ISMAY
                    (numbly, backing away)
                 Yes, quite right. Sorry.

                                                              CUT TO:

170   EXT. BOAT DECK/ PORT SIDE   170

SECOND OFFICER LIGHTOLLER is loading the boat nearest Cal and Rose...
Boat 6.

                            LIGHTOLLER
                 Women and children only! Sorry sir, no men yet.

Another rocket bursts overhead, lighting the crowd. Startled faces turn upward. Fear
now in the eyes.

DANIEL MARVIN has his Biograph camera set up, cranking away... hoping to get
an exposure off the rocket's light. He has Mary posed in front of the scene at the
boats.

                              MARVIN
                 You're afraid, darling. Scared to death. That's it!   *Deleted
                                                                        before principal
Either she suddenly learned to act or she is petrified.   photography*

ROSE watches the farewells taking place right in front of her as they step closer to
the boat. Husbands saying goodbye to wives and children. Lovers and friends
parted. Nearby MOLLY is getting a reluctant woman to board the boat.

                              MOLLY
                 Come on, you heard the man. Get in the boat, sister.

                               RUTH
                 Will the lifeboats be seated according to class? I
                 hope they're not too crowded—

                               ROSE
                 Oh, Mother shut up!
                    (Ruth freezes, mouth open)
                 Don't you understand? The water is freezing and there
                 aren't enough boats... not enough by half. Half of the
                 people on this ship are going to die.

                               CAL
                 Not the better half.

PUSH IN ON ROSE'S FACE as it hits her like a thunderbolt. Jack is third class. He
doesn't stand a chance. Another rocket bursts overhead, bathing her face in white
light.

                               ROSE
                 You unimaginable bastard.

                                                              (CONTINUED)

CAMERON: "During pre-production rehearsals, Kate suggested that, rather than poke him with a hatpin, Rose should spit in Cal's face. I loved the suggestion immediately because getting back at Cal using a skill she learned from Jack has that perfect dramatic symmetry. It's a great indicator for how much she's grown as a character." The rest of the scene (and Scene 171) was deleted as unnecessary. Cal is too shocked to run after her because Rose has made her point so powerfully.

                              MOLLY
           Come on Ruth, get in the boat. These are the first
           class seats right up here. That's it.

Molly practically hands her over to Lightoller, then looks around for some other
women who might need a push.

                              MOLLY
           Come on, Rose. You're next, darlin'.

Rose steps back, shaking her head.

                              RUTH
           Rose, get in the boat!

                              ROSE
           Goodbye, Mother.

Ruth, standing in the tippy lifeboat, can do nothing. Cal grabs Rose's arm but she
pulls free and walks away through the crowd. Cal catches up to Rose and grabs her
again, roughly.

                              CAL
           Where are you going? To him? Is that it? To be a
           whore to that gutter rat?

                              ROSE
           I'd rather be his whore than your wife.

He clenches his jaw and squeezes her arm viciously, pulling her back toward the
lifeboat. Rose pulls out a hairpin and jabs him with it. He lets go with a curse and she
runs into the crowd.

                              LIGHTOLLER
           Lower away!!

                              RUTH
           Rose! ROSE!!

                              MOLLY
           Stuff a sock in it, would ya, Ruth. She'll be along.

The boat lurches downward as the falls are paid out.

TRACKING WITH ROSE, as she runs through the clusters of people. She looks
back and a furious Cal is coming after her. She runs breathlessly up to two proper
looking men.

                              ROSE
           That man tried to take advantage of me in the crowd!

Appalled they turn to see Cal running toward them. Rose runs on as the two men
grab Cal, restraining him. She runs through the First Class entrance.

                                                          (CONTINUED)

Deleted in post

This scene was shot
as a series of long
takes to allow the
room to flood. This
gave Cameron plenty
of material to intercut
with Rose's scenes,
even though these
beats are not refer-
enced in the script.

170   CONTINUED: (2)   170

Cal breaks free and runs after her. He reaches the entrance, but runs into a knot of
people coming out. He pushes rudely through them...

                                                                        CUT TO:

171   INT. BOAT DECK FOYER/ STAIRCASE/ A-DECK FOYER   171

Cal runs in, and down to the landing, pushing past the gentlemen and ladies who are
filing up the stairs. He scans the A-Deck foyer. Rose is gone.

                                                                        CUT TO:

172   EXT. OCEAN/ TITANIC/ BOAT 6   172

The hull of Titanic looms over Boat 6 like a cliff. Its enormous mass is suddenly threatening to those in the tiny boat. Quartermaster Hitchins, at the tiller,
wants nothing but to get away from the ship. Unfortunately his two seamen can't row.
They flail like a duck with a broken wing.

                              HITCHINS
                Keep pulling... away from the ship. Pull.

                              MOLLY
                Ain't you boys ever rowed before? Here, gimme
                those oars. I'll show ya how it's done.

She climbs over Ruth to get at the oars, stepping on her feet.

Around them the evacuation is in full swing, with boats in the water, others being lowered.

                                                                        CUT TO:

173   INT. MASTER AT ARMS OFFICE/ CORRIDOR   173

Jack pulls on the pipe with all his strength. It's not budging. He hears a gurgling
sound. Water pours under the door, spreading rapidly across the floor.

                              JACK
                Shit.

He tries to pull one hand out of the cuffs, working it until the skin is
raw... no good.

                              JACK
                Help!! Somebody!! Can anybody hear me?!
                    (to himself)
                This could be bad.

174   THE CORRIDOR outside is deserted. Flooded a couple of inches deep. Jack's voice   174
comes faintly through the door, but there is no one to hear it.

                                                                        CUT TO:

In the film, Andrews gives more complicated directions to a flustered Rose.

CAMERON: "By the time we filmed that scene I understood the geography of the real ship better. I wanted to exploit this for dramatic effect because the actual path Rose would have had to take was more maze-like than I could have imagined."

175   INT. FIRST CLASS CORRIDOR   175

Thomas Andrews is opening stateroom doors, checking that people are out.

                              ANDREWS
                    Anyone in here?

Rose runs up to him, breathless.

                              ROSE
                    Mr. Andrews, thank God! Where would the Master at
                    Arms take someone under arrest!?

                              ANDREWS
                    What? You have to get to a boat right away!

                              ROSE
                    No! I'll do this with or without your help, sir. But
                    without will take longer.

                              ANDREWS
                       (beat)

                    Take the elevator to the very bottom, go left, down
                    the crewman's passage, then make a right.

                              ROSE
                    Bottom, left, right. I have it.

                              ANDREWS
                    Hurry, Rose.

                                                                CUT TO:

176   INT. FOYER / ELEVATORS   176

Rose runs up as the last Elevator Operator is closing up his lift to
leave.

                              OPERATOR
                    Sorry, miss, lifts are closed—

Without thinking she grabs him and shoves him back into the lift.

                              ROSE
                    I'm through being polite, goddamnit!! I may never be
                    polite the rest of my life! Now take me down!!

The operator fumbles to close the gate and start the lift.

                                                                CUT TO:

177   EXT. OCEAN/ BOAT 6   177

Molly and the two seamen are rowing, and they've made it a hundred feet or so.
Enough to see that the ship is angled down into the water, with the bow rail less than ten
feet above the surface.

                         MOLLY
              Come on girls, join in, it'll keep ya warm. Let's go
              Ruth. Grab an oar!

Ruth just stares at the spectacle of the great liner, its rows of lights blazing, slanting
down into the sullen black mirror of the Atlantic.

                                                                      CUT TO:

178   INT. FIRST CLASS ELEVATOR/ CORRIDORS   178

Through the wrought iron door of the elevator car Rose can see the decks going past.
The lift slows. Suddenly ICEWATER is swirling around her legs. She SCREAMS
in surprise. So does the operator.

The car has landed in a foot of freezing water, shocking the hell out of her. She claws
the door open and splashes out, hiking up her floor-length skirt so she can move. The
lift goes back up, behind her, as she looks around.

                         ROSE
              Left, crew passage.

She spots it and slogs down the flooded corridor. The place is understandably
deserted. She is on her own.

                         ROSE
              Right, right... right.

She turns into a cross-corridor, splashing down the hall. A row of doors on each
side.

                         ROSE
              Jack? Jaaacckk??

                                                                      CUT TO:

179   INT. MASTER AT ARMS OFFICE/ CORRIDOR   179

Jack is hopelessly pulling on the pipe again, straining until he turns red. He collapses
back on the bench, realizing he's screwed. Then he hears her through the door.

                         JACK
              ROSE!! In here!

180   IN THE HALL Rose hears his voice behind her. She spins and runs back, locating   180
       the right door, then pushes it open, creating a small wave.

She splashes over to Jack and puts her arms around him.

                                                          (CONTINUED)

Deleted prior to shooting.
Replaced with first shot
from scene 191

                              ROSE
              Jack, Jack, Jack... I'm sorry, I'm so sorry.

They are so happy to see each other it's embarrassing.

                              JACK
              That guy Lovejoy put it in my pocket.

                              ROSE
              I know, I know.

                              JACK
              See if you can find a key for these. Try those
              drawers. It's a little brass one.

She kisses his face and hugs him again, then starts to go through the
desk.

                              JACK
              So... how did you find out I didn't do it?

                              ROSE
              I didn't.
                 (she looks at him)
              I just realized I already *knew*.

They share a look, then she goes back to ransacking the room, searching drawers
and cupboards. Jack sees movement out the porthole and looks out.

A LIFEBOAT hits the surface of the water, seen from below.

                                                              CUT TO:

181   EXT. TITANIC / BOAT ONE   181

While the seamen detach the falls, Boat One rocks next to the hull. Lucile and Sir
Cosmo Duff-Gordon sit with ten others in a boat made for <u>four</u> times that many.

                              LUCILE
              I despise small boats. I just know I'm going to be
              seasick. I always get seasick in small boats. Good
              Heavens, there's a man down there.

In a lit porthole beneath the surface she sees Jack looking up at her... a face in a bubble
of light under the water.

                                                              CUT TO:

182   INT. MASTER AT ARMS OFFICE   182

Rose stops trashing the room, and stands there, breathing hard.

                              ROSE
              There's no key in here.

                                                              (CONTINUED)

While the script refers to Rose tearing off part of her dress, wardrobe choices dictated that she should discard her heavy topcoat instead. Also Cameron felt that this action played better when she tries to get back to Jack in Scene 185.

They look around at the water, now almost two feet deep. Jack has pulled his feet up onto the bench.

> JACK
> You have to go for help.

> ROSE
> (nodding)
> I'll be right back.

> JACK
> I'll wait here.

She runs out, looking back at him once from the doorway, then splashes away. Jack looks down at the swirling water.

                                                              CUT TO:

183   INT. STAIRWELL AND CORRIDORS   183

 Rose splashes down the hall to a stairwell going up to the next deck. She climbs the stairs, her long skirt leaving a trail like a giant snail. The weight of it is really slow-ing her down. She rips at the buttons and shimmies quickly out of the thing. She bounds up the stairs in her stockings and knee-length slip, to find herself in—

184   A LONG CORRIDOR... part of the labyrinth of steerage hallways forward. She is   184
      alone here. A long groan of stressed metal echoes along the hall as the ship continues to
      settle. She runs down the hall, unimpeded now.

> ROSE
> Hello? Somebody?!

She turns a corner and runs along another corridor in a daze. The hall slopes down into water which, shimmers, reflecting the lights. The margin of the water creeps toward her. A young man appears, running through the water, sending up geysers of spray. He pelts past her without slowing, his eyes crazed...

> ROSE
> Help me! We need help!

He doesn't look back. It is like a bad dream. The hull gongs with terrifying sounds.

The lights flicker and go out, leaving utter darkness. A beat. Then they come back on. She finds herself hyperventilating. That one moment of blackness was the most terrifying of her life.

A steward runs around the nearest corner, his arms full of lifebelts. He is upset to see someone still in his section. He grabs her forcefully by the arm, pulling her with him like a wayward child.

> STEWARD
> Come on, then, let's get you topside, miss, that's
> right.

                                                          (CONTINUED)

Rose's line, "See you there buster," was cut in post because Cameron felt her punch was the stronger of the two moments.

> ROSE
> Wait. <u>Wait!</u> <u>I need your help!</u> There's—

> STEWARD
> No need for panic, miss. <u>Come along</u>!

> ROSE
> <u>No, let me go!</u> <u>You're going the wrong way</u>!

He's not listening. And he won't let her go.

She SHOUTS in his ear, and when he turns, she punches him squarely in the nose. Shocked, he lets her go and staggers back.

> STEWARD
> To Hell with you!

> ROSE
> See you there, buster!

The steward runs off, holding his bloody nose. She spits after him. Just the way Jack taught her.

She turns around, SEES: a glass case with a fire-axe in it. She breaks the glass with a battered suitcase which is lying discarded nearby, and seizes the axe, running back the way she came.

185   AT THE STAIRWELL she looks down and gasps. The water has flooded the bottom five   185
steps. She goes down and has to crouch to look along the corridor to the room where
Jack is trapped.

Rose plunges into the water, which is up to her waist... and powers forward, holding
the axe above her head in two hands. She grimaces at the pain from the literally
freezing water.

Added second shot from scene 191 in post   CUT TO:

186   INT. MASTER AT ARMS OFFICE   186

Jack has climbed up on the bench, and is hugging the waterpipe. Rose wades in,
holding the axe above her head.

> ROSE
> Will this work?

> JACK
> We'll find out.

They are both terrified, but trying to keep panic at bay. He positions the chain connecting the two cuffs, stretching it taut across the steel pipe. The chain is of course
very short, and his exposed wrists are on either side of it.

(CONTINUED)

As shot, Scene 186 eliminated some of the scripted dialogue. Cameron: "Leo always naturalized his dialogue. During rehearsals he stopped saying the 'Nice work, there, Paul Bunyan,' so I assumed he felt uncomfortable doing that line. I didn't miss it. There's actually a great deal of humor in that scene without that kind of dialogue. Think about it; you have a guy chained to a pipe whose only hope for being rescued is this little first-class woman who has transformed herself into this axe-wielding bundle of energy. I showed a cut of the scene to Kate and she laughed. She said she never knew the scene was funny because she'd never looked at it out of character."

                              JACK
                    Try a couple practice swings.

Rose hefts the axe and thunks it into a wooden cabinet.

                              JACK
                    Now try to hit the same mark again.

She swings hard and the blade thunks in four inches from the mark.

                              JACK
                    Okay, that's enough practice.

He winces, bracing himself as she raises the axe. She has to hit a target about an inch
wide with all the force she can muster, with his hands on either side.

                              JACK
                        (sounding calm)
                    You can do it, Rose. Hit it as hard as you can, I
                    trust you.

Jack closes his eyes. *So does she.*

The axe comes down. K-WHANG! Rose gingerly opens her eyes and looks...
Jack is grinning with two separated cuffs.

Rose drops the axe, all the strength going out of her.

                              JACK
                    Nice work, there, Paul Bunyan.

He climbs down into the water next to her. He can't breathe for a second.

                              JACK
                    Shit! Excuse my French. Ow ow ow, that is <u>cold</u>!
                    Come on, let's go.

They wade out into the hall. Rose starts toward the stairs going up, but Jack stops
her. There is only about a foot of the stairwell opening visible.

                              JACK
                    Too deep. We gotta find another way out.

                                                                       CUT TO:

187   EXT. BOAT 6 AND TITANIC   187

TIGHT ON THE LETTERS **TITANIC** painted two feet high on the bow of the
doomed steamer. Once 50 feet above the waterline, they now quietly slip below the
surface. We see them, gold on black, rippling and dimming to a pale green as they
go deeper.

Deleted in post

CAMERON: "Up to this point in the movie I've emphasized how huge the ship is. Now, we see the ship tiny and isolated in a vast, dark environment, its rocket pathetically ineffective and futile."

188   IN BOAT SIX, Ruth looks back at the Titanic, transfixed by the sight of the   188
dying liner. The bowsprit is now barely above the waterline. Another of
Boxhall's rockets EXPLODES overhead. K-BOOM! It lights up the whole area,
and we see half a dozen boats in the water, spreading out from the ship.

                              MOLLY
              Now there's somethin' you don't see every day.

Moved parts of scene 190 here   CUT TO:

189   INT. SCOTLAND ROAD / E-DECK   189

The widest passageway in the ship, it is used by crew and steerage alike, and runs
almost the length of the ship. Right now steerage passengers move along it like
refugees, heading aft.

CRASH! A wooden doorframe splinters and the door bursts open under the force
of Jack's shoulder. Jack and Rose stumble through, into the corridor. A STEW-
ARD, who was nearby herding people along, marches over.

                              STEWARD
              Here you! You'll have to pay for that, you know.
              That's White Star Line property—

                         JACK AND ROSE   *Deleted in post*
                      (turning together)   *for pacing*
              Shutup!

Jack leads her past the dumbfounded steward. They join the steerage stragglers going
aft. In places the corridor is almost completely blocked by large families carrying
all their luggage.

AN IRISH WOMAN gives Rose a blanket, more for modesty than because she is
blue-lipped and shivering.

                            IRISHWOMAN
                 Here, lass, cover yerself.

Jack rubs her arms and tries to warm her up as they walk along. The woman's husband offers them a flask of whiskey.

                            IRISHMAN
                 This'll take the chill off.

Rose takes a mighty belt and hands it to Jack. He grins and follows suit. Jack
tries a number of DOORS and IRON GATES along the way, finding them all locked.

                                                               CUT TO:

190   EXT. BOAT DECK   190

ON THE BOAT DECK, the action has moved to the aft group of boats, numbers 9, 11, 13,
and 15 on the starboard side, and 10, 12, 14 and 16 on the port side. The pace of work is

                                                          (CONTINUED)

Having spent so much time below decks with Jack and Rose, Cameron wanted to quickly present how chaotic events had become in their absence. By having some of Lightoller and Lowe's lifeboat activity (as well as Cal and Lovejoy's discussion) prior to Scene 189, the larger picture of what's happening on board is established.

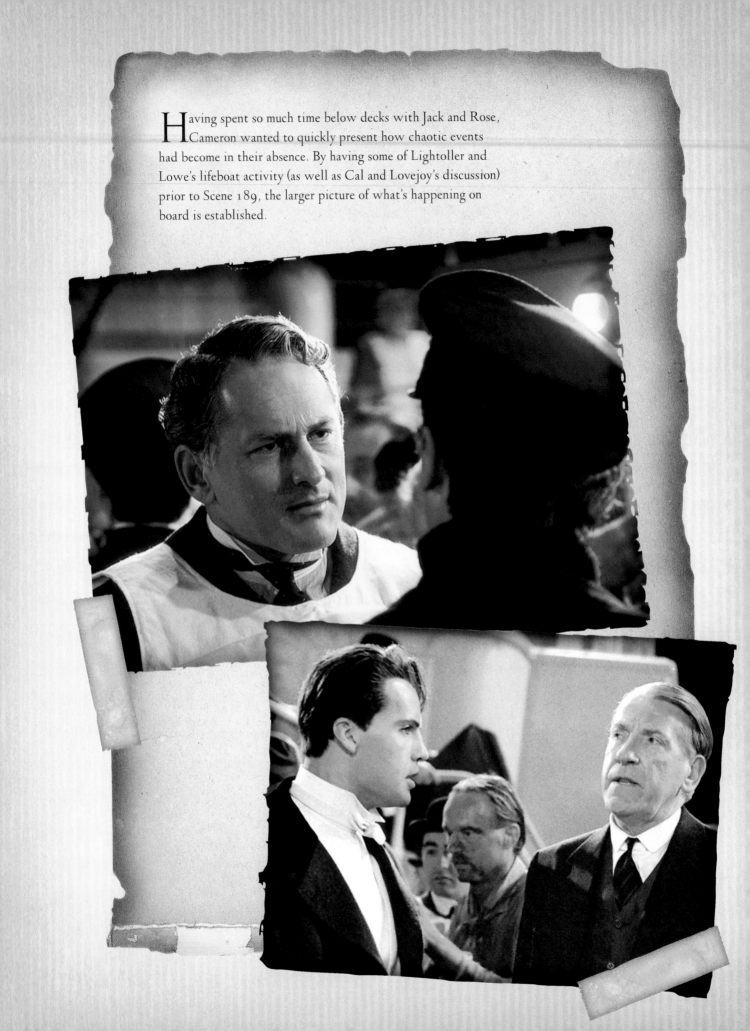

more frantic. You see crew and officers running now to work the davits, their previous complacency gone.

CAL pushes through the crowd, scanning for Rose. Around him is chaos and confusion. A woman is calling for a child who has become separated in the crowd. A man is shouting over people's heads. A woman takes hold of Second Officer Lightoller's arm as he is about to launch Boat 10.

>   WOMAN
>   Will you hold the boat a moment? I just have to run
>   back to my room for something—

Lightoller grabs her and shoves her bodily into the boat. Thomas Andrews rushes up to him just then.

>   ANDREWS
>   Why are the boats being launched half full?!

Lightoller steps past him, helping a seaman clear a snarled fall.

>   LIGHTOLLER
>   Not now, Mr. Andrews.

>   ANDREWS
>   (pointing down at the water)
>   There, look... twenty or so in a boat built for sixty
>   five. And I saw one boat with only twelve. Twelve!

>   LIGHTOLLER
>   Well... we were not sure of the weight—

>   ANDREWS
>   Rubbish! They were tested in Belfast with the weight
>   of 70 men. Now fill these boats, Mr. Lightoller. For
>   God's sake, man!

The shot HANDS OFF to Cal, who sees Lovejoy hurrying toward him through the aisle connecting the port and starboard sides of the boat deck.

>   LOVEJOY
>   She's not on the starboard side either.

>   CAL
>   We're running out of time. And this strutting
>   martinet...
>   (indicating Lightoller)
>   ...isn't letting any men in at all.

>   LOVEJOY
>   The one on the other side is letting men in.

>   CAL
>   Then that's our play. But we're still going to need
>   some insurance.
>   (MORE)

                                                   (CONTINUED)

Deleted in post ←

During production, an unscripted scene was shot showing Fabrizio peering out of one of the third-class gangway doors to explain how he knows what is happening with the lifeboats in Scene 192. In the final film, it takes the place of Scene 191, which was utilized in two separate places.

                              CAL (cont'd)
                    (he starts off forward)
              Come on.

Cal charges off, heading forward, followed by Lovejoy. The SHOT HANDS OFF
to a finely dressed elderly couple, IDA and ISADOR STRAUSS.

                              ISADOR
              Please, Ida, get into the boat.

                               IDA
              No. We've been together for forty years, and where
              you go, I go. Don't argue with me, Isador, you know
              it does no good.

He looks at her with sadness and great love. They embrace gently.

                             LIGHTOLLER
              Lower away!!

                                         Replaced scene 181

                                                              CUT TO:

191   EXT. BRIDGE/FORWARD WELL DECK/ FOC'SLE   191

AT THE BOW... the place where Jack and Rose first kissed... the bow railing goes
under water. Water swirls around the capstans and windlasses on the foc'sle deck.

Smith strides to the bridge rail and looks down at the well deck. Water is shipping over
the sides and the well deck is awash. Two men run across the deck, their feet sending
up spray. Behind Smith, Boxhall fires another rocket. WHOOSH!

                      Moved prior
                                                              CUT TO:

192   INT. E-DECK CORRIDORS AND STAIRWELL   *to scene 185*   192

Fabrizio, standing with Helga Dahl and her family, hears Jack's voice.

                               JACK
              Fabrizio! _Fabri_!

Fabrizio turns and sees Jack and Rose pushing through the crowd. He and Jack hug
like brothers.

                             FABRIZIO
              The boats are all going.

                               JACK
              We gotta get up there or we're gonna be gargling salt-
              water. Where's Tommy?

Fabrizio points over the heads of the solidly packed crowd to the stairwell.

TOMMY has his hands on the bars of the steel gate which blocks the head of the stairwell. The crew open the gate a foot or so and a few women are squeezing through.

                                                  (CONTINUED)

As shot, the order of Scene 192 differs slightly in the film. Fabrizio joins the scene after the mob scene at the gate for a better dramatic flow.

                          STEWARD #2
              Women only. No men. No men!!

But some terrified men, not understanding English, try to rush through the gap, forcing
the gate open. The crewmen and stewards push them back, shoving and punching them.

                          STEWARD #2
              Get back! Get back you lot!
                  (to the crewmen)
              Lock it!!

They struggle to get the gate closed again, while Steward #2 brandishes a small
revolver. Another holds a fire axe. They lock the gate, and a cry goes up among the
crowd, who surge forward, pounding against the steel and shouting in several languages.

                          TOMMY
              For the love of God, man, there are children down
              here! Let us up, so we can have a chance!

But the crewmen are scared now. They have let the situation get out of hand, and
now they have a mob. Tommy gives up and pushes his way back through the crowd,
going down the stairs. He rejoins Jack, Rose and Fabrizio.

                          TOMMY
              It's hopeless that way.

                          JACK
              Well, whatever we're goin' to do, we better do it fast.

Fabrizio turns to Helga, praying he can make himself understood.

                          FABRIZIO
                  (with a lot of hand gestures)
              Everyone... all of you... come with me now. We go
              to boats. We go to boats. Capito? Come now!

They can't understand what he's saying. They can see his urgency, but OLUF DAHL,
the patriarch of the family, shakes his head. He will not panic, and will not let his
family go with this boy. Fabrizio turns to Helga.

                          FABRIZIO
              Helga ... per favore... please ... come with me, I am
              lucky. Is my destiny to go to America.

She kisses him, then steps back to be with her family. Jack lays a hand on his shoulder, his eyes saying "Let's go".

                          FABRIZIO
              I will never forget you.

He turns to Jack, who leads the way out of the crowd. Looking back Fabrizio sees her
face disappear into the crowd.

                                                          CUT TO:

Deleted in post

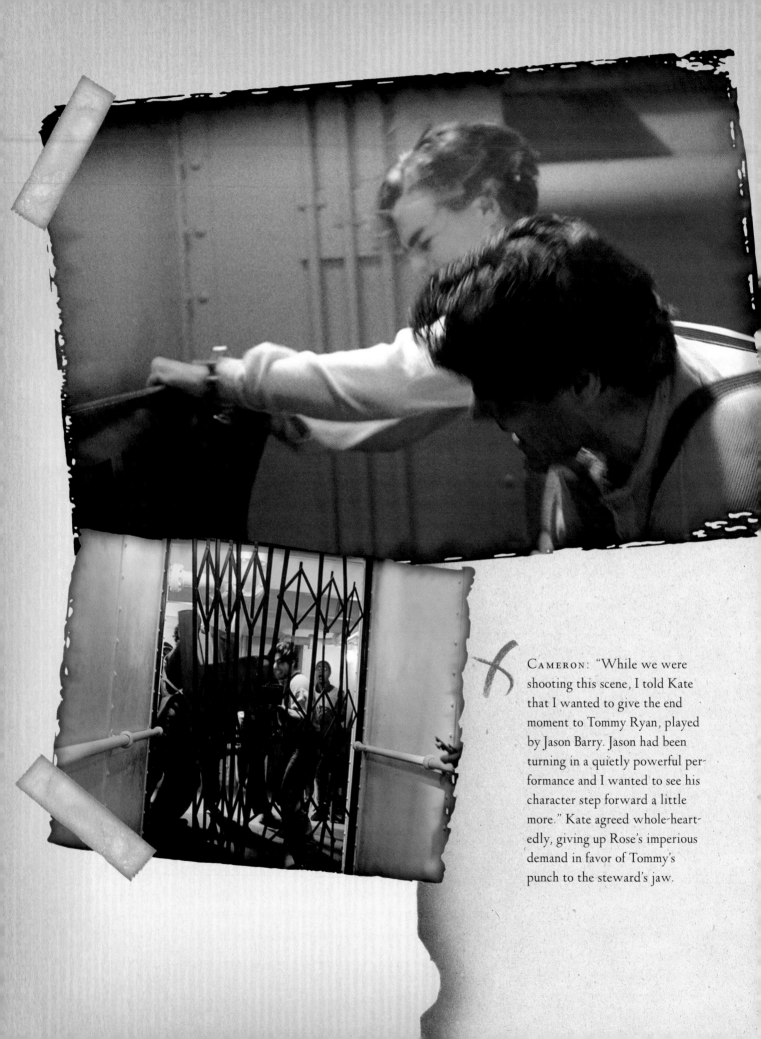

CAMERON: "While we were shooting this scene, I told Kate that I wanted to give the end moment to Tommy Ryan, played by Jason Barry. Jason had been turning in a quietly powerful performance and I wanted to see his character step forward a little more." Kate agreed whole-heartedly, giving up Rose's imperious demand in favor of Tommy's punch to the steward's jaw.

193   INT. CAL AND ROSE'S SUITE   193

CLUNK! Cal opens his safe and reaches inside. As Lovejoy watches, he pulls out
two stacks of bills, still banded by bank wrappers. Then he takes out the "Heart of
the Sea", putting it in the pocket of his overcoat, and locks the safe.

                              CAL
                    (holding up stacks of bills)
                I make my own luck.

                              LOVEJOY
                    (patting the .45 in his waistband)
                So do I.

Cal grins, putting the money in his pocket as they go out.

                                                            CUT TO:

194   INT. STEERAGE, AFT   194

Jack, Rose, Fabrizio and Tommy are lost, searching for a way out. They push
past confused passengers... past a mother changing her baby's diaper on top of an
upturned steamer trunk ... past a woman arguing heatedly with a man in Serbo-
Croatian, a wailing child next to them ... past a man kneeling to console a woman
who is just sitting on the floor, sobbing ... and past another man with an
English/Arabic dictionary, trying to figure out what the signs mean, while his wife and
children wait patiently.

Jack et al come upon a narrow stairwell and they go up two decks before they are
stopped by a small group pressed up against a steel gate. The steerage men are yelling
at a scared STEWARD.

                              STEWARD
                Go to the main stairwell, with everyone else. It'll
                all get sorted out there.

Jack takes one look at this scene and finally just *loses* it.

                              JACK
                <u>God damn it to Hell son of a bitch!!</u>

He grabs one end of a bench bolted to the floor on the landing. He starts pulling on it,
and Tommy and Fabrizio pitch in until the bolts shear and it breaks free. Rose figures out what they are doing and clears a path up the stairs between the waiting
people.

                              ROSE
                Move aside! Quickly, move aside!

Jack and Tommy run up the steps with the bench and RAM IT INTO THE GATE with
all their strength. It rips loose from its track and falls outward, narrowly missing the
steward. Led by Jack, the crowd surges through. <u>Rose steps up to the cowering steward and says in her most imperious tone:</u>

                                                        (CONTINUED)

194 CONTINUED: 194

                              ROSE
          If you have any intention of keeping your pathetic job
          with the White Star Line, I suggest you escort these
          good people to the boat deck... *now.*

Class wins out. He nods dumbly and motions for them to follow.

                                                            CUT TO:

195   EXT. BOAT 6/ TITANIC - NIGHT   195

Ruth rows with Molly Brown, two other women and the incompetent sailors. She rests
on her oars, exhausted, and looks back at the ship.

It slants down into the water, still ablaze with light. Nothing is above water forward of
the bridge except for the foremast. Another rocket goes off, lighting up the entire
area... there are a dozen boats moving outward from the ship.

196   AT THE BOAT DECK RAIL Captain Smith is shouting to Boat 6 through a large metal   196
      megaphone.

                              SMITH
              <u>Come back</u>! <u>Come back to the ship!</u>

CHIEF OFFICER WILDE joins him, blowing his silver whistle.

197   FROM BOAT 6 the whistle comes shrilly across the water. Quartermaster Hitchins   197
      grips the rudder in fear.

                            HITCHINS
          The suction will pull us right down if we don't keep
          going.

                          MOLLY BROWN
          We got room for lots more. I say we go back.

                            HITCHINS
          No! It's our lives now, not theirs. And I'm in charge
          of this boat! <u>Now row!!</u>

Deleted in post

198   CAPTAIN SMITH, at the rail of the boat deck, lowers his megaphone slowly.   198

                              SMITH
          The fools.

                                                            CUT TO:

199   INT. A-DECK FOYER   199

As Cal and Lovejoy cross the foyer they encounter Benjamin Guggenheim and his
valet, both dressed in white tie, tail-coats and top hats.

Deleted before shooting

                                                        (CONTINUED)

Not every decision is a purely creative one. Scene 199 was shot very close to the December/January hiatus when the production was focused on imploding the Grand Staircase (a sequence which did not involve the three main cast members). Cameron wanted to give the cast as much vacation time as possible, so he decided to remove the fictional Cal's interaction with Guggenheim and preserve history intact. The moment plays just as it was reported to the U.S. Senate inquiry, with one exception. Guggenheim asking for a brandy was an ad lib.

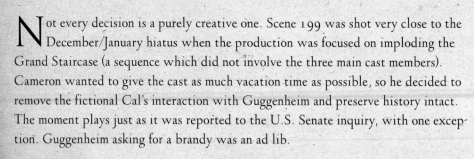

[Note: Shooting the scene, Cameron added an exchange between Guggenheim and J.J. Astor in which Astor tells Guggenheim that he's looking for his dog. The scene made reference to the fact that Astor was reported by one witness to have gone below decks to open up the kennels, thus giving the dogs on *Titanic* a fighting chance. Cameron liked the moment because it showed two of the most powerful men on the ship who, unlike Cal, made no attempt to use their position to save themselves and accepted their fate with grace. The scene was cut for reasons of pacing.]

The actors playing the ship's officers were given information about the disaster, shown the procedures for filling and lowering a lifeboat by an on-set naval historian, and then left alone to improvise their dialogue and commands based on whatever aspect of the sinking Cameron was staging at the time.

CAMERON: "I often told them to stay in character and keep order for me while I was off shooting some other angle. They went hoarse from screaming orders at the background performers. When Jonathan Phillips (Lightoller) whipped around with that gun and roared 'I'll shoot you all like dogs,' I loved it. I ran up and told him it was great and that he should do it again. And he said, 'What did I say?' He was so into it by that point he didn't even remember."

Deleted

                         CAL
        Ben, what's the occasion?

                     GUGGENHEIM
        We have dressed in our best and are prepared to go
        down like gentlemen.

Moved before scene 223

                         CAL
        That's admirable, Ben.
              (walking on)
        I'll be sure and tell your wife... when I get to New
        York.

                                                        CUT TO:

Never shot

200   INT. FIRST CLASS SMOKING ROOM   200

        There are still two cardgames in progress. The room is quiet and civilized. A
        silver serving cart, holding a large humidor, begins to roll slowly across the room.
        One of the cardplayers takes a cigar from it as it rolls by.

                      CARDPLAYER
        It seems we've been dealt a bad hand this time.

                                                        CUT TO:

Shot but deleted

201   EXT. / INT. A-DECK PROMENADE   201

        Cal and Lovejoy are walking aft with a purposeful stride. They pass CHIEF
        BAKER JOUGHIN, who is working up a sweat tossing deck chairs over the rail. After
        they go by, Joughin takes a break and pulls a bottle of scotch from a pocket, upending
        it. He drains it, and tosses it over the side too, then stands there a little unsteadily.

                                                        CUT TO:

202   EXT. BOAT DECK AND A-DECK, AFT   202

        PANIC IS SETTING IN around the remaining boats aft. The crowd here is now a mix
        of all three classes. Officers repeatedly warn men back from the boats. The crowd
        presses in closer.

        Seaman SCAROTT brandishes the tiller of boat 14 to discourage a close press of men
        who look ready to rush the boat. Several men break ranks and rush forward.

        Lightoller pulls out his Webley revolver and aims it at them.

                     LIGHTOLLER
        Get back! Keep order!

        The men back down. Fifth Officer Lowe, standing in the boat, yells to the
        crew.

                        LOWE
        Lower away left and right!

                                                (CONTINUED)

CONTINUED:

Lightoller turns away from the crowd and, out of their sight, breaks his pistol open. Letting out a long breath, he starts to LOAD IT.

                                                        CUT TO:

203   EXT. BOAT DECK, STARBOARD SIDE, AFT   203

CAL AND LOVEJOY arrive in time to see Murdoch lowering his last boat.

                         CAL
            We're too late.

                       LOVEJOY
            There are still some boats forward. Stay with this
            one... Murdoch. He seems to be quite... *practical.*

204   IN THE WATER BELOW there is another panic. Boat 13, already in the water but   204
       still attached to its falls, is pushed aft by the discharge water being pumped out
       of the ship. It winds up directly under boat 15, which is coming down right on top
       of it.

       The passengers shout in panic to the crew above to stop lowering. They are ignored.
       Some men put their hands up, trying futilely to keep the 5 tons of boat 15 from
       crushing them.

       Fred Barrett, the stoker, gets out his knife and leaps to the after falls, climbing rudely
       over people. He cuts the aft falls while another crewman cuts the forward lines. 13 drifts
       out from beneath 15 just seconds before it touches the water with a slap.

       CAL, looking down from the rail hears GUNSHOTS—

                                                        CUT TO:

205   EXT. BOAT DECK/ A-DECK, PORT, AFT   205

       Fifth Officer Lowe, in Boat 14 is firing his gun as a warning to a bunch of
       men threatening to jump into the boat as it passes the open promenade on
       A-Deck.

                         LOWE
            Stay back you lot!

       BLAM! BLAM!

                                                        CUT TO:

206   EXT. BOAT DECK, STARBOARD, AFT   206

       The shots echo away.

                         CAL
            It's starting to fall apart. We don't have much time.

       Cal sees three dogs run by, including the black French bulldog. Someone has released
       the pets from the kennels.

                              Deleted in post   (CONTINUED)

During production, Cameron realized he needed an extra beat to account for the time it would take Jack and the others to run two hundred feet down the Boat Deck to where the band was playing. He and Jonathan Evans Jones (Wallace Hartley) improvised the "they don't listen to us at dinner, either" dialogue expressly for this purpose. Cameron feels it had the added benefit of shoring up the band's motivation to continue playing, helping to alleviate audience concerns discussed earlier (See notes for Scenes 17 and 165).

Cal sees Murdoch turn from the davits of boat 15 and start walking toward the bow. He catches up and falls in beside him.

                              CAL
                    Mr. Murdoch, I'm a businessman, as you know, and I
                    have a business proposition for you.

                                                                     CUT TO:

207   EXT. BOAT DECK, PORT   207

Jack, Rose et al burst out onto the boat deck from the crew stairs just aft of the third funnel. They look at the empty davits.

                              ROSE
                    The boats are gone!

She sees Colonel Gracie chugging forward along the deck, escorting two first class ladies.

                              ROSE
                    Colonel! Are there any boats left?

                              GRACIE
                    (staring at her bedraggled state)
                    Yes, miss... there are still a couple of boats all the
                    way forward. This way, I'll lead you!

Jack grabs her hand and they sprint past Gracie, with Tommy and Fabrizio close behind.

ANGLE ON THE BAND... incredibly they are still playing. Jack, Rose and the others run by.

                              TOMMY
                    Music to drown by. Now I _know_ I'm in First Class.

                                                                     CUT TO:

208   EXT. BOAT DECK, STARBOARD, FORWARD   208

Water pours like a spillway over the forward railing on B-Deck. CAMERA SWEEPS UP past A-Deck to the Boat Deck where Murdoch and his team are loading Collapsible C at the forward-most davits.

NOTE: There are four so-called collapsibles, or Engelhardt boats, including two which are stored on the roof of the officers quarters.

The crowd here is sparse, with most people still aft. Cal slips his hand out of the pocket of his overcoat and into the waist pocket of Murdoch's greatcoat, leaving the stacks of bills there.

                              CAL
                    So we have an understanding then?

                                                             (CONTINUED)

Murdoch's line, "As you've said," was eliminated. Cameron did not want Murdoch accepting Cal's bribe outright. Cameron: "It's ambiguous territory. I wanted to imply that he was too preoccupied with other matters to deal with it at that moment." As staged, Murdoch glances at Cal's money in his pocket and then walks off.

In the film, Cameron splits Scene 208 by cutting to the port side, where Lightoller fires his gun to keep the crowds at bay. Cameron: "At the inquiries, Lightoller denied firing his gun, but he also said the ship didn't break in two so it is possible to question his testimony. And later in life he admitted to using his gun in a private letter. Since there was supporting historical evidence and because it is more dramatic, I chose to show him shooting. Lightoller was presented as a young British hero in "A Night to Remember." Our Lightoller is hanging on by his fingernails."

                            MURDOCH
                    (nodding curtly)
                As you've said.

Cal, satisfied, steps back. He finds himself waiting next to J. Bruce Ismay. Ismay
does not meet his eyes, nor anyone's. Lovejoy comes up to Cal at that moment.

                            LOVEJOY
                I've found her. She's just over on the port side. With
                <u>him</u>.

                            MURDOCH
                Women and children? Any more women and children?
                    (glancing at Cal)
                Any one else, then?

Cal looks longingly at his boat... his moment has arrived.

                              CAL
                God damn it to hell! Come on.

He and Lovejoy head for the port side, taking a short-cut through the
bridge.

Bruce Ismay, seeing his opportunity, steps quickly into Collapsible C. He stares
straight ahead, not meeting Murdoch's eyes.

                            MURDOCH
                    (staring at Ismay)
                Take them down.

                                                              CUT TO:

209   EXT. BOAT DECK / PORT SIDE - NIGHT   209

ON THE PORT SIDE Lightoller is getting people into boat 2. He keeps his pistol in
his hand at this point. Twenty feet below them the sea is pouring into the doors and
windows of B deck staterooms. They can hear the roar of water cascading into the
ship.

                            LIGHTOLLER
                Women and children please. Women and children
                <u>only</u>. Step back, sir.

Even with Jack's arms wrapped around her, Rose is shivering in the cold. Near her
a woman with two young daughters looks into the eyes of a husband she knows she
may not see again.

                            HUSBAND
                Goodbye for a little while... only for a little while.
                    (to his two little girls)
                Go with mummy.

The woman stumbles to the boat with the children, hiding her tears from them.
Beneath the false good cheer, the man is choked with emotion.

                                                          (CONTINUED)

As shot, Cal's line about there being boats on the other side was changed to read, "Look, I have an arrangement with an officer on the other side of the ship." Cameron: "I wanted Cal's lie to be more specific so it would be more believable to Rose. A lie always works best when you're more specific."

                            HUSBAND
            Hold mummy's hand and be a good girl. That's right.

Some of the women are stoic, others are overwhelmed by emotion and have to be
helped into the boats. A man scribbles a note and hands it to a woman who is about
to board.   *Deleted*

                              MAN
            Please get this to my wife in Des Moines, Iowa.

Jack looks at Tommy and Fabrizio.

                             JACK
            You better check the other side.   *Moved to after
                                                            Cal's bribe attempt*

They nod and run off, searching for a way around the deckhouse.

*Moved to   ROSE
the end of   I'm not going without you.
scene 207*
                             JACK
            Get in the boat, Rose.

Cal walks up just then.

                             CAL
            Yes. *Get in the boat, Rose.*

She is shocked to see him. She steps instinctively to Jack. Cal looks at her,
standing there shivering in her wet slip and stockings, a shocking display in 1912.

                             CAL
            My God, look at you.
               (taking off his coat)
            Here, put this on.

She numbly shrugs into it. He is doing it for modesty, not the cold.

                          LIGHTOLLER
            Quickly, ladies. Step into the boat. Hurry, please!

                             JACK
            Go on. I'll get the next one.

                             ROSE
            No. Not without you!

She doesn't even care that Cal is standing right there. He sees the emotion between
Jack and Rose and his jaw clenches. But then he leans close to her and says...

                             CAL
               (low)
            There are boats on the other side that are allowing
            men in. Jack and I can get off safely. Both of us.

                                                          (CONTINUED)

                                    JACK
                    (he smiles reassuringly)
               I'll be alright. Hurry up so we can get going... we
               got our own boat to catch.

                                    CAL
               Get in... hurry up, it's almost full.

Lightoller grabs her arm and pulls her toward the boat. She reaches out for Jack and
her fingers brush his for a moment. Then she finds herself stepping down into the boat.
It's all a rush and blur.

                                    LIGHTOLLER
               Lower away!

The two men watch at the rail as the boat begins to descend.

                                    CAL
                    (low)
               You're a good liar.

                                    JACK
               Almost as good as you.

                                    CAL
               I always win, Jack. One way or another.
                    (looks at him, smiling)
               Pity I didn't keep that drawing. It's going to be
               worth a lot more by morning.

Moved to scene 170

Jack knows he is screwed. He looks down at Rose, not wanting to waste a second of
his last view of her.

210   ROSE'S PERCEPTION... IN SLOW MOTION: *The ropes going through the pulleys*   210
       as the seamen start to lower. All sound going away... Lightoller giving orders,
       his lips moving... but Rose hears only the blood pounding in her ears... this can-
       not be happening... a rocket bursts above in slow-motion, outlining Jack in a halo
       of light... Rose's hair blowing in slow motion as she gazes up at him, descending
       away from him...she sees his hand trembling, the tears at the corners of his eyes, and
       cannot believe the unbearable pain she is feeling...

Rose is still staring up, tears pouring down her face.

SUDDENLY SHE IS MOVING. She lunges across the women next to her. Reaches
the gunwale, climbing it...

Hurls herself out of the boat to the rail of the A-Deck promenade, catching it,
and scrambling over the rail. The Boat 2 continues down. But Rose is back on
Titanic.

                                    JACK
               No Rose! NOOOO!!

Jack spins from the rail, running for the nearest way down to A-Deck.

                                                                    (CONTINUED)

Hockley too has seen her jump. She is willing to die for this man, this gutter scum. He is overwhelmed by a rage so all consuming it eclipses all thought.

CUT TO:

211   INT. GRAND STAIRCASE   211

TRACKING WITH JACK as he bangs through the doors to the foyer and sprints down the stairs. He sees her coming into the A-deck foyer, running toward him, Cal's long coat flying out behind her as she runs.

They meet at the bottom of the stairs, and collide in an embrace.

> JACK
> Rose, Rose, you're so stupid, you're such an idiot--

And all the while he's kissing her and holding her as tightly as he can.

> ROSE
> You jump, I jump, right?

> JACK
> Right.

HOCKLEY comes in and runs to the railing. Looking down he sees them locked in their embrace. Lovejoy comes up behind Cal and puts a restraining HAND on him, but Cal whips around, grabbing the pistol from Lovejoy's waistband in one cobra-fast move.

He RUNS along the rail and down the stairs. As he reaches the landing above them he raises the gun. SCREAMING in rage, he FIRES.

The carved cherub at the foot of the center railing EXPLODES. Jack pulls Rose toward the stairs going down to the next deck. Cal fires again, running down the steps toward them. A bullet blows a divet out of the oak panelling behind Jack's head as he pulls Rose down the next flight of stairs.

Hockley steps on the skittering head of the cherub statue and goes sprawling. The gun clatters across the marble floor. He gets up, and reeling drunkenly goes over to retrieve it.

CUT TO:

212   INT. D-DECK RECEPTION ROOM   212

The bottom of the grand staircase is flooded several feet deep. Jack and Rose come down the stairs two at a time and run straight into the water, fording across the room to where the floor slopes up, until they reach dry footing at the entrance to the dining saloon.

STEADICAM WITH HOCKLEY as he reels down the stairs in time to see Jack and Rose splashing through the water toward the dining saloon. He FIRES twice. Big gouts of spray near them, but he's not a great shot.

The water boils up around his feet and he retreats up the stairs a couple of steps. Around him the woodwork groans and creaks.

(CONTINUED)

CAMERON: "Audiences hated this scene. Even when I was writing it I knew it was a bit of a forced excursion, but I thought audiences would want to see Jack being heroic and winning out against Lovejoy. Of course, after it was shot the scene had its own reasons for staying in. It was visually impressive. It was expensive to shoot. But these reasons have nothing to do with dramatic validity. We were holding onto something that the audience wasn't buying and we simply couldn't see it. So then I thought, all right, maybe it's just too long. I cut the scene in half and we screened the film again. No change. The audience still hated the scene.

"Reading the second test audience's comments, I realized that by introducing guns and fist fights I had committed a tonal violation. Audiences didn't want the additional jeopardy because they were so completely focused on the dangers of the sinking. The scene had to come out.

                                        CAL
                    (calling to them)
                Enjoy your time together!!

Lovejoy arrives next to him. Cal suddenly remembers something and starts to
laugh.

                                      LOVEJOY
                What could possibly be funny?

                                        CAL
                I put the diamond in my coat pocket.
                And I put my coat... *on her.*

He turns to Lovejoy with a sickly expression, his eyes glittering.

                                        CAL
                I give it you... if you can get it.

He hands Lovejoy the pistol and goes back up the stairs. Lovejoy thinks about it...
then slogs into the water. The icewater is up to his waist as he crosses the pool to
the dining saloon.

                                                                      CUT TO:

213   INT. DINING SALOON   213

Lovejoy moves among the tables and ornate columns, searching... listening... his
eyes tracking rapidly. It is a sea of tables, and they could be anywhere. A silver serv-
ing trolley rolls downhill, bumping into tables and pillars.

He glances behind him. The water is following him into the room, advancing in a hundred foot wide tide. The reception room is now a roiling lake, and the grand staircase is submerged past the first landing. Monstrous groans echo through the ship.

ON JACK AND ROSE, crouched behind a table, somewhere in the middle. They see
the water advancing toward them, swirling over the floor. They crawl ahead of it to
the next row of tables.

                                        JACK
                    (whispering)
                Stay here.

He moves off as--

Lovejoy moves over one row and looks along the tables. Nothing.

The ship GROANS and CREAKS. He moves another row.

ANGLE ON A METAL CART... five feet tall and full of stacks of china dishes. It
starts to roll down the aisle between tables.

ON ROSE as the cart rolls toward her. It hits a table and the stacks of dishes topple
out, EXPLODING across the floor and showering her.

                                                                      (CONTINUED)

Deleted in post

"For the next screening I removed the fight scene entirely and I was convinced it wouldn't fly. Jack and Rose just sort of ran in and out and the next time you see them they're on the stairs and you have no clue as to why. The audience went *nuts*. They loved the movie. And we got no negative responses *at all*."

A brief reshoot enabled Cameron to smooth out the continuity by having Kate and Leo run through a section of rebuilt hallway. Also, Lovejoy was digitally removed from one of the shots of the flooding first-class Dining Room so that audiences could still experience the visceral thrill of what Cameron called "elegance submerged."

CAMERON: "The whole process was so revealing of how an audience thinks. If you can get them to play by your rules—and it takes time and effort to do that—then you'd better not break your own rules. The audience won't stand for it. They'll become the concept police."

213   CONTINUED: 213

She scrambles out of the way and--

Lovejoy spins, seeing her. He moves rapidly toward her, keeping the gun
aimed—

That's when Jack tackles him from the side. They slam together into a table, crashing
over it, and toppling to the floor. They land in the water which is flowing rapidly
between the tables.

Jack and Lovejoy grapple in the icy water. Jack jams his knee down on Lovejoy's
hand, breaking his grip on the pistol, and kicks it away. Lovejoy scrambles up and
lunges at him, but Jack GUTPUNCHES him right in the solar plexus, doubling him
over.

                              JACK
          Compliments of the Chippewa Falls Dawsons.

He grabs Lovejoy and slams him into an ornate column. Lovejoy drops to the floor
with a splash, stunned.

                              JACK
              Let's go.

Jack and Rose run aft... uphill... entering the galley. Behind them the tables have
become islands in a lake... and the far end of the room is flooded up to the ceiling.

Lovejoy gets up and looks around for his gun. He pulls it up out of the water and
wades after them.

                                                             CUT TO:

214   INT. GALLEY / STAIRWELL   214

They run through the galley and Rose spots the stairs. She starts up and Jack grabs
her hand. He leads her DOWN.

They crouch together on the landing as Lovejoy runs to the stairs. Assuming they
have gone up (who wouldn't?) he clomps up them two at a time.   *Delete*

They wait for the footsteps to recede. A long CREAKING GROAN. Then they hear
it... a CRYING CHILD. Below them. They go down a few steps to look along the
next deck.

                                                             CUT TO:

215   INT. E-DECK CORRIDORS   215

The corridor is awash, about a foot deep. Standing against the wall, about 50 feet away,
is a little BOY, about 3. The water swirls around his legs and he is wailing.

                              ROSE
              We can't leave him.

Jack nods and they leave the promise of escape up the stairwell to run to the child.
Jack scoops up the kid and they run back to the stairs but—

                                                          (CONTINUED)

A torrent of water comes pouring down the stairs like a rapids. In seconds it is too powerful for them to go against.

                              JACK
              Come on.

Charging the other way down the flooding corridor, they blast up spray with each foot-step. At the end of the hall are heavy double doors. As Jack approaches them he sees water spraying through the gap between the doors right up to the ceiling. The doors groan and start to crack under the tons of pressure.

                              JACK
              Back! Go back!!

Rose pivots and runs back the way they came, taking a turn into a cross-corridor. A MAN is coming the other way. He sees the boy in Jack's arms and cries out, grabbing him away from Jack. Starts cursing him in Russian. He runs on with the boy--

                              ROSE
           No! Not that way! Come back!

216   DOUBLE DOORS BLAST OPEN. A wall of water thunders into the corridor. The   216
       father and child DISAPPEAR instantly.

Jack and Rose run as a wave blasts around the corner, foaming from floor to ceiling. It gains on them like a locomotive. They make it to a stairway going up.

                                                                    CUT TO:

217   INT. STAIRWELL   217

Jack and Rose pound up the steps as white water swirls up behind them. PULL BACK to reveal that a steel gate blocks the top of the stairs. Jack SLAMS against the gate, grip-ping the bars.

A terrified steward standing guard on the landing above turns to run at the sight of the water thundering up the stairs.

                              JACK
              Wait! Wait! Help us! Unlock the gate.

The steward runs on. The water wells up around Jack and Rose, pouring through the gate and slamming them against it. In seconds it is up to their waist.

                              ROSE
           Help us! Please!

The steward stops and looks back. He sees Jack and Rose at the gate, their arms reaching through... sees the water POURING through the gate onto the landing.

                              STEWARD
              Fucking 'ell!

                                                                (CONTINUED)

As staged, the steward drops the keys and runs off, leaving Jack to retrieve them from underwater and open the gate at the last moment. Cameron wanted to give the heroic beat to Jack while at the same time ratcheting up the tension.

He runs back, slogging against the current. He pulls a key ring from his belt and struggles to unlock the padlock as the water fountains up around them.

The lights short out and the landing is plunged into darkness.

The water rises over the lock and he's doing it by feel.

> JACK
> Come on! come on!

 Jack and Rose are right up against the ceiling...

Suddenly the gate gives and SWINGS OPEN. They are pushed through by the force of the water. They make it to stairs on the other side of the landing and follow the steward up to the next deck.

CUT TO:

218   EXT. BOAT DECK, STARBOARD SIDE   218

Cal comes reeling out of the first class entrance, looking wild-eyed. He lurches down the deck toward the bridge. Waltz music wafts over the ship. Somewhere the band is still playing.

CAL'S POV: A little girl, maybe two years old, is crying alone in an alcove. She looks up at Cal beseechingly. Cal moves on without a glance back... reaching a large crowd clustered around COLLAPSIBLE A just aft of the bridge. He sees Murdoch and a number of crewmen struggling to drag the boat to the davits, with no luck.

Cal pushes forward, trying to signal Murdoch, but the officer ignores him. Nearby TOMMY AND FABRIZIO are being pushed forward by the crowd behind. PURSER MCELROY pushes them back, getting a couple of seamen to help him. He brandishes his gun, waving it in the air, yelling for the crowd to stay back.

Moved until after Murdoch's suicide   CUT TO:

219   EXT. BOAT DECK, PORT SIDE/ ROOF OF OFFICERS' QUARTERS   219

Lightoller, with a group of crew and passengers, is trying to get Collapsible B down from the roof. They slide it down a pair of oars leaned against the deck house.

> LIGHTOLLER
> Hold it! <u>Hold it!</u>

The weight of the boat snaps the oars and it crashes to the deck, upside down. The two Swedish cousins, OLAUS and BJORN GUNDERSEN, jump back as the boat nearly hits them.

CUT TO:

220   INT. STAIRWELL AND CORRIDORS   220

Jack and Rose run up seemingly endless stairs as the ship groans and torques around them.

(CONTINUED)

As seen in the final film, Scene 221 was changed so that Murdoch flings the bribe money into Cal's face and says, "Your money can't save you any more than it can save me."

CAMERON: "I re-wrote the scene because I wanted to make it clearer that Murdoch saw his own situation as hopeless. He's accepting full responsibility for the chaos around him. Murdoch was an honorable man who felt the burden of responsibility for the deaths which were to come."

CUT TO:

221   EXT. BOAT DECK, STARBOARD SIDE   221

Murdoch, at Collapsible A, is no longer in control. The crowd is threatening to rush the boat. They push and jostle, yelling and shouting at the officers. The pressure from behind pushes them forward, and one guy falls off the edge of the deck into the water less than ten feet below.

                              TOMMY
                Give us a chance to live, you limey bastards!

Murdoch fires his Webley twice in the air, then points it at the crowd.

                              MURDOCH
                I'll shoot any man who tries to get past me.

Cal steps up to him.

                              CAL
                We had a deal, damn you.

Murdoch pushes him back, pointing the pistol at Cal.

                              MURDOCH
            Get back!

A man next to Tommy rushes forward, and Tommy is shoved from behind. Murdoch SHOOTS the first man, and seeing Tommy coming forward, puts a bullet into his chest.

Tommy collapses, and Fabrizio grabs him, holding him in his arms as his life flows out over the deck.

Murdoch turns to his men and salutes smartly. Then he puts the pistol to his temple and... BLAM! He drops like a puppet with the strings cut and topples over the edge of the boat deck into the water only a few feet below.

Cal stares in horror at Murdoch's body bobbing in the black water. The MONEY FLOATS out of the pocket of his greatcoat, the bills spreading across the surface.

The crew rush to get the last few women aboard the boat.

                         PURSER MCELROY
                   (calling above the confusion)
                Any more women or children?!

THE CHILD crying in the alcove. Cal scoops her up and runs forward, cradling her in his arms.

                              CAL
                   (forcing his way through the crowd)
                Here's a child! I've got a child!
                              (MORE)

                                                            (CONTINUED)

                              CAL (cont'd)
                    (to McElroy)
               Please... I'm all she has in the world.

McElroy nods curtly and pushes him into the boat. He spins with his gun, brandishing
it in the air to keep the other men back. Cal gets into the boat, holding the little
girl. He takes a seat with the women.

                              CAL
               There, there.

                                                                       CUT TO:

222   INT. FIRST CLASS SMOKING ROOM   222

Thomas Andrews stands in front of the fireplace, staring at the large painting above
the mantel. The fire is still going in the fireplace.

The room is empty except for Andrews. An ashtray falls off a table. Behind him Jack
and Rose run into the room, out of breath and soaked. They run through, toward the
aft revolving door... then Rose recognizes him. She sees that his lifebelt is off,
lying on a table.

                              ROSE
               Won't you even make a try for it, Mr. Andrews?

                              ANDREWS
                    (a tear rolls down his cheek)
               I'm sorry that I didn't build you a stronger ship,
               young Rose.

                              JACK
                    (to her)
               It's going fast... we've gotta keep moving.

Andrews picks up his lifebelt and hands it to her.

                              ANDREWS
               Good luck to you, Rose.

                              ROSE
                    (hugging him)
               And to you, Mr. Andrews.

Jack pulls her away and they run through the revolving door.

                         Scene 224 moved here   CUT TO:

223   EXT. BOAT DECK AND VARIOUS LOCATIONS   223

The band finishes the waltz. Wallace Hartley looks at the orchestra members.

                              HARTLEY
               Right, that's it then.

                                                                   (CONTINUED)

Cameron added an unscripted beat to the scene during production. A foreign mother, holding her infant, pleads with Captain Smith for help. Smith is overcome with horror and simply walks away in an almost catatonic state.

CAMERON: "I wanted to externalize his guilt. Smith was last seen walking toward the Bridge, and by this time third-class passengers could have made their way forward and approached him. Whether or not such an exchange occurred, it provided a way for audiences to get inside the moment."

With their earlier scene deleted for pacing, Ida and Isador Strauss, two of *Titanic's* most famous passengers, are never identified in the film for who they are.

CAMERON: "In its own way that fact speaks to the universality of their love. Audiences don't need to know *Titanic* history to appreciate the bond between these two people who will not be separated, even in death."

Prior to shooting, Cameron decided he wanted the Irish mother to be telling her children a bedtime fable. Performer Brian Walsh (the piper in the Irish band from the third-class party scene) knew several pieces of Gaelic folklore and shared them with Jenette Goldstein (a Cameron ensemble regular - "Aliens," "T2") who played the mother. Jenette proposed several of Brian's stories to Cameron, who chose the legend of *Tir Na Nog* for its last line, which referred to a land of eternal youth and beauty and was highly resonant to the scene.

They leave him, walking forward along the deck. Hartley puts his violin to his chin and bows the first notes of "Nearer My God to Thee". One by one the band members turn, hearing the lonely melody.

Without a word they walk back and take their places. They join in with Hartley, filling out the sound so that it reaches all over the ship on this still night. The vocalist begins: "If in my dreams I be, nearer my God to thee..."

THE HYMN PLAYS OVER THE FOLLOWING SEQUENCE:

224   A seaman pulls off his lifebelt and catches up to Captain Smith as he walks to the   224
       bridge. He proffers it, but Smith seems to stare through him. Without a word he
       turns and goes onto the bridge. He enters the enclosed WHEELHOUSE and closes
       the door. He is alone, surrounded by the gleaming brass instruments. He seems
       to inwardly collapse.

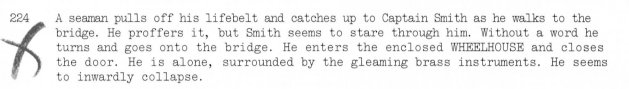

225   IN THE FIRST CLASS SMOKING ROOM Andrews stands like a statue. He pulls out   225
       his pocketwatch and checks the time. Then he opens the face of the mantel clock and
       adjusts it to the correct time: 2:12 a.m. Everything must be correct.

226   IN CAL'S PARLOUR SUITE water swirls in from the private promenade deck.   226
       Rose's paintings are submerged. The Picasso transforms under the water's
       surface. Degas' colors run. Monet's water lilies come to life.

227   DOWNANGLE on two figures lying side by side, fully clothed, on a bed in a   227
       FIRST CLASS CABIN. Elderly Ida and Isador Strauss stare at the ceiling, holding
       hands like young lovers. Water pours into the room through a doorway. It swirls
       around the bed, two feet deep and rising fast.

228   IN A STEERAGE CABIN somewhere in the bowels of the ship, the young IRISH   228
       MOTHER, seen earlier stoically waiting at the stairs, is tucking her two young chil-
       dren into bed. She pulls up the covers, making sure they are all warm and cozy. She
       lies down with them on the bed, speaking soothingly and holding them.

                                                                          CUT TO:

EXT. BOAT DECK/ BRIDGE

229   IN A WIDE SHOT we see a wave travel up the boat deck as the bridge house sinks into   229
       the water.

230   ON THE PORT SIDE Collapsible B is picked up by the water. Working frantically, the   230
       men try to detach it from the falls so the ship won't drag it under. Colonel Gracie
       hands Lightoller a pocket knife and he saws furiously at the ropes as the water swirls
       around his legs. The boat, still upside down, is swept off the ship. Men start diving
       in, swimming to stay with it.

231   IN COLLAPSIBLE A Cal sits next to the wailing child, whom he has completely   231
       forgotten. He watches the water rising around the men as they work, scrambling to get
       the ropes cut so the ship won't drag the collapsible under.

       Fabrizio removes the lifebelt from Tommy's body and struggles to put it on as the
       water rises around him.

The end of "Nearer My God to Thee" was moved prior to the Bridge implosion (Scene 232) because Smith's demise was a better "trigger" for the final death throes of the ship.

232   CAPTAIN SMITH, standing near the wheel, watches the black water climbing   232
       the windows of the enclosed wheelhouse. He has the stricken expression of a damned
       soul on Judgment Day. The windows burst suddenly and a wall of water edged with
       shards of glass slams into Smith. He disappears in a vortex of foam.

233   Collapsible A is hit by a wave as the bow plunges suddenly. It partially swamps the   233
       boat, washing it along the deck. Over a hundred passengers are plunged into the
       freezing water and the area around the boat becomes a frenzy of splashing, screaming
       people.

       As men are trying to climb into the collapsible, Cal grabs an oar and pushes them back
       into the water.

                                   CAL
                  Get back! You'll swamp us!

       Fabrizio, swimming for his life, gets swirled under a davit. The ropes and pulleys
       tangle around him as the davit goes under the water, and he is dragged down.
       Underwater he struggles to free himself, and then kicks back to the surface. He sur-
       faces, gasping for air in the freezing water.

234   WALLACE HARTLEY sees the water rolling rapidly up the deck toward them. He holds   234
       the last note of the hymn in a sustain, and then lowers his violin.

                                   HARTLEY
                  Gentlemen, it has been a privilege playing with you
                  tonight.

                                                        Moved prior to scene 232

                                                                          CUT TO:

235   EXT. A-DECK AFT, PORT SIDE   235

       Jack and Rose run out of the PALM COURT into a dense crowd. Jack pushes his way to
       the rail and looks at the state of the ship. The bridge is under water and there is chaos
       on deck. Jack helps her put her lifebelt on. People stream around them, shout-
       ing and pushing.

                                   JACK
                  Okay... we keep moving aft. We have to stay on the
                  ship as long as possible.

       They push their way aft through the panicking crowd.

                                                                          CUT TO:

236   EXT. FORWARD FUNNEL   236

       Collapsible A is whirled like a leaf in the currents around the sinking ship. It slams
       against the side of the forward funnel.

                                   CAL
                  (to the crew in the boat)
                  Row! Row you bastards!!

       Deleted for pacing

Fabrizio's "near-miss" was replaced with an unscripted scene in which he is almost sucked into a first class window. Actor Danny Nucci, performing this stunt himself, had one chance to pull it off and got it exactly right on the single last sinking take.

While Fabrizio's original death scene was shot (see Scene 267), it was changed for reasons of pacing and to keep Cal's character from being too overly negative.

CAMERON: "Once he uses the little steerage girl to get a place in a lifeboat, we hate him enough to last the rest of the film."

237   NEARBY: Fabrizio is drawn up against the grating of a STOKEHOLD VENT   237
       as water pours through it. The force of tons of water roaring down into the ship
       traps him against it, and he is dragged down under the surface as the ship sinks.
       He struggles to free himself but cannot.

       Suddenly there is a concussion deep in the bowels of the ship as a furnace explodes
       and a blast of hot air belches out of the ventilator, ejecting Fabrizio. He surfaces in a
       roar of foam and keeps swimming.

                                                                          CUT TO:

238   EXT. A-DECK/ B-DECK/ WELL DECK, AFT   238

       Jack and Rose clamber over the A-Deck aft rail. Then, using all his strength, he lowers
       her toward the deck below, holding on with one hand. She dangles, then falls. Jack
       jumps down behind her.

       They join a crush of people literally clawing and scrambling over each other to get
       down the narrow stairs to the well deck... the only way aft.

       Seeing that the stairs are impossible, Jack climbs over the B-Deck railing and helps
       Rose over. He lowers her again, and she falls in a heap. BAKER JOUGHIN, now three
       sheets to the wind, happens to be next to her. He hauls Rose to her feet. Jack
       drops down and the three of them push through the crowd across the well deck. Near
       them, at the rail, people are jumping into the water.

       The ship GROANS and SHUDDERS. The man ahead of Jack is walking like a zom-
       bie.

                              MAN
                 Yeah, though I walk through the valley of the shadow
                 of death--

                              JACK
                 You wanna walk a little faster through that valley,
                 fella?
                          Moved to the end of scene 239
                                                                          CUT TO:

239   EXT. FORWARD FUNNEL   239

       The stay cables along the top of the funnel snap, and they lash like steel whips down
       into the water. Cal watches as the funnel topples from its mounts. Falling like a tem-
       ple pillar twenty eight feet across it whomps into the water with a tremendous splash.
       People swimming underneath it disappear in an instant.

       Fabrizio, a few feet away, is hurled back by a huge wave. He comes up, gasping...
       still swimming. The water pouring into the open end of the funnel draws in several
       swimmers. The funnel sinks, disappearing, but—

       Hundreds of tons of water pour down through the 30 foot hole where the funnel
       stood, thundering down into the belly of the ship. A whirlpool forms, a hole in the
       ocean, like an enormous toilet-flush. T. W. McCauley, the gym instructor, swims in
       a frenzy as the vortex draws him in. He is sucked down like a spider going down
       a drain.
                   Deleted prior to shooting
                                                                       (CONTINUED)

Move Fabrizio's death to here

While the death of the Cartmell family was photographed, Cameron decided that the scene was too intense. Historically, 52 children were lost on *Titanic*, all of them third-class passengers.

CONTINUED:

Fabrizio, nearby, swims like Hell as more people are sucked down behind him.
He manages to get clear. He's going to live no matter what it takes.

CUT TO:

240   INT. BOAT DECK FOYER/ GRAND STAIRCASE   240

Water roars through the doors and windows, cascading down the stairs like a
rapids. John Jacob Astor is swept down the marble steps to A-Deck, which is already
flooded... a roiling vortex. He grabs the headless cherub at the bottom of the staircase and wraps his arms around it.

Astor looks up in time to see the 30 foot glass dome overhead EXPLODE INWARD
with the wave of water washing over it. A Niagara of sea water thunders down into
the room, blasting through the first class opulence. It is the Armageddon of elegance.

CUT TO:

241   INT. BELOWDECKS   241

The flooding is horrific. Walls and doors are splintered like kindling. Water roars
down corridors with pile-driver force.

The CARTMELL FAMILY are at the top of a stairwell, jammed against a locked gate
like Jack and Rose were. Water boils up the stairwell behind them. Bert Cartmell
shakes the gate futilely, shouting for help. Little Cora wails as the water boils up
around them all.

CUT TO:

Deleted in post for Pacing

242   EXT. STERN   242

Rose and Jack struggle to climb the well deck stairs as the ship tilts. Drunk Baker
Joughin puts a hand squarely on Rose's butt and shoves her up onto the deck.

                                    JOUGHIN
                Sorry, miss!

Hundreds of people are already on the poop deck, and more are pouring up every second. Jack and Rose cling together as they struggle across the tilting deck.

243   As the bow goes down, the STERN RISES. IN BOAT TWO, which is just off the stern,   243
passengers gape as the giant bronze propellers rise out of the water like gods of the
deep, FILLING FRAME behind them.

People are JUMPING from the well deck, the poop deck, the gangway doors. Some
hit debris in the water and are hurt or killed.

244   EXT. STERN   244

ON THE POOP DECK Jack and Rose struggle aft as the angle increases. Hundreds
of passengers, clinging to every fixed object on deck, huddle on their knees around
FATHER BYLES, who has his voice raised in prayer. They are praying, sobbing, or just
staring at nothing, their minds blank with dread.

(CONTINUED)

In the film, Rose says a line inspired by the scene description: "Jack, this is where we first met."

CAMERON: "That was a demanding moment for Kate. The only way to play Rose's sense of fated destiny was to say it, but without sacrificing the character's fear and realization that they were probably going to die there. It was a fragile idea that could easily have not worked, especially since it was suggested on the spot.

"She did it just right and it became what I feel to be one of the best moments in the film."

In the film, prior to Scene 247, we see an underwater shot of a drowned woman floating eerily in front of the chandelier in the first-class Lounge. Cameron had designed the shot but did not know exactly where he intended to use it. Co-editor Richard Harris placed it after Scene 246, where Cameron thought it played hauntingly after Father Byles' reading from the New Testament Book of Revelations.

REV. 6/06/96

246 FORMERLY 145.1

Pulling himself from handhold to handhold, Jack tugs Rose aft along the deck.

                          JACK   *Deleted*
            Come on, Rose. We can't expect God to do all the   *in post*
            work for us.

They struggle on, pushing through the praying people. A MAN loses his footing ahead and slides toward them. Jack helps him up.

245   THE PROPELLERS are twenty feet above the water and rising faster.   245

246   JACK AND ROSE make it to the stern rail, right at the base of the flagpole. They   246
       grip the rail, jammed in between other people. It is the spot where Jack pulled her back
       onto the ship, just two nights... and a lifetime... ago.

Above the wailing and sobbing, Father Byles' voice carries, cracking with emotion.

                     FATHER BYLES
            ...and I saw new heavens and a new earth. The
            former heavens and the former earth had passed away
            and the sea was no longer.

The lights flicker, threatening to go out. Rose grips Jack as the stern rises into a night sky ablaze with stars.

                     FATHER BYLES
            I also saw a new Jerusalem, the holy city coming
            down out of heaven from God, beautiful as a bride
            prepared to meet her husband. I heard a loud voice
            from the throne ring out this is God's dwelling among
            men. He shall dwell with them and they shall be his
            people and He shall be their God who is always with
            them.

Rose stares about her at the faces of the doomed. Near them are the DAHL FAMILY, clinging together stoically. Helga looks at her briefly, and her eyes are infinitely sad.

Rose sees a young mother next to her, clutching her five year old son, who is crying in terror.

                      MOTHER
            Shhh. Don't cry. It'll be over soon, darling. It'll
            all be over soon.

                     FATHER BYLES
            He shall wipe every tear from their eyes. And there
            shall be no more death or mourning, crying out or
            pain, for the former world has passed away.

Added drowned woman here   CUT TO:

INT. SHIP— VARIOUS

As the ship tilts further everything not bolted down inside shifts.

247   CUPBOARDS burst open in the pantry, showering the floor with tons of china. A   247
        PIANO slides across the floor, crashing into a wall. FURNITURE tumbles across
        the Smoking Room floor.

248   ON THE A-DECK PROMENADE passengers lose their grip and slide down the   248
        wooden deck like a bobsled run, hundreds of feet before they hit the water.
        TRUDY BOLT, Rose's maid, slips as she struggles along the railing and slides
        away screaming.

249   AT THE STERN the propellers are 100 feet out of the water and rising. Panicking   249
        people leap from the poop deck rail, fall screaming and hit the water like mortar
        rounds. A man falls from the poop deck, hitting the bronze hub of the starboard pro-
        peller with a sickening smack.

250   SWIMMERS LOOK UP and see the stern towering over them like a monolith,   250
        the propellers rising against the stars. 110 feet. 120.

251   AT THE STERN RAIL a man jumps. IN HIS POV we fall seemingly forever, right   251
        past one of the giant screws. The water rushes up—

                P.O.V. never shot   CUT TO:

EXT. TITANIC/ BOAT 6

252   TRACKING SLOWLY IN on Ruth as the sounds of the dying ship and the   252
        screaming people come across the water.

253   REVERSE/ HER POV: IN A WIDE SHOT we see the spectacle of the Titanic, her   253
        lights blazing, reflecting in the still water. Its stern is high in the air, angled up
        over forty five degrees. The propellers are 150 feet out of the water. Over a thousand
        passengers cling to the decks, looking from a distance like a swarm of bees.

        The image is shocking, unbelievable, unthinkable. Ruth stares at the spectacle, unable
        to frame it or put it into any proportion.

                        MOLLY BROWN
            God Almighty.

        The great liner's lights flicker.

                                            CUT TO:

254   INT. ENGINE ROOM   254

        In darkness Chief Engineer Bell hangs onto a pipe at the master breaker panel.
        Around him men climb through tilted cyclopean machines with electric hand-torches. It
        is a black hell of breaking pipes, spraying water, and groaning machinery threatening to
        tear right out of its bedplates.

        Water sprays down, hitting the breaker panel, but Bell will not leave his post.
        CLUNK. The breakers kick. He slams them in again and— WHOOM! a blast of light!
        Something melts and arcing fills the engine room with nightmarish light—

                                              CUT TO:

255   EXT. TITANIC   255

WIDE SHOT. The lights go out all over the ship. Titanic becomes a vast black silhouette against the stars.

IN COLLAPSIBLE C: BRUCE ISMAY has his back to the ship, unable to watch the
great steamer die. He is catatonic with remorse, his mind overloaded. He can avert
his eyes, but he can't block out the sounds of dying people and machinery.

A loud CRACKING REPORT comes across the water.   *Moved prior
                                                  to scene 254*   CUT TO:

256   EXT. BOAT DECK   256

Near the third funnel a man clutches the ship's rail. He stares down as the DECK
SPLITS right between his feet. A yawning chasm opens with a THUNDER of breaking
steel.

LOVEJOY is clutching the railing on the roof of the Officers' Mess. He watches in
horror as the ship's structure RIPS APART right in front of him. He gapes down
into a widening maw, seeing straight down into the bowels of the ship, amid
a BOOMING CONCUSSION like the sound of artillery. People falling into the
widening crevasse look like dolls.

The stay cables on the funnel part and snap across the decks like whips, ripping off
davits and ventilators. A man is hit by a whipping cable and snatched OUT OF
FRAME. Another cable smashes the rail next to Lovejoy and it rips free. He falls backward
into the pit of jagged metal.

Fires, explosions and sparks light the yawning chasm as the hull splits down through
nine decks to the keel. The sea pours into the gaping wound—

                                                                  CUT TO:

257   INT. ENGINE ROOM   257

It is a thundering black hell. Men scream as monstrous machinery comes apart
around them, steel frames twisting like taffy. Their torches illuminate the roaring,
foaming demon of water as it races at them through the machines. Trying to climb, they
are overtaken in seconds.

                                                                  CUT TO:

258   EXT. TITANIC - NIGHT   258

The STERN HALF of the ship, almost four hundred feet long, falls back toward the
water. On the poop deck everyone screams as they feel themselves plummeting. The
sound goes up like the roar of fans at a baseball stadium when a run is scored.

Swimming in the water directly under the stern a few unfortunates shriek as they see
the keel coming down on them like God's bootheel. The massive stern section falls
back almost level, thundering down into the sea and pushing out a mighty wave of dis-
placed water.

CAMERON: "Not letting go is a thematic element in the relationship between Jack and Rose from the moment they meet to the moment Jack dies. In post I actually copied the voice track from Scene 61 where Jack is pulling Rose back onto the ship after her suicide attempt ("I've got you. I won't let go.") and copied it into this scene to make it the strongest possible rhyming sequence."

Baker Joughin's line was deleted from the final film because it disrupted the suspense and horror of the scene.

259   Jack and Rose struggle to hold onto the stern rail. They feel the ship seemingly   259
RIGHT ITSELF. Some of those praying think it is salvation.

                         SEVERAL PEOPLE
        We're saved!

Jack looks at Rose and shakes his head, grimly.

260   Now the horrible mechanics play out. Pulled down by the awesome weight of the   260
flooded bow, the buoyant stern tilts up rapidly. They feel the RUSH OF ASCENT as
the fantail angles up again. Everyone is clinging to benches, railings, ventilators...
anything to keep from sliding as the stern lifts.

The stern goes up and up, past 45 degrees, then past sixty.

261   People start to fall, sliding and tumbling. They skid down the deck, screaming and flailing   261
to grab onto something. They wrench other people loose and pull them down as
well. There is a pile-up of bodies at the forward rail. The DAHL FAMILY falls one
by one.

                        JACK
        We have to move!

He climbs over the stern rail and reaches back for Rose. She is terrified to move.
He grabs her hand.

                        JACK
        Come on! I've got you!

Jack pulls her over the rail. *It is the same place he pulled her over the rail two
nights earlier, going the other direction.* She gets over just as the railing is going
HORIZONTAL, and the deck VERTICAL. Jack grips her fiercely.

The stern is now straight up in the air... a rumbling black monolith standing against
the stars. It hangs there like that for a long grace note, its buoyancy stable.

Rose lies on the railing, looking down fifteen stories to the boiling sea at the base of
the stern section. People near them, who didn't climb over, hang from the railing, their
legs dangling over the long drop. They fall one by one, plummeting down the vertical
face of the poop deck. Some of them bounce horribly off deck benches and ventilators.

Jack and Rose lie side by side on what was the vertical face of the hull, gripping
the railing, which is now horizontal. Just beneath their feet are the gold letters
TITANIC emblazoned across the stern.

Rose stares down terrified at the black ocean waiting below to claim them. Jack looks
to his left and sees Baker Joughin, crouching on the hull, holding onto the railing.
It is a surreal moment.

                      JOUGHIN
           (nodding a greeting)
        Helluva night.

                                      (CONTINUED)

As originally filmed, Scene 263 showed Jack and Rose struggling underwater against the darkness of the ocean depths. Cameron: "Billy Zane was watching me edit that sequence and he said, 'You know, you should see the ship sinking into the depths behind them in that shot.' I thought it was a brilliant idea, so we added the stern falling away from them digitally."

As photographed, Scenes 263 and 264 were slightly different than scripted. Cameron realized it would be more horrifying if Jack and Rose were separated by the suction and Rose surfaced into the total chaos, alone.

The final relentless plunge begins as the stern section floods. Looking down a hundred feet to the water, we drop like an elevator with Jack and Rose.

> JACK
> (talking fast)
> Take a deep breath and hold it right before we go into
> the water. The ship will suck us down. Kick for the
> surface and keep kicking. Don't let go of my hand.
> We're gonna make it Rose. Trust me.

She stares at the water coming up at them, and grips his hand harder.

> ROSE
> I trust you.

Below them the poop deck is disappearing. The plunge gathers speed... the
boiling surface engulfs the docking bridge and then rushes up the last thirty
feet.

262   IN A HIGH SHOT, we see the stern descend into the boiling sea. The name   262
TITANIC disappears, and the tiny figures of Jack and Rose vanish under
the water.

Where the ship stood, now there is nothing. Only the black ocean.

                                                                    CUT TO:

263   EXT. OCEAN/ UNDERWATER AND SURFACE   263

Bodies are whirled and spun, some limp as dolls, others struggling spasmodically,
as the vortex sucks them down and tumbles them.

264   Jack rises INTO FRAME F.G. kicking hard for the surface... holding tightly to   264
Rose, pulling her up.

265   AT THE SURFACE: a roiling chaos of screaming, thrashing people. Over a   265
thousand people are now floating where the ship went down. Some are stunned,
gasping for breath. Others are crying, praying, moaning, shouting... screaming.

Jack and Rose surface among them. They barely have time to gasp for air before
people are clawing at them. People driven insane by the water, 4 degrees below
freezing, a cold so intense it is indistinguishable from death by fire.

A man pushes Rose under, trying to climb on top of her... senselessly trying to get
out of the water, to climb onto anything. Jack PUNCHES him repeatedly, pulling her
free.

> JACK
> Swim, Rose! SWIM!

She tries, but her strokes are not as effective as his because of her lifejacket. They
break out of the clot of people. He has to find some kind of flotation, anything to get
her out of the freezing water.

                                                                  (CONTINUED)

                              JACK
               Keep swimming. Keep moving. Come on, you can
               do it.

All about them there is a tremendous wailing, screaming and moaning... a chorus of tormented souls. And beyond that... nothing but black water stretching to
the horizon. The sense of isolation and hopelessness is overwhelming.

                                                                    CUT TO:

266   EXT. OCEAN   266

Jack strokes rhythmically, the effort keeping him from freezing.

                              JACK
               Look for something floating. Some debris... wood...
               anything.

                              ROSE   *Deleted in post*
               It's so cold.

                              JACK
               I know. I know. Help me, here. Look around.

His words keep her focused, taking her mind off the wailing around them. Rose scans
the water, panting, barely able to draw a breath. She turns and... SCREAMS.

A DEVIL is right in front of her face. It is the black FRENCH BULLDOG, swimming right at her like a seamonster in the darkness, its coal eyes bugging. It motors
past her, like it is heading for Newfoundland.

Beyond it Rose sees something in the water.

                              ROSE
               What's that?

Jack sees what she is pointing to, and they make for it together. It is a piece of
wooden debris, intricately carved. He pushes her up and she slithers onto it belly
down.

But when Jack tries to get up onto the thing, it tilts and submerges, almost dumping
Rose off. It is clearly only big enough to support her. He clings to it, close to her,
keeping his upper body out of the water as best he can.

Their breath floats around them in a cloud as they pant from the exertion. A MAN
swims toward them, homing in on the piece of debris. Jack warns him back.

                              JACK
               It's just enough for this lady... you'll push it
               under.

                              MAN
               Let me try at least, or I'll die soon.

                                                                  (CONTINUED)

Deleted in post

　CONTINUED:　

>   JACK
>   You'll die quicker if you come any closer.

>   MAN
>   Yes, I see. Good luck to you then.
>   (swimming off)
>   God bless.

                                        CUT TO:

267　EXT. COLLAPSIBLE A/ OCEAN　267

The boat is overloaded and half-flooded. Men cling to the sides in the water. Others, swimming, are drawn to it as their only hope. Cal, standing in the boat, slaps his oar in the water as a warning.

>   CAL
>   <u>Stay back</u>! <u>Keep off</u>!

Fabrizio, exhausted and near the limit, makes it almost to the boat. Cal CLUBS HIM with the oar, cutting open his scalp.

>   FABRIZIO
>   You don't... understand... I have...
>   to get... to America.

>   CAL
>   (pointing with the oar)
>   It's that way!

Deleted in post (see notes for scene 239)

CLOSE ON FABRIZIO as he floats, panting, each breath agony. You see the spirit leave him.

FABRIZIO'S POV: Cal in SLOW MOTION, yelling and wielding the oar. A demon in a tuxedo. The image fades to black.

                                        CUT TO:

268　EXT. OCEAN　268

JACK AND ROSE still float amid a chorus of the damned. Jack sees a ship's officer nearby, CHIEF OFFICER WILDE. He is blowing his whistle furiously, knowing the sound will carry over the water for miles.

>   JACK
>   The boats will come back for us, Rose. Hold on just a
>   little longer. They had to row away for the suction
>   and now they'll be coming back.

She nods, his words helping her. She is shivering uncontrollably, her lips blue and her teeth chattering.

                                        (CONTINUED)

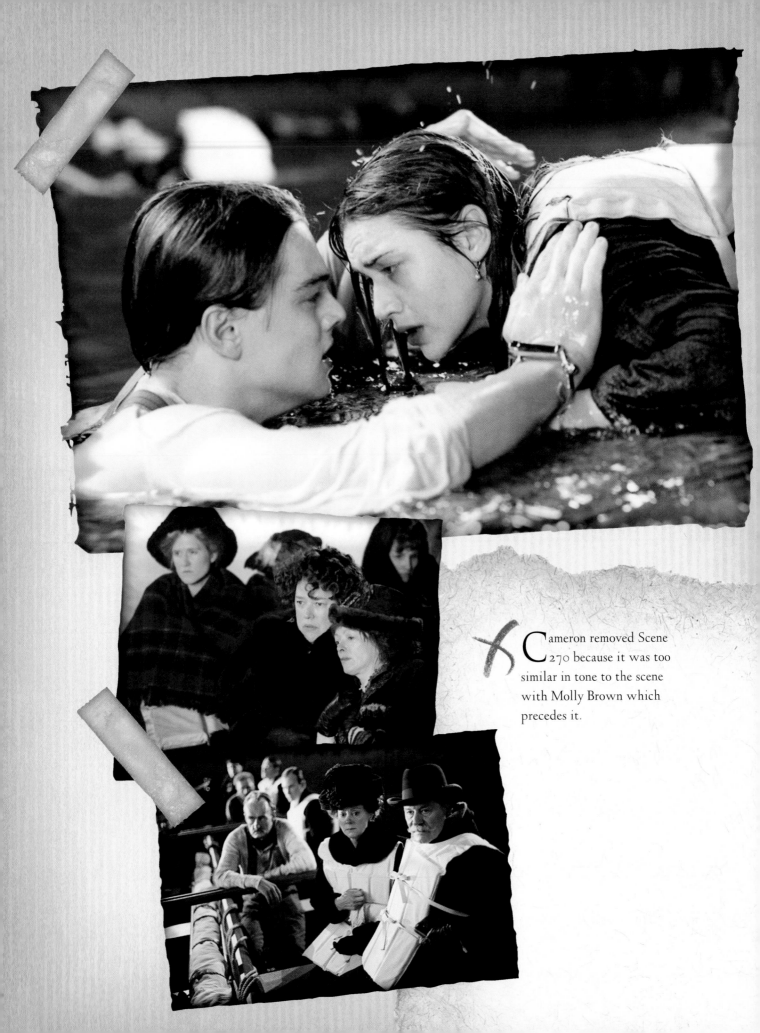

Cameron removed Scene 270 because it was too similar in tone to the scene with Molly Brown which precedes it.

                              ROSE
          Thank God for you Jack.

People are still screaming, calling to the lifeboats.

                              WOMAN
          Come back! Please! We know you can hear us. For
          God's sake!

                              MAN
          Please... help us. Save one life! SAVE ONE LIFE!

                                                        CUT TO:

269   EXT. LIFEBOATS/ OCEAN   269

IN BOAT 6: Ruth has her ears covered against the wailing in the darkness. The
first class women in the boat sit, stunned, listening to the sound of hundreds
screaming.

                              HITCHINS
          They'll pull us right down I tell ya!

                              MOLLY
          Aw knock it off, yer scarin' me. Come on girls, grab
          your oars. Let's go.
               (nobody moves)
          Well come on!

The women won't meet her eyes. They huddle into their ermine wraps.

                              MOLLY
          I don't understand a one of you. What's the matter
          with you? It's your men back there! We got plenty a'
          room for more.

                              HITCHINS
          If you don't shut that hole in yer face, there'll be
          one less in this boat!

Ruth keeps her ears covered and her eyes closed, shutting it all out.

270   IN BOAT ONE: Sir Cosmo and Lucile Duff-Gordon sit with ten other people in a boat   270
       that is two thirds empty. They are two hundred yards from the screaming in the
       darkness.

                              FIREMAN HENDRICKSON
          We should do something.

Lucile squeezes Cosmo's hand and pleads to him with her eyes. She is terrified.

                              SIR COSMO
          It's out of the question.

                                                        (CONTINUED)

270   CONTINUED:

270

The crewmembers, intimidated by a nobleman, acquiesce. They hunch guiltily, hoping the sound will stop soon.

TWENTY BOATS, most half full, float in the darkness. None of them make a move.

Moved scene 272 here

CUT TO:

271   EXT. OCEAN

271

Jack and Rose drift under the blazing stars. The water is glassy, with only the faintest undulating swell. Rose can actually see the stars reflecting on the black mirror of the sea.

Jack squeezes the water out of her long coat, tucking it in tightly around her legs. He rubs her arms. His face is chalk white in the darkness. A low MOANING in the darkness around them.

                    ROSE
          It's getting quiet.

                    JACK
          Just a few more minutes. It'll take them a while to
          get the boats organized...

Rose is unmoving, just staring into space. She knows the truth. There won't be any boats. Behind Jack she sees that Officer Wilde has stopped moving. He is slumped in his lifejacket, looking almost asleep. He has died of exposure already.

                    JACK
          I don't know about you, but I intend to write a
          strongly worded letter to the White Star Line about
          all this.

He laughs weakly, but it sounds like a gasp of fear. Rose finds his eyes in the dim light.

                    ROSE
          I love you Jack.

He takes her hand.

                    JACK
          No... don't say your good-byes, Rose. Don't you
          give up. Don't do it.

                    ROSE
          I'm so cold.

                    JACK
          You're going to get out of this... you're going to go
          on and you're going to make babies and watch them
          grow and you're going to die an old old lady, warm in
          your bed. Not here. Not this night. Do you
          understand me?

                                        (CONTINUED)

As filmed, Jack kisses her hand at the end of the scene, a grim reference to Scene 75 when he kisses her hand on the Grand Staircase. It is the last thing Jack ever does.

> ROSE
> I can't feel my body.

> JACK
> Rose, listen to me. Listen. Winning that ticket was
> the best thing that ever happened to me.

Jack is having trouble getting the breath to speak.

> JACK
> It brought me to you. And I'm thankful, Rose. I'm
> thankful.

His voice is trembling with the cold which is working its way to his heart. But his eyes
are unwavering.

> JACK
> You must do me this honor... promise me you will
> survive... that you will never give up... no matter
> what happens... no matter how hopeless... promise
> me now, and never let go of that promise.

> ROSE
> I promise.

> JACK
> Never let go.

> ROSE
> I promise. I will never let go, Jack. I'll never let
> go.

She grips his hand and they lie with their heads together. It is quiet now, except for
the lapping of the water.

> CUT TO:

272   EXT. LIFEBOATS / OCEAN - NIGHT   272

Fifth Officer Lowe, the impetuous young Welshman, has gotten Boats 10, 12
and Collapsible D together with his own Boat 14. A demon of energy, he's had
everyone hold the boats together and is transferring passengers from 14 into the others,
to empty his boat for a rescue attempt.

As the women step gingerly across into the other boats, Lowe sees a shawled figure in
too much of a hurry. He rips the shawl off, and finds himself staring into the face of
a man. He angrily shoves the stowaway into another boat and turns to his crew of
three.

> LOWE   *Deleted in post*
> Right, man the oars.   *for Pacing*

> CUT TO:

Cameron never shot Lowe's beam illuminating the trail of debris because he felt the reveal of the bodies was more powerful.

Shot but not included in the final film were unscripted beats of Lowe rescuing a Chinese passenger, one of the five passengers he pulled from the water. (Two of them did not survive the night.) The Chinese man (Ling Yi) was played by Van Ling, a longtime Cameron collaborator who wrote the annotated script book for "T2", whose performance ironically ended up on the cutting room floor.

The beam of an electric torch plays across the water like a searchlight as Boat 14 comes toward us.

ANGLE FROM THE BOAT as the torch illuminates floating debris, a poignant trail of flotsam: a violin, a child's wooden soldier, a framed photo of a steerage family. Daniel Marvin's wooden Biograph camera.

Deleted during production

Then, their white lifebelts bobbing in the darkness like signposts, the first bodies come into the torch's beam. The people are dead but not drowned, killed by the freezing water. Some look like they could be sleeping. Others stare with frozen eyes at the stars.

Soon bodies are so thick the seamen cannot row. They hit the oars on the heads of floating men and women... a wooden thunk. One seaman throws up. Lowe sees a mother floating with her arms frozen around her lifeless baby.

                              LOWE
                (the worst moment of his life)
              We waited too long.

                                                          CUT TO:

274   EXT. OCEAN   274

IN A HOVERING DOWNANGLE we see Jack and Rose floating in the black water. The stars reflect in the mill pond surface, and the two of them seem to be floating in interstellar space. They are absolutely still. Their hands are locked together. Rose is staring upwards at the canopy of stars wheeling above her. The music is transparent, floating... as the long sleep steals over Rose, and she feels peace.

CLOSE ON Rose's face. Pale, like the faces of the dead. She seems to be floating in a void. Rose is in a semi-hallucinatory state. She knows she is dying. Her lips barely move as she sings a scrap of Jack's song:

                              ROSE
              "Come Josephine in my flying machine..."

ROSE'S POV: The stars. Like you've never seen them. The Milky Way a glorious band from horizon to horizon.

A SHOOTING STAR flares... a line of light across the heavens.

TIGHT ON ROSE again. We see that her hair is dusted with frost crystals. Her breathing is so shallow, she is almost motionless. Her eyes track down from the stars to the water.

ROSE'S POV... SLOW MOTION: The silhouette of a boat crossing the stars. She sees men in it, rowing so slowly the oars lift out of the syrupy water, leaving weightless pearls floating in the air. The VOICES of the men sound slow and DISTORTED.

Then the lookout flashes his torch toward her and the light flares across the water, silhouetting the bobbing corpses in between. It flicks past her motionless form and moves on. The boat is 50 feet away, and moving past her. The men look away.

                                                      (CONTINUED)

Rose lifts her head to turn to Jack. We see that her hair has frozen to the wood under her.

                              ROSE
                    (barely audible)
              Jack.

She touches his shoulder with her free hand. He doesn't respond. Rose gently turns his face toward her. It is rimed with frost.

He seems to be sleeping peacefully.

But he is not asleep.

Rose can only stare at his still face as the realization goes through her.

                              ROSE
              Oh, Jack.

All hope, will and spirit leave her. She looks at the boat. It is further away now, the voices fainter. Rose watches them go.

She closes her eyes. She is so weak, and there just seems to be no reason to even try.

And then...her eyes snap open.

She raises her head suddenly, cracking the ice as she rips her hair off the wood. She calls out, but her voice is so weak they don't hear her. The boat is invisible now, the torch light a star impossibly far away. She struggles to draw breath, calling again.

275   IN THE BOAT Lowe hears nothing behind him. He points to something ahead, turning   275
        the tiller.

276   ROSE struggles to move. Her hand, she realizes, is actually frozen to Jack's. She   276
        breathes on it, melting the ice a little, and gently unclasps their hands, breaking away a
        thin tinkling film.

                              ROSE
                    I won't let go. I promise.

She releases him and he sinks into the black water. He seems to fade out like a spirit returning to some immaterial plane.

Rose rolls off the floating staircase and plunges into the icy water. She swims to Chief Officer Wilde's body and grabs his whistle. She starts to BLOW THE WHISTLE with all the strength in her body. Its sound slaps across the still water.

277   IN BOAT 14 Lowe whips around at the sound of the whistle.   277

                              LOWE
                    (turning the tiller)
              Row back! That way! <u>Pull</u>!

                                                                    (CONTINUED)

CAMERON: "Most of the transitions between the present and the past were engineered to be seamlessly smooth, but I wanted this one to shock the audience for effect. We've been wrapped up in the past since before the iceberg, so it's important to re-establish Old Rose as the storyteller.

"Interestingly, I had written Old Rose's speech about the lifeboats not coming back as if she had made her peace with the disaster years ago, but when Gloria read the lines she found herself getting angry. I realized that even at her character's advanced age the injustice of it would probably still resonate, so I told Gloria to play the anger, but as if it hadn't ruined her life or saddened her completely. She put real steel in her voice at that point."

Rose keeps blowing as the boat comes to her. She is still blowing when Lowe takes the whistle from her mouth as they haul her into the boat. She slips into uncon-sciousness and they scramble to cover her with blankets...

                                                              DISSOLVE TO:

278   INT. IMAGING SHACK / KELDYSH   278

EXTREME CLOSEUP of Rose's ancient, wrinkled face. Present day.

                          OLD ROSE
          Fifteen hundred people went into the sea when Titanic
          sank from under us. There were twenty boats floating
          nearby and only one came back. One. Six were saved
          from the water, myself included. Six out of fifteen
          hundred.

As she speaks THE CAMERA TRACKS slowly across the faces of Lizzy and the salvage crew on KELDYSH. Lovett, Bodine, Buell, the others... the reality of what happened here 84 years before has hit them like never before. With her story Rose has put them on Titanic in its final hours, and for the first time, they do feel like graverobbers.

Lovett, for the first time, has even forgotten to ask about the diamond.

                          OLD ROSE
          Afterward, the seven hundred people in the boats had
          nothing to do but wait... wait to die, wait to live,
          wait for an absolution which would never come.

                                                              DISSOLVE TO:

279   EXT. LIFEBOATS/OPEN SEA - PRE-DAWN   279

MATCHING MOVE as the camera tracks along the faces of the saved.

DISSOLVE TO: ANOTHER BOAT, and then ANOTHER, seeing faces we know among the sur-vivors: Ismay in a trance, just staring and trembling... Cal, sipping from a hip flask offered to him by a black-faced stoker... Ruth hugging herself, rocking gently.

280   IN BOAT 14: CLOSE ON ROSE, lying swaddled. Only her face is visible, white as the   280
moon. The man next to her jumps up, pointing and yelling. Soon everyone is looking and shouting excitedly. In Rose's POV it is all silent, SLOW MOTION.

IN SLOW-MOTION SILENCE we see Lowe light a green flare and wave it as everyone shouts and cheers. Rose doesn't react. She floats beyond all human emotion.

                                                              DISSOLVE TO:

Cameron shot all of Scene 282 but removed it to help pacing and to remain focused on Rose, feeling her loss.

281   EXT. LIFEBOATS OPEN SEA - DAWN   281

Golden light washes across the white boats, which float in a calm sea reflecting the
rosy sky. All around them, like a flotilla of sailing ships, are icebergs. The
CARPATHIA sits nearby, as boats row toward her.

                                                            DISSOLVE TO:

282   EXT. LIFEBOATS/ OCEAN/ CARPATHIA MONTAGE - DAY   282

IMAGES DISSOLVE into one another: a ship's hull looming, with the letters
CARPATHIA visible on the bow... Rose watching, rocked by the sea, her face
blank... seamen helping survivors up the rope ladder to the Carpathia's gangway
doors... two women crying and hugging each other inside the ship... ALL SILENT,
ALL IN SLOW-MOTION. There is just music, so gentle and sad, part elegy, part
hymn, part aching song of love lost forever.

THE IMAGES CONTINUE to music ... Rose, outside of time, outside of herself,
coming into Carpathia, barely able to stand... Rose being draped with warm blankets
and given hot tea... BRUCE ISMAY climbing aboard. He has the face and eyes of a damned
soul.

As Ismay walks along the hall, guided by a crewman toward the doctor's cabin, he
passes rows of seated and standing widows. He must run the gauntlet of their accus-
ing gazes. It's the longest walk of his life.

                                                            CUT TO:

283   EXT. DECK / CARPATHIA - DAY   283

It is the afternoon of the 15th. Cal is searching the faces of the widows lining the
deck, looking for Rose. The deck of Carpathia is crammed with huddled people, and even
the recovered lifeboats of Titanic. On a hatch cover sits an enormous pile of
lifebelts.

He keeps walking toward the stern. Seeing Cal's tuxedo, a steward approaches
him.

                        CARPATHIA STEWARD
            You won't find any of your people back here, sir. It's
            all steerage.

Cal ignores him and goes amongst this wretched group, looking under shawls and blankets at one bleak face after another.

Rose is sipping hot tea. Her eyes focus on him as he approaches her. He
barely recognizes her. She looks like a refugee, her matted hair hanging
in her eyes.

                        ROSE
            Yes, I lived. How awkward for you.

                        CAL
            Rose... your mother and I have been looking for you--

She holds up her hand, stopping him.

                                                            (CONTINUED)

Deleted

                                                                    147

The night before shooting, Cameron decided to play the scene silently, with Cal never finding Rose among the passengers. He thought after everything Rose had been through, it was too soon for her to show so much resolve.

CAMERON: "The way I wrote the scene didn't pay correct respect to the disaster. She is in mourning along with every survivor onboard that ship. She's a strong character now, but the inspiration for her strength is gone."

Sacrificed with the dialogue was one powerful rhyming sequence: Rose asking Cal "Is this in any way unclear?" was a direct payback for his treatment of her in Scene 84 at the breakfast table.

285 - CARPATHIA DOCKED @ PIER 54; MOVE OFF SHIP TO REVEAL CROWD (PULL BACK)
6/17/96

283   CONTINUED: 283

                              ROSE
              Please don't. Don't talk. Just listen. We will make a
              deal, since that is something you understand. From
              this moment you do not exist for me, nor I for you.
              You shall not see me again. And you will not attempt
              to find me. In return I will keep my silence. Your
              actions last night need never come to light, and you
              will get to keep the honor you have so carefully
              purchased.

      She fixes him with a glare as cold and hard as the ice which changed their
      lives.

                              ROSE
              Is this in any way unclear?

                              CAL
                  (after a long beat)
              What do I tell your mother?

                              ROSE
              Tell her that her daughter died with the Titanic.

      She stands, turning to the rail. Dismissing him. We see Cal stricken with emo-
      tion.

                              CAL
              You're precious to me, Rose.

                              ROSE
              Jewels are precious. Goodbye, Mr. Hockley.

      We see that in his way, the only way he knows, he does truly love her.

      After a moment, he turns and walks away.

                              OLD ROSE (V.O.)
              That was the last time I ever saw him. He married, of
              course, and inherited his millions. The crash of 28 hit
              his interests hard, and he put a pistol in his mouth
              that year. His children fought over the scraps of his
              estate like hyenas, or so I read.

284   ANGLE ON ROSE, at the railing of the Carpathia, 9pm April 18th. She gazes up at   284
      the Statue of Liberty, looking just as it does today, welcoming her home with her
      glowing torch. It is just as Fabrizio saw it, so clearly, in his mind.

285   LATER CARPATHIA DISGORGES THE SURVIVORS at the Cunard pier, Pier 54.   285
      Over 30,000 people line the dock and fill the surrounding streets. The magnesium
      flashes of the photographers go off like small bombs, lighting an amazing tableau.

      Several hundred police keep the mob back. The dock is packed with friends and rela-
      tives, officials, ambulances, and the press--

                                                                 (CONTINUED)

Deleted

Staging Scene 285 as written would have required re-creating *Carpathia* docked in New York with thousands of spectators and hundreds of reporters in the rain at night—an expensive proposition for such a brief amount of screen time, especially as the production neared the end of its arduous schedule.

CAMERON: "All the scene was really about is Rose saying, 'Dawson. Rose Dawson.' So I decided we could do the scene more elegantly on the deck of *Carpathia* as she steams past Liberty Island. The statue becomes a personal symbol for Rose's new freedom."

Old Rose's final voice-over was deleted when Cameron decided he wanted the butterfly theme not be stated so directly.

Reporters and photographers swarm everywhere... 6 deep at the foot of the gang-
ways, lining the tops of cars and trucks... it is the 1912 equivalent of a media circus.
They jostle to get close to the survivors, tugging on them as they pass and shouting over
each other to ask them questions.

Rose is covered with a woollen shawl and walking with a group of steerage passengers. Immigration officers are asking them questions as they come off the gangway.

                          IMMIGRATION OFFICER
        Name?
                                ROSE   *Moved to the end
        Dawson. Rose Dawson.   of scene 284*

The officer steers her toward a holding area for processing. Rose walks forward with
the dazed immigrants. The BOOM! of photographers' magnesium flashes cause them
to flinch, and the glare is blinding. There is a sudden disturbance near her as two
men burst through the cordon, running to embrace an older woman among the survivors, who cries out with joy. The reporters converge on this emotional scene, and
flashes explode.

Rose uses this moment to slip away into the crowd. She pushes through the
jostling people, moving with purpose, and none challenges her in the confusion.

                          OLD ROSE (V.O.)
                *Can you exchange one life for another? A caterpillar
                turns into a butterfly. If a mindless insect can do it,
                why couldn't I? Was it any more unimaginable than
                the sinking of the Titanic?*

TRACKING WITH HER as she walks away, further and further until the flashes and
the roar are far behind her, and she is still walking, determined.

                                                              CUT TO:

286   INT. IMAGING SHACK/ KELDYSH   286

Old Rose sits with the group in the Imaging shack, lit by the blue glow of the screens.
She holds the haircomb with the jade butterfly on the handle in her gnarled hands.

                          BODINE
                We never found anything on Jack. There's no record
                of him at all.

                          OLD ROSE
                No, there wouldn't be, would there? And I've never
                spoken of him until now, not to anyone.
                     (to Lizzy)
                Not even your grandfather. A woman's heart is a deep
                ocean of secrets. But now you all know there was a
                man named Jack Dawson, and that he saved me, in
                every way that a person can be saved.
                     (closing her eyes)
                                (MORE)

                                                              (CONTINUED)

As shot, Brock's dialogue was substantially more emotional, telling Lizzy, "For three years, I thought of nothing but *Titanic*. But I never got it. I never let it in."

Cameron shot footage for the wrap party mentioned in the scene description, but never used it for reasons of pacing.

286   CONTINUED: 286

                                    OLD ROSE (cont'd)
                        I don't even have a picture of him. He exists now
                        only in my memory.

                                                                                CUT TO:

287   EXT. OCEAN FLOOR/ TITANIC WRECK   287

       The Mir submersibles make their last pass over the ship. We hear Yuri the pilot on
       the UQC:

                                        YURI
                        Mir One returning to surface.

       The sub rises off the deck of the wreck, taking its light with it, leaving the Titanic
       once again in its fine and private darkness.

                                                                                CUT TO:

288   EXT. KELDYSH DECK   288

       A desultory wrap party for the expedition is in progress. There is music and some of
       the (co-ed) Russian crew are dancing. Bodine is getting drunk in the aggressive style
       of Baker Joughin.

       Lovett stands at the rail, looking down into the black water. Lizzy comes to him, offer-
       ing him a beer. She puts her hand on his arm.

                                        LIZZY   *Deleted*
                        I'm sorry.

                                        BROCK
                        We were pissin' in the wind the whole time.

       Lovett notices a figure move through the lights far down at the stern of the
       ship.

                                        LOVETT
                        Oh shit.

                                                                                CUT TO:

289   EXT. KELDYSH STERN DECK   289

       Rose walks through the shadows of the deck machinery. Her nightgown blows in
       the wind. Her feet are bare. Her hands are clutched at her chest, almost as if she is
       praying.

       ON BROCK AND LIZZY running down the stairs from the top deck, hauling ass.

       ROSE reaches the stern rail. Her gnarled fingers wrap over the rail. Her ancient foot
       steps up on the gunwale. She pushes herself up, leaning forward. Over her shoulder,
       we see the black water glinting far below.

       BROCK AND LIZZY run up behind her.

                                                                                (CONTINUED)

Deleted

For reasons already discussed [See Cameron's interview, page ix], Scene 289 was rewritten completely to make Old Rose's moment at the stern a private one.

                                    LIZZY
              Grandma, wait!! Don't--

ROSE TURNS her head, looking at them. She turns further, and we see she
has something in her hand, something she was about to drop overboard.

It is the "Heart of the Ocean".

Keep

Lovett sees his holy grail in her hand and his eyes go wide. Rose keeps it over the
railing where she can drop it anytime.

                                    ROSE
              Don't come any closer.

                                    LOVETT
              You had it the entire time!?

*FLASH CUT TO: A SILENT IMAGE OF YOUNG ROSE walking away from Pier 54.
The photographers' flashes go off like a battle behind her. She has her hands
in her pockets. She stops, feeling something, and pulls out the necklace. She
stares at it in amazement.*

BACK ON KELDYSH, Rose smiles at Brock's incomprehension.

                                    ROSE
              The hardest part about being so poor, was being so
              rich. But every time I thought of selling it, I
              thought of Cal. And somehow I always got by without
              his help.

*Keep – change
to reflect
re-written
scene*

She holds it out over the water. Bodine and a couple of the other guys come up
behind Brock, reacting to what is in Rose's hand.

                                    BODINE
              Holy shit.

                                    LOVETT
              Don't drop it Rose.

                                    BODINE
                   (a fierce whisper)
              Rush her.

                                    LOVETT
                   (to Bodine)
              It's hers, you schmuck.
                   (to her)
              Look, Rose, I... I don't know what to say to a woman
              who tries to jump off the Titanic when it's not sink-
              ing, and jumps back onto it when it is... we're not
              dealing with logic here, I know that... but please...
              think about this a second.

                                                              (CONTINUED)

                              ROSE
          I have. I came all the way here so this could go back
          where it belongs.

The massive diamond glitters. Brock edges closer and holds out his hand...

                              BROCK
          Just let me hold it in my hand, Rose. Please. Just
          once.

He comes closer to her. It is reminiscent of Jack slowly moving up to her at the stern
of Titanic.

Surprisingly, she calmly places the massive stone in the palm of his hand, while
still holding onto the necklace. Brock gazes at the object of his quest. An infinity
of cold scalpels glint in its blue depths. It is mesmerizing. It fits in his hand just like
he imagined.

                              BROCK
          My God.

His grip tightens on the diamond.

He looks up, meeting her gaze. Her eyes are suddenly infinitely wise and
deep.

                              ROSE
          You look for treasure in the wrong place, Mr. Lovett.
          Only life is priceless, and making each day count.

His fingers relax. He opens them slowly. Gently she slips the diamond out of his
hand. He feels it sliding away.   *Keep*

Then, with an impish little grin, Rose tosses the necklace over the rail. Bodine
gives a strangled cry and rushes to the rail in time to see it hit the water and disappear forever.

                              BODINE
          Aww!! That really sucks, lady!

Brock Lovett goes through ten changes before he settles on a reaction... HE
LAUGHS. He laughs until the tears come to his eyes. Then he turns to Lizzy.

                              LOVETT
          Would you like to dance?

Lizzy grins at him and nods. Rose smiles. She looks up at the stars.

290   IN THE BLACK HEART OF THE OCEAN, the diamond sinks, twinkling end over end,   290
      into the infinite depths.

                                                            CUT TO:

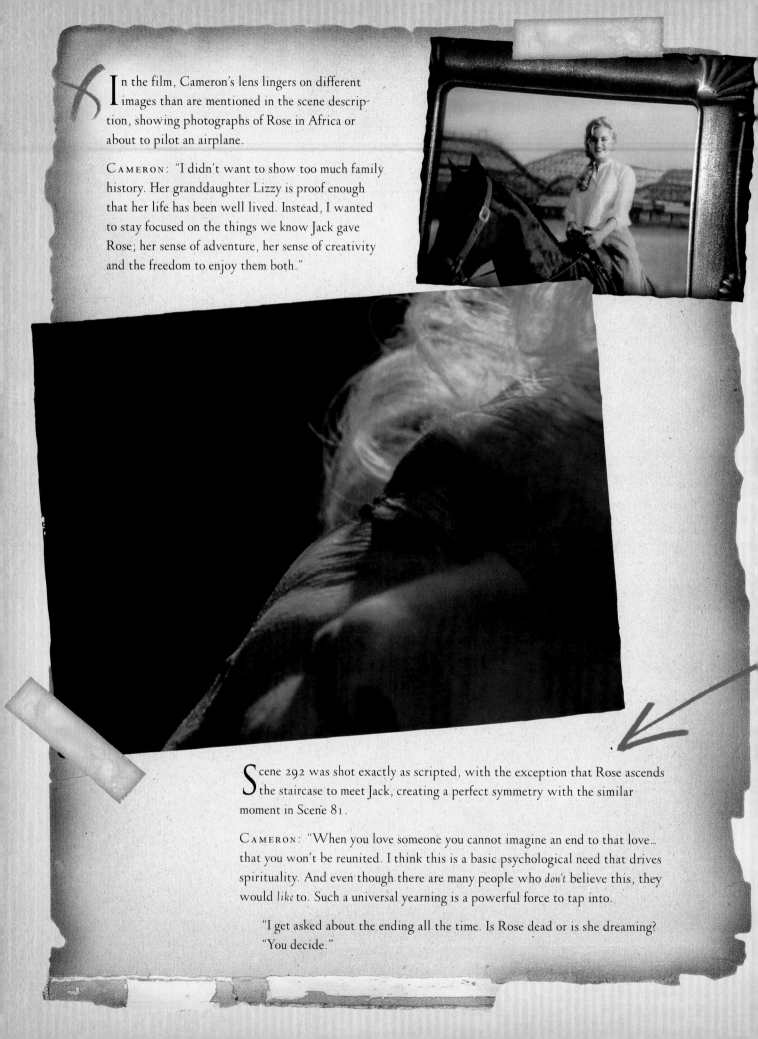

In the film, Cameron's lens lingers on different images than are mentioned in the scene description, showing photographs of Rose in Africa or about to pilot an airplane.

CAMERON: "I didn't want to show too much family history. Her granddaughter Lizzy is proof enough that her life has been well lived. Instead, I wanted to stay focused on the things we know Jack gave Rose; her sense of adventure, her sense of creativity and the freedom to enjoy them both."

Scene 292 was shot exactly as scripted, with the exception that Rose ascends the staircase to meet Jack, creating a perfect symmetry with the similar moment in Scene 81.

CAMERON: "When you love someone you cannot imagine an end to that love... that you won't be reunited. I think this is a basic psychological need that drives spirituality. And even though there are many people who *don't* believe this, they would *like* to. Such a universal yearning is a powerful force to tap into.

"I get asked about the ending all the time. Is Rose dead or is she dreaming? "You decide."

291   INT. ROSE'S CABIN/KELDYSH   291

A GRACEFUL PAN across Rose's shelf of carefully arranged pictures:

Rose as a young actress in California, radiant... a theatrically lit studio publicity
shot... Rose and her husband, with their two children... Rose with her son at his college
graduation... Rose with her children and grandchildren at her 70th birthday. A collage of
images of a life lived well.

THE PAN STOPS on an image filling frame. Rose, circa 1920. She is at the
beach, sitting on a horse at the surfline. The Santa Monica pier, with its roller-
coaster, is behind her. She is grinning, full of life.

We PAN OFF the last picture to Rose herself, warm in her bunk. A profile shot.
She is very still. She could be sleeping, or maybe something else.

                                                        CUT TO:

BLACKNESS.

292   THE WRECK OF TITANIC looms like a ghost out of the dark. It is lit by a kind   292
of moonlight, a light of the mind. We pass over the endless forecastle deck
to the superstructure, moving faster than subs can move... almost like we
are flying.

WE GO INSIDE, and the echoing sound of distant waltz music is heard. The rust
fades away from the walls of the dark corridor and it is transformed... WE
EMERGE onto the grand staircase, lit by glowing chandeliers. The music is vibrant
now, and the room is populated by men in tie and tails, women in gowns. It is
exquisitely beautiful.

IN POV we sweep down the staircase. The crowd of beautiful gentlemen and ladies
turn as we descend toward them. At the bottom a man stands with his back to us...
he turns and it is Jack. Smiling he holds his hand out toward us.

IN A SIDE ANGLE Rose goes into his arms, a girl of 17. The passengers, officers
and crew of the RMS Titanic smile and applaud in the utter silence of the
abyss.

C A S T

JACK DAWSON	LEONARDO DiCAPRIO
ROSE DEWITT BUKATER	KATE WINSLET
CAL HOCKLEY	BILLY ZANE
MOLLY BROWN	KATHY BATES
RUTH DEWITT BUKATER	FRANCES FISHER
OLD ROSE	GLORIA STUART
BROCK LOVETT	BILL PAXTON
CAPTAIN SMITH	BERNARD HILL
SPICER LOVEJOY	DAVID WARNER
THOMAS ANDREWS	VICTOR GARBER
BRUCE ISMAY	JONATHAN HYDE
LIZZY CALVERT	SUZY AMIS
LEWIS BODINE	LEWIS ABERNATHY
BOBBY BUELL	NICHOLAS CASCONE
ANATOLY MILKAILAVICH	DR. ANATOLY M. SAGALEVITCH
FABRIZIO	DANNY NUCCI
TOMMY RYAN	JASON BARRY
1ST OFFICER MURDOCH	EWAN STEWART
FIFTH OFFICER LOWE	IOAN GRUFFUDD
2ND OFFICER LIGHTOLLER	JONNY PHILLIPS
CHIEF OFFICER WILDE	MARK LINDSAY CHAPMAN
QUARTERMASTER ROWE	RICHARD GRAHAM
QUARTERMASTER HICHENS	PAUL BRIGHTWELL
MASTER AT ARMS	RON DONACHIE

JOHN JACOB ASTOR	ERIC BRAEDEN
MADELEINE ASTOR	CHARLOTTE CHATTON
COL. ARCHIBALD GRACIE	BERNARD FOX
BENJAMIN GUGGENHEIM	MICHAEL ENSIGN
MADAME AUBERT	FANNIE BRETT
IRISH MOMMY	JENETTE GOLDSTEIN
HELGA DAHL	CAMILLA OVERBYE ROOS
3RD CLASS WOMAN	LINDA KERNS
TRUDY BOLT	AMY GAIPA
SIR DUFF GORDON	MARTIN JARVIS
LADY DUFF GORDON	ROSALIND AYRES
COUNTESS OF ROTHES	ROCHELLE ROSE
WALLACE HARTLEY	JONATHAN EVANS-JONES
IRISH MAN	BRIAN WALSH
BERT CARTMELL	ROCKY TAYLOR
CORA CARTMELL	ALEXANDRE OWENS
4TH OFFICER BOXHALL	SIMON CRANE
6TH OFFICER MOODY	EDWARD FLETCHER
FREDERICK FLEET	SCOTT G. ANDERSON
LOOKOUT LEE	MARTIN EAST
HAROLD BRIDE	CRAIG KELLY
JACK PHILLIPS	GREGORY COOKE
CHIEF BAKER JOUGHIN	LIAM TUOHY
FATHER BYLES	JAMES LANCASTER

IDA STRAUS	ELSA RAVEN
ISIDOR STRAUS	LEW PALTER
IRISH LITTLE BOY	REECE P. THOMPSON III
IRISH LITTLE GIRL	LARAMIE LANDIS
CAL'S CRYING GIRL	AMBER and ALISON WADDELL
YALEY	MARK RAFAEL TRUITT
1ST CLASS HUSBAND	JOHN WALCUTT
CHIEF ENGINEER BELL	TERRY FORRESTAL
LEADING STOKER BARRETT	DEREK LEA
CARPENTER JOHN HUTCHINSON	RICHARD ASHTON
ELEVATOR OPERATOR	SEAN M. NEPITA
SCOTLAND ROAD STEWARD	BRENDAN CONNOLLY
CREWMAN	DAVID CRONNELLY
1ST CLASS WAITER	GARTH WILTON
PROMENADE DECK STEWARD	MARTIN LAING
STEWARD #1	RICHARD FOX
STEWARD #2	NICK MEANEY
STEWARD #3	KEVIN OWERS
STEWARD #4	MARK CAPRI
HOLD STEWARD #1	MARC CASS
HOLD STEWARD #2	PAUL HERBERT
1ST CLASS STEWARD	EMMETT JAMES
STAIRWELL STEWARD	CHRISTOPHER BYRNE
STEWARD BARNES	OLIVER PAGE

TITANIC PORTER	JAMES GARRETT
OLAF DAHL	ERIK HOLLAND
BJORN GUNDERSON	JARI KINNUNEN
OLAUS GUNDERSON	ANDERS FALK
SLOVAKIAN FATHER	MARTIN HUB
SLOVAKIAN 3 YEAR OLD BOY	SETH ADKINS
PRAYING MAN	BARRY DENNEN
MAN IN WATER	VERN URICH
MOTHER AT STERN	REBECCA JANE KLINGLER
WOMAN	TRICIA O'NEIL
WOMAN IN WATER	KATHLEEN DUNN
SYRIAN MAN	ROMEO FRANCIS
SYRIAN WOMAN	MANDANA MARINO
CHINESE MAN	VAN LING
OLAF	BJØRN
SVEN	DAN PETTERSSON
PUBKEEPER	SHAY DUFFIN
CARPATHIA STEWARD	GREG ELLIS
NEWS REPORTER	DIANA MORGAN
TITANIC ORCHESTRA	I SALONISTI
STEERAGE BAND	GAELIC STORM

C R E D I T S

WRITTEN AND DIRECTED BY	JAMES CAMERON
PRODUCED BY	JAMES CAMERON AND JON LANDAU
EXECUTIVE PRODUCER	RAE SANCHINI
DIRECTOR OF PHOTOGRAPHY	RUSSELL CARPENTER, A.S.C.
PRODUCTION DESIGNER	PETER LAMONT
EDITED BY	CONRAD BUFF, A.C.E.
	JAMES CAMERON
	RICHARD A. HARRIS
COSTUME DESIGNER	DEBORAH L. SCOTT
VISUAL EFFECTS SUPERVISOR	ROBERT LEGATO
MUSIC COMPOSED BY	JAMES HORNER
CASTING BY	MALI FINN, C.S.A.
MUSIC SUPERVISOR	RANDY GERSTON
CO-PRODUCERS	AL GIDDINGS
	GRANT HILL, SHARON MANN
ASSOCIATE PRODUCER	PAMELA EASLEY HARRIS
UNIT PRODUCTION MANAGERS	GRANT HILL, ANNA ROTH
	SHARON MANN, JON LANDAU
FIRST ASSISTANT DIRECTOR	JOSH McLAGLEN
SECOND ASSISTANT DIRECTORS	SEBASTIAN SILVA
	KATHLEEN "BO" BOBAK
ASSOCIATE EDITOR	ROGER BARTON
SECOND UNIT DIRECTOR	STEVEN QUALE
PRODUCTION SUPERVISOR	GIG RACKAUSKAS
SPECIAL EFFECTS BY	THOMAS L. FISHER
CAMERA OPERATOR/STEADICAM	JIM MURO
SUPERVISING ART DIRECTOR	CHARLES LEE
ART DIRECTOR	MARTIN LAING
GAFFER	JOHN BUCKLEY
RIGGING GAFFER	MIKE AMORELLI

KEY GRIP	LLOYD MORIARITY
RIGGING KEY GRIP	PHILIP SLOAN
STUNT COORDINATOR	SIMON CRANE
SCRIPT SUPERVISOR	SHELLEY CRAWFORD
UNIT MANAGER	KEVIN DeLANOY
AQUATIC SUPERVISOR/RESEARCHER	CHARLIE ARNESON
SET DECORATOR	MICHAEL FORD
CONSTRUCTION COORDINATORS	W. LES COLLINS
	TONY GRAYSMARK
MARINE COORDINATOR	LANCE JULIAN
TRANSPORTATION COORDINATORS	ROGER HANNA
	TOM GORDON
MEDICAL COORDINATOR	L. DOUGLAS FENTON
SPECIAL ENGINEER	DUNCAN FERGUSON
KEY SCAFFOLDING ENGINEER	HARRY HEEKS
KEY MAKE-UP ARTIST	TINA EARNSHAW
KEY HAIRDRESSERS	SIMON THOMPSON
	KAY GEORGIOU

CAMERA / SOUND DEPARTMENTS

SOUND MIXER	MARK ULANO, C.A.S.
BOOM OPERATOR	DONAVAN DEAR
2ND BOOM OPERATOR	JIMMY OSBURN
B CAMERA 1ST ASSISTANT	GERARDO MANJARREZ
CAMERA FILM LOADERS	SCOTT RONNOW
	HECTOR MEDINA
VIDEO ASSIST	CHUCK WEISS
AUDIO SYSTEM OPERATOR	BRENDAN BEEBE
CAMERA 1ST ASSISTANT	MARK JACKSON
CAMERA 2ND ASSISTANT	KIRK BLOOM
B CAMERA OPERATOR	GUILLERMO "MEMO" ROSAS

B CAMERA 2ND ASSISTANTS	JOAQUIN CERVERA
	CESAR R. SOLIS
CAMERA PRODUCTION ASSISTANT	GLENN BROWN
ASSISTANT VIDEO ASSIST	MITCH BRYAN
2ND UNIT DIRECTORS OF PHOTOGRAPHY	ROY UNGER
	JOHN STEPHENS
	AARON E SCHNEIDER
SPECIAL DEEP OCEAN CAMERA SYSTEM	MICHAEL CAMERON

PRODUCTION DEPARTMENT

LOCATION MANAGER	NICOLE KOLIN
ADDITIONAL 1ST ASSISTANT DIRECTOR	TOBY PEASE
2ND ASSISTANT DIRECTOR	JOAQUIN SILVA
ADDITIONAL ASSISTANT DIRECTOR	T. C. BADALATO
3RD ASSISTANT DIRECTOR	GISELLE GURZA
PRODUCTION EXECUTIVE	LOUIS G. FRIEDMAN
KEY PRODUCTION COORDINATOR	STACY PLAVOUKOS
ASSISTANT PRODUCTION COORDINATORS	ROSANNA SUN
	CARLA RAYGOZA
2ND UNIT SCRIPT SUPERVISOR	BERTHA MEDINA
PRODUCTION ASSOCIATE	GEOFF BURDICK
LIGHTSTORM FINANCIAL	CAROL HENRY
2ND UNIT 1ST ASSISTANT DIRECTOR	JONATHAN SOUTHARD
TITANIC VISUAL HISTORIAN	KEN MARSCHALL
ADDITIONAL PRODUCTION SUPERVISOR	MICHAEL LEVINE
KEY 2ND ASSISTANT DIRECTOR	JACINTA HAYNE
2ND 2ND ASSISTANT DIRECTOR	A. HUGO GUTIERREZ CUELLAR
ASSISTANT UNIT PRODUCTION MANAGER	MARK INDIG
PRODUCTION COORDINATOR	BELINDA URIEGAS
L. A. PRODUCTION COORDINATOR	EVE HONTHANER

ASSISTANT TO JON LANDAU	CYNTHIA ANN SCRIMA
ASSISTANTS TO JAMES CAMERON	NANCY HOBSON
	PERRY SANTOS
ASSISTANT TO RAE SANCHINI	KIM E. F. TROY
ASSISTANT TO GRANT HILL	ROBERT CATRON
LIGHTSTORM PRODUCTION	AL RIVES, MIKE TRAINOTTI
SET COORDINATOR	RAFAEL CUERVO
NAVAL CONSULTANT	KIT BONNER
TITANIC HISTORIAN	DON LYNCH

PROPS / SET DRESSING DEPARTMENTS

PROPMASTERS	BARRY WILKINSON
	ANTONIO MATA
SUPERVISING FLOOR PROPMAN	SIMON WILKINSON
FLOOR PROPMEN	GARY IXER, BEN WILKINSON
CHARGE HAND PROPSMEN	ANDY PALMER
	JAMIE WILKINSON
DRAPES MASTER	CLEO NETHERSOLE
ASSISTANT SET DECORATORS	ROSALIND SHINGLETON
	RICHARD ROBERTS
SUPERVISING DRESS PROPMEN	JOHN PALMER
	MARTIN G. KINGSLEY
ASSISTANT SET DRESSER	ENRIQUE ESTEVEZ
DRAPES ASSISTANTS	RICARDO OSORIO
	JESUS OSORIO, MARCO CARRANZA, MANUEL ORDAZ
PROPS ASSISTANTS	RAMIRO MARTINEZ L.
	MARIO TORRES, MARTIN GUTIERREZ
	ANTONIO GODINEZ, GUSTAVO CASTELLANOS
	ANDRES SANTANA, ADRIAN ZAMUDIO

ART DEPARTMENT

ADDITIONAL ART DIRECTORS	NEIL LAMONT, BOB LAING

ART DEPARTMENT SUPERVISOR ....THOM COLWELL
SET DESIGNERS ....MARCO NIRO
DOMINIC MASTERS, PETER FRANCIS
SUPERVISING STOREKEEPER ....DEREK CREEDON
STAND-BY PAINTER ....MARILYN McAVOY
ASSISTANT ART DIRECTORS ....STEVE LAWRENCE
HECTOR ROMERO
ART DEPARTMENT COORDINATOR ....AMANDA SALLYBANKS
JUNIOR SET DESIGNERS ....FRANCISCO GARCIA
EUGENIO CASTA

ASSISTANT ART DEPARTMENT
COORDINATOR ....LUISA GOMEZ DE SILVA

WARDROBE DEPARTMENT
ASSISTANT COSTUME DESIGNER ....DAVID LE VEY
DEPARTMENT COORDINATOR ....BETH KOENIGSBERG
MEN'S COSTUME SUPERVISORS ....ADOLFO RAMIREZ
TOM NUMBERS
KEY MEN'S SET COSTUMERS ....MURRAY LANTZ
ISMAEL JARDON
FLOOR SUPERVISOR ....WILLIAM McPHAIL
HEAD BEADER ....PAULE A. DRISSI
COSTUME MANUFACTURING FOREMAN ......SALVADOR PEREZ
COSTUME SHOP ....DIANE PUHALLA
DAVID JARDON, LOURDES LOPEZ MARTINEZ
ASSISTANT COSTUME DESIGNER ....LAHLY POORE
WOMEN'S COSTUME SUPERVISOR ....SARAH TOUAIBI
KEY WOMEN'S SET COSTUMERS ....AMY ARNOLD
LEIGH LEVERETT
TEXTILE ARTIST ....MATT REITSMA
HEAD CUTTER / FITTER ....DALE WIBBEN
TAILOR SHOP SUPERVISOR ......SANDRA LAURA RAMOS
CUTTER / FITTER ....KAREN NASER
MILLINERS ....SHARON KING
KIRSTEN OSTHUS, JOSEPHINE WILLIS
COSTUMERS ....JOSE LUIS MONTERO
JAVIER DELGADO, CARLOS MUNGUIA
MICHAEL LONG, SCOTT GABA
PHILIP MALDONADO, ROCIO CEJA
CYNTHIA MARTINEZ, MARIA LUISA ANDRADE
KANANI WOLF, MARSHA BOZEMAN
CECILIA STANFORD, JEANIE BAKER
DEBORAH (CHA) BLEVINS, ENRIQUE VILLAVIENCIO

ELECTRICAL DEPARTMENT
BEST BOYS ELECTRIC ....JOHN WEEKS
ENRIQUE SANCHEZ
DIMMER BOARD OPERATOR ....SUSAN A. TURCOT
RIGGING BEST BOYS ELECTRIC ....ISMAEL (IZZY) GONZALEZ
JACK McLEAN, BILL GREENBERG, PAUL AMORELLI
REYES SANTAMARIA, ROSALIO CANO
JESSE POGOLER, JESUS GONZALEZ
LAMP OPERATORS ....MALCOLM BRYCE
CESAR CAMACHO, ANGEL SANCHES CASTRO
PAUL CHEUNG, JORGE ENRIQUEZ
GARY FREDRICKSON, MANUEL GARCIA G.
SERGIO GONSALEZ, KHAN GRIFFITH, HAL GROSHON
JON HANEY, RON HOFFMAN, ENRIQUE LARA
LUIS SANCHEZ LARA, JASON LEEDS, MARC MARINO
LEONARDO M. MARRON, BILL MAYBERRY
MARC MEISENHEIMER, ROLANDO MICHEL
SALVADOR GUTIERREZ MORENO
EDUARDO J. OVIEDO, JASON PARRILLO
ROBERTO PICHARDO, JUAN JOSE CASILLAS RIVERA
CARLOS SANCHEZ, JOSE LUIS SANCHEZ
RALPH SANDERS, RENE TANNOS

MARCO A. LEON TUPIA, JUAN JOSE VALENCIA
MARCO VALLARINO, MICHAEL YOPE
RIGGING ELECTRICS ....RENE TORRES ACOSTA
LEOPOLDO VEGA ALVARADO, JOSE L. BARAJAS P.
JOSE L. CANEDO, JAVIER SANCHEZ CARRERA
ROMAN COVARRUBIAS, ALFREDO LUNA GALINDO
FELIPE DE JESUS GUTIERREZ, ROBERTO GUTIERREZ
SAUL DOMINGUEZ HERNANDEZ
RIGGING ELECTRICS (cont'd) ....CARLOS CHACON INOTA
JOAQUIN ALCANTARA JIMENEZ
EDGAR HURTADO LOPEZ, BENITO AGUILAR PEREZ
JORGE F. SOLORIO, JORGE GONZALEZ URIBE
NESTOR MARTINEZ VILLANUEVA
PRACTICAL ELECTRIC SUPERVISORS ....ERIC MELVILLE
BILL FINE, STEVE HARVEY, JIM ROPER
FIXTURE ELECTRICS ....ROB CHEUNG, KEVIN BOTHAM
BOB SMITH, BOB FISHER
GENERATOR OPERATORS ....JONATHAN McCREA HARMON
STEVEN C. EAKINS, CHIP ROBINSON
BUDDY BOTHAM
MUSCO TECHNICIAN ....PAUL CIANCETTA
NIGHTSUN TECHNICIAN ....THOMAS BARR O'DONNELL

GRIP DEPARTMENT
KEY GRIP MEXICO ....GUSTAVO COVARRUBIAS .
BEST BOY GRIP ....EUGENE BRIAN KERRY .
DOLLY GRIPS ....DOUGLAS CHARTIER
RICARDO COVARRUBIAS
RIGGING BEST BOY GRIPS ....TIMOTHY COLLINS
ANTONIO VARGAS PEREZ
GRIPS ....DANIEL ANAYA, RICARDO ARVIZU
TONY BENDT, BRUCE BYALL
MIKE CATANZARITE, KEVIN COOK
MICHAEL DRONGE, JORGE COVARRUBIAS GARCIA
MARCOS HERNANDEZ, GARY "GARO T" KINGSTON
JESUS LABASTIDA, PATRICIO PEREDA
HUMBERTO SANCHEZ, RON SANTOYO
BOB SNOWDON, GLENN WADE
PAUL WILKOWSKY, ROBERT ZULLO
RIGGING GRIPS ....ALVARDO BORTOLINI CAMACHO
CARLOS MENDOZA CAMPOS
JOSE ANTONIO CARMONA, BRUCE CAROTHERS
RAUL CORTEZ, ROMEL ESQUIVEL
SALVADOR ORENDAIN ESTRADA
FERNANDO FERNANDEZ ARZOTE, TODD GRIFFITH
JOHN HARMON, RICK HERRES
RICHARD JONES, DENNIS KUNEFF
MARCELINO LUNA, CESAR ROJO MEDINA
MANUEL PEREZ MENDOZA
JULIO REYES MUNOZ, ISMAEL PAREDES
PEDRO PEDRAZA, JUAN CARLOS RODRIGUEZ
ALFREDO AUDEL ROMAN
ANDRES JOAQUIN SOLANO
EVERARDO PEREDA SOLORZANO
WESCAM OPERATOR ....KURT SODERLING S.O.C.
WESCAM TECHNICIAN ....STEVEN J. WINSLOW
TECHNOCRANE OPERATOR ....DANIEL HEGARTY
AKELA CRANE OPERATORS ....JOHN BONNIN
CHARLEY REFFITT, HORACE REYNOLDS
RICK JOHNSON, DAN BONNIN

PRODUCTION CONSULTANT ....MARTY KATZ
OLD ROSE SPECIAL EFFECTS MAKE-UP ....GREG CANNOM
CHOREOGRAPHER / ETIQUETTE COACH ....LYNNE HOCKNEY
CASTING ASSOCIATE ....EMILY SCHWEBER

HAIR / MAKE-UP DEPARTMENTS
MAKE-UP ARTISTS ....SIAN GRIEGG
POLLY EARNSHAW, ENZO MASTRANTONIO
REBECCA LAFFORD, LISA McDEVITT
HAIRDRESSERS ....BETTY GLASOW
JOHN HENRY GORDON, ZOE TAHIR
HAIR CROWD SUPERVISORS ....DEBORAH BALL
THELMA MILLER
ADDITIONAL MAKE-UP ....RAUL SARMIENTO PINA
DEBBIE GOWER, MEL GIBSON, TONI RIKI
DIYAN ROGERS, TERESA PATTERSON
ANITA E. BRABEC, GUADALUPE PEREZ P.
HUMBERTO ESCAMILLA
ASSISTANT HAIRDRESSERS ....CATHERINE LEBLANC
CHRISTINE LEAUSTIC, ISABEL AMEZCUA
GUADALUPE RAMIREZ, MARTHA RAMOS
ESPERANZA GOMEZ S., RAUL COVARRUBIAS
GEORGIA DUNN, LAUREL KELLY
MICHAEL GUTIERREZ
CARLOS HORCASITAS, LUIS HORCASITAS

SPECIAL EFFECTS DEPARTMENT
SFX CO-COORDINATOR ....SCOTT FISHER
SFX ADMINISTRATOR ....PAULA FISHER .
SFX FOREMEN ....JAY B. KING, SERGIO JARA SR.
SFX RIGGING FOREMAN ....ANDREW JESSE MILLER
SFX TECHNICIANS ......NEIL GARLAND, ROBERT SLATER
ROBERT EARL TOWNSEND
STEVEN CURTIS TOWNSEND, SERGIO JARA JR.
LUIS EDUARDO AMBRIZ, VICTOR RAMIREZ
WELDERS ....ALVIN LICOAN, IAN C. McARTHUR
JOE LIVOLSI, DAVID ROMERO

CONSTRUCTION DEPARTMENT
STEEL FABRICATION SUPERVISORS ......ROGER BEAUDOIN
J. BARNEY CLAREY
CONSTRUCTION FOREMEN ....JIM HANSON
MARK McCARTHY, VINNIE BOWEN, RANDALL GROVES
CONSTRUCTION ESTIMATOR ....GERALD SCAIFE
SCENIC ARTIST ....STEVE SALLYBANKS
HEAD SIGN WRITER ....ARTURO MENDEZ
SAFETY OFFICER ....EDWARD ZUBRITSKY
SUPERVISING PLASTERER ....PAUL TAGGART
CONSTRUCTION BUYER ....HARVEY T. COLLINS
MIGUEL PINEDA
STAGEHAND ....GRAHAM JOHN BLINCO
RIGGING FOREMAN ....ROBERT HAROLD COOPER
ASSISTANT CONSTRUCTION COORDINATORS ......RUFUS BEST
T. KEVIN FISHER, MARK PETRAK, PAUL HAYES
CONSTRUCTION SUPERVISORS ....CHRIS BROWN
DEREK DAWSON, JOHN KIRSOP
CONSTRUCTION GANG BOSSES ....JEREMY HARFORD
DANNY KISER, ROBIN JONES, DAVE MOSALL
LEAD SCENICS ....M. DOMINIC CETANI
GENESSA GOLDSMITH PROCTOR, CHERYL JOHNSON
LEAD SCENIC INTERIORS ....DAVID WESCOTT
SIGN WRITER ....STEVE HEDINGER
HEAD PLASTERER ....DAVID COLDHAM
MACHINIST ....STEVE RICHARDS
HEAD SHIPPING & REC'G ....OZMANDIAS
CONSTRUCTION OFFICE COORDINATOR ....LAUREEN A. CLARKE
STEEL RIGGER GANG BOSS ....JAMES MARKS
SITE ENGINEER ....ANDREW KIRBY
CONSTRUCTION GROUP HEADS ......SERGIO FUENTES GARCIA
FLORENTINO AGUILAR
FRANCISCO MARTINEZ RIVERA

CARLOS MENDEZ, RAFAEL RODRIGUEZ PALACIOS
MARGARITO LOPEZ, JESUS LABASTIDA
FEDERICO MEDINA, DAVID GOMEZ FRIAS
RICARDO NAJERA, LUIS ALTAMIRANO
SALVADOR DE GANTE
FELIX PEREZ, JAIME SANCHEZ
WELDING FOREMEN / GANG BOSSES ....STEPHEN BOURGEOIS
PATRICK H. MALISAUSKAS, RICHARD PECORA
CARLOS COLINA, LLOYD BURKE JR.
PETER D. DUFFY, JOHN ERIC SEAY
SCENIC FOREMEN / GANG BOSSES ....LOUIS BOWEN
MARCUS CETANI, JOSE GONZALEZ
CARL KELLER, ELIZABETH FISHER
LYNN JOHANSON, JAMES DELAPLANE
RODNEY DELAPLANE, DANIEL WALKER
SCAFFOLDING ENGINEERS ....LEONARD HARRIS
JUSTIN HEATH, PAUL SKINNER
ANDREW SYKES, GARY WATSON
ROY WEATHERLY, DAVID SKINNER

ACCOUNTING
PRODUCTION CONTROLLERS ......KEN RYAN, NICOLE FURIA
PRODUCTION ACCOUNTANT MEXICO .....ARMANDO AMADOR
ACCOUNTING ESTIMATORS ....CRAIG CANNOLD
HEATHER McINTOSH
PRODUCTION ACCOUNTANTS ....MAYDA RENIZZI-HOLT
JOANIE SPATES
1ST ASSISTANT ACCOUNTANTS ......SHAWN K. GILLESPIE
KORIN A. TARIN
CONSTRUCTION ACCOUNTANT ....PATRICK SHIFFRAR
ASSISTANT ACCOUNTANTS ....ERIC LAYNE, EDDIE ADOLPH
TIMOTHY JOSEPH FLOREEN
M. ROSS MICHAELS
ASSISTANT ACCOUNTANTS (cont'd) ....MARY JANE FARIS
ALBERT (JAY) PITKETHLY, MICHAEL MORGENTHAL
JANETTE EVANS, JULIE ANN MOYEDA
HAL HOPKINS, ENRIQUETA AMADOR
ANGIE RYAN, JUDI WEAVER, GREGG STUART

CASTING
LONDON CASTING .....SUZANNE CROWLEY, GILLY POOLE
EXTRAS CASTING COORDINATOR ....CHUCHO GUERRERO
DIALECT COACH ....SUSAN HEGARTY
CHILDREN'S GUARDIAN ....MARITZA CORRALES
EXTRAS CASTING ....AMY CATON-FORD
TINA LOUISE KERR
DEEDRA RICKETTS
ASSISTANT CASTING COORDINATORS ....EDNA ARRIOLA
JORGE GUERRERO
STUDIO TEACHER ....CECILIA CARDWELL
ASSISTANT TO CHOREOGRAPHER ......LANCE MACDONALD
CASTING ASSOCIATES ....MAGUI JIMENEZ
RODOLFO "RUDY" JOFFROY, GEMMA JOFFROY
JESUS IGNACIO SANTANA

STILLS / PUBLICITY ETC.
UNIT PUBLICIST ....EILEEN PETERSON
STILLS PHOTOGRAPHER ....MERIE W. WALLACE
DOCUMENTARIAN ....ED W. MARSH
DOCUMENTARY DIRECTOR OF PHOTOGRAPHY ....ANDERS FALK

TRANSPORTATION
TRANSPORTATION CAPTAINS ....ARTURO CURIEL
ROCKEY REED
TRANSPORTATION CO-CAPTAIN ....HUGO CHEW
DRIVERS ....LARRY ALICATA
TOM BRIGGS, JOSE CASTILLO
ROSEMARY ECHEVERRIA, WAYNE EDWARDS

WILLIAM ESPARZA, RIGO GONZALES
RAYMOND E. KEHOE, BOB LIMON
JUAN LOPEZ, ANGELO OREFICE
JULIAN SAAVEDRA, STEVE SCHULTZ

MARINE DEPARTMENT

ASSISTANT MARINE COORDINATOR ....NICK SPETSIOTIS
MARINE TANK / CRANE SUPERVISOR ....JOE DONALDSON
MARINE TECHNICIAN ....AL PERRY
TOWER CRANE OPERATOR ....LARRY WEBBER
MARINE RIGGER ....HARRY JULIAN
MARINE MECHANIC ....BRIAN BRADLEY
MARINE TECHNICIAN ....BILL GLESNE
TOWER CRANE FLAGMAN ....JASON MAXEY

POST PRODUCTION / EDITORIAL

1ST ASSISTANT EDITOR ....DAVID BROBERG
1ST ASSISTANT EDITOR ....LADD LANFORD
VISUAL EFFECTS EDITORS ....BRYAN CARROLL
                                        STEVE R. MOORE
POST PRODUCTION CONTROLLER ....PAULA CATANIA
ADDITIONAL ASSISTANT EDITORS ......DAVID CROWTHER
JOHN MORRISEY, JAMES DURANTE
EDGAR PAVON, ALEX HEPBURN
PAUL WAGNER, WARREN PAEFF
EDITORIAL APPRENTICE ....DANIEL ROBERT BOCCOLI
POST PRODUCTION SUPERVISOR .....LISA ANN DENNIS
ASSISTANT VFX EDITOR ....JASON GAUDIO
EDITORAL PRODUCTION ASSISTANT ......IGNACIO GUZMAN
POST PRODUCTION SOUND SERVICES
PROVIDED BY ....**SKYWALKER SOUND**
A DIVISION OF LUCAS DIGITAL LTD. MARIN COUNTY, CALIFORNIA
RE-RECORDING MIXERS ....GARY RYDSTROM
TOM JOHNSON, GARY SUMMERS
CHRISTOPHER BOYES, LORA HIRSCHBERG
SUPERVISING SOUND EDITOR ....TOM BELLFORT
SOUND DESIGNER ....CHRISTOPHER BOYES
ASSISTANT SOUND DESIGNER ....SHANNON MILLS
SOUND EFFECTS EDITORS ....ETHAN VAN DER RYN
SCOTT GUITTEAU, CHRISTOPHER SCARABOSIO
SUPERVISING ADR EDITOR ....HUGH WADDELL
ADR EDITORS ...SUZANNE FOX, HARRIET FIDLOW WINN
RICHARD G. CORWIN, CINDY MARTY, LEE LEMONT
DIALOGUE EDITORS ....GWENDOLYN YATES WHITTLE
CLAIRE SANFILIPPO
J. H. ARRUFAT, RICHARD QUINN
SUPERVISING FOLEY EDITOR ....THOMAS SMALL
FOLEY EDITORS ....SCOTT CURTIS
TAMMY FEARING, DAVE HORTON, JR.
SUPERVISING ASSISTANT SOUND EDITOR ....SCOTT KOUÉ
SUPERVISING ASSISTANT ADR EDITOR ....JONATHAN NULL
ASSISTANT SOUND EDITORS ....BEAU BORDERS
JESSICA BELLFORT, MARY WORKS
MICHAEL AXINN
PARAMOUNT FOLEY MIXER ....RANDY K. SINGER
FOLEY ARTISTS ....SARAH MONAT, ROBIN HARLAN
ADR MIXERS ....DEAN DRABIN
BRIAN RUBERG, TONY ANSCOMBE
RECORDISTS ....CARY STRATTON, ANN HADSELL
JOAN CHAMBERLAIN, SCOTT JONES
DARREN McQUADE
RE-RECORDISTS ....RONALD C. ROUMAS
SCOTT LEVY, AL NELSON, MARK PENDERGRAFT
MACHINE ROOM OPERATORS ....DAVID TURNER
STEVE ROMANKO, CHRISTOPHER BARRON
MIX TECHNICIANS ....GARY A. RIZZO, TONY SERENO

SEAN ENGLAND, KENT SPARLING
JURGEN SCHARPF
TRANSFER SUPERVISOR ....MARNI L. HAMMETT
DIGITAL AUDIO TRANSFER ....JONATHAN GREBER
DEE SELBY, MICHAEL RIVO
VIDEO SERVICES ....CHRISTIAN VON BURKLEO
JOHN "JT" TORRIJOS

MUSIC

SCORE ORCHESTRATIONS ....JAMES HORNER
SUPERVISING MUSIC EDITOR ....JIM HENRIKSON
ASSISTANT MUSIC EDITORS ....LESLEY LANGS
NANCY FOGARTY
CONTRACTOR ....SANDY De CRESCENT
INSTRUMENTAL SOLOISTS ....SIMON FRANGLEN
TONY HINNIGAN, IAN UNDERWOOD
RANDY KERBER, ERIC RIGLER
JAMES HORNER
MUSIC COORDINATORS ....MICHAL LALI KAGAN
AMY ROSEN
SCORING ENGINEER ....SHAWN MURPHY
MUSIC EDITOR ....JOE E. RAND
ADDITIONAL ORCHESTRATIONS ....DON DAVIS
VOCAL PERFORMANCES BY ....SISSEL
COURTESY OF POLYGRAM A.S., NORWAY
MUSIC PREPARATION ....BOB BORNSTEIN
ASSISTANT ENGINEERS ....ANDY BASS
DAVID MARQUETTE, JAY SELVESTER

TITANIC DEEP DIVE

DIRECTOR OF PHOTOGRAPHY ....JAMES CAMERON
TECHNOLOGY SUPERVISOR ....MICHAEL CAMERON
LEAD DESIGN ENGINEER ....VINCE CATLIN
PRODUCTION COORDINATOR ....ANTHONY ALLEGRE
TECHNOLOGY COORDINATOR ....RALPH WHITE
ASSISTANT TECHNOLOGY COORDINATOR ....VALERIE MOORE
SENIOR TECHNICIAN/ROV PILOT ....JEFFREY N. LEDDA
VIDEO CREW ....JEFFREY CREE, JON DODSON
VINCE PACE, RANDY WIMBERG
PRE-VIS PREP MODEL ....LOU ZUTAVERN
BIG Z MINIATURES
ACCOUNTANT ....KATHY GRANT

THE DEEP DIVE COULD NOT HAVE BEEN ACCOMPLISHED
WITHOUT THE HELP OF THE FOLLOWING:
DR. ANATOLY M. SAGALEVITCH AND THE ENTIRE CREW
OF AKADEMIK MSTISLAV KELDYSH
P. P. SHIRSHOV INSTITUTE OF
OCEANOLOGY, RUSSIAN ACADEMY OF SCIENCES
PANAVISION, BENTHOS, INC.
MEDIA LOGIC, DEEP SEA POWER & LIGHT, IMAX
WESTERN SPACE AND MARINE, INC.
HARD SUITS, INC., AND PISCES DESIGN

VISUAL EFFECTS

VISUAL EFFECTS PRODUCER ....CAMILLE CELLUCCI
VISUAL EFFECTS WRANGLER ....ROB YAMAMOTO
VISUAL EFFECTS CONSULTANT ....JOHN BRUNO
VISUAL EFFECTS COORDINATOR ....BLERIME TOPALLI
ASSISTANT VFX COORDINATORS ....ROBYN BREEN
SEAN STANEK
SPECIAL VISUAL EFFECTS AND DIGITAL
ANIMATION BY ....**DIGITAL DOMAIN** VENICE, CALIFORNIA
VISUAL EFFECTS PRODUCER ....CRYSTAL DOWD
DIGITAL EFFECTS SUPERVISORS ....MARK LASOFF
JUDITH CROW

VISUAL EFFECTS DIRECTOR OF PHOTOGRAPHY ......ERIK NASH
VISUAL EFFECTS LINE PRODUCER ....CARI THOMAS
DIGITAL COMPOSITING SUPERVISORS ......MICHAEL KANFER
MARK FORKER
DIGITAL EFFECTS PRODUCER ....KAREN M. MURPHY
COMPOSITING CONSULTANT ....PRICE PETHEL
LEAD COMPOSITORS ....RICK DUNN, BRYAN GRILL
SIMON HASLETT
SPECIAL EFFECTS COORDINATOR ....MARK NOEL
CHARACTER INTEGRATION SUPERVISOR ......UMESH SHUKLA
DATA INTEGRATION
SUPERVISOR ....MATTHEW "TEAL" BUTLER
MOTION CAPTURE SUPERVISOR ....ANDRÉ BUSTANOBY
DIGITAL STUNT SEQUENCE SUPERVISORS ......MARK BROWN
ANDY JONES
DIGITAL PARAPHERNALIA SUPERVISOR ....KELLY PORT
MOTION EDITING & TRACKING SOFTWARE ....DOUG ROBLE
CHARACTER TEXTURE PAINTERS ....JOHN HART
CHRIS CORTESE
CHARACTER INTEGRATION ARTISTS ......ROCCO PASSIONINO
FREDERIC SOUMAGNAS, JEFF BASINSKI
JON AGHASSIAN, MIKE EDLAND, DAN LEMMON
LEAD MORPH ARTIST ....CHRISTINE LO
VISUAL EFFECTS PRODUCTION MANAGER ....DEAN WRIGHT
MODEL SUPERVISOR ....LESLIE EKKER
KEY COMPOSITORS .....CLAAS HENKE, BRENT PREVATT
SCOTT RADER, ANDREA SHOLER
ANIMATION SUPERVISOR ....DANIEL ROBICHAUD
CG TECHNICAL SUPERVISOR ....BILL SPITZAK
DIGITAL OCEAN SUPERVISOR ....RICHARD KIDD
DIGITAL OCEAN ARTISTS ....JOHN GIBSON
DAVID ISYOMIN, NIKOS KALAITZIDIS
ZSOLT KRAJCSIK, DARREN POE, SANDOR RABB
TOSHI SHIOZAWA, PAUL VAN CAMP
CHARACTER SUPERVISOR ....DANIEL LOEB
CHARACTER MODELER ....SHAWNA OLWEN
DIGITAL SHIP ARTISTS .....FRANK AALBERS, ALAN CHAN
KARL DENHAM, RUSTY IPPOLITO
ANDY LESNIAK, PETER NYE
DIGITAL SHIP MODEL LEAD ....FRED TEPPER
VISUAL EFFECTS EDITOR ....MICHAEL BACKAUSKAS
MODEL CREW CHIEFS ....GEORGE STEVENS
GENE RIZZARDI
NIGHT COMPOSITING SUPERVISOR ....CAREY VILLEGAS
MIR SEQUENCE COMPOSITING SUPERVISOR ......JAMIE FRIDAY
VISUAL EFFECTS ART DIRECTOR ....KENNETH MIRMAN
DIGITAL SHIP EXTENSION
SUPERVISOR ....RICHARD A. PAYNE JR.
DATA INTEGRATION DIGITAL ARTISTS ....SEAN FADEN
CANDIDA NUNEZ, FRANCO PIETRANTONI
ZACK TUCKER
DIGITAL OCEAN SOFTWARE ....HANK DRISKILL
LUCIO FLORES, KEN MUSGRAVE, JIM ROTHROCK
DATA INTEGRATION LEADS ....MIKE O'NEAL
CHRIS SPRINGFIELD, DAVID SANTIAGO
MOTION CAPTURE ANIMATION ....DAN MA
MICHAEL SANDERS
CHARACTER INTEGRATION SOFTWARE ......DARYLL STRAUSS
MARCUS MITCHELL
DIGITAL PARAPHERNALIA ARTISTS ....DAVID BLEICH
FILLIPO CONSTANZO, JOHN COURTE
FRANCISCO DEJESUS, ALAN KAPLER, MARCUS KURTZ,
FRANKLIN LONDIN
DAVID PRESCOTT , KYLE STRAWITZ

CHARACTER ANIMATORS ....KEIJI YAMAGUCHI
BERND ANGERER, STEPHANE COUTURE
MARTINE DELAGE, ROBIN FINN
GONZALO GARRAMUNO, GIANCARLO LARI
CHARACTER ANIMATORS (cont'd) ....HAE-JEON LEE
SUNNY LEE, JAY RANDALL
CHRIS RODA, KEITH SMITH
FUMIHIKO SORI, LIZA SOROTZKIN
CHRIS WALSH
DIGITAL COMPOSITORS .....JEFF OLM, JONATHAN EGSTAD
DAVID STERN, PAUL KIRWIN
RON SHOCK, CHARLES MEREDITH
CRAIG HALPERIN, DAVE LOCKWOOD
JOHN SASAKI, DENNIS DAVIS, MIMI ABERS
MARC SCOTT, SONJA BURCHARD, TREENA LORIA
DONOVAN SCOTT, LARRY BUTCHER
CHIEF LIGHTING TECHNICIAN / ADDITIONAL
PHOTOGRAPHY ....VICTOR ABBENE
CAMERA OPERATOR / ADDITIONAL
PHOTOGRAPHY ....JOHN PASZKIEWICZ
DIGITAL MATTE PAINTERS ....PETER BAUSTAEDTER
CHARLES DARBY, MARTHA MACK
1ST ASSISTANT CAMERA OPERATORS .....HEATHER ROBERTS
AARON KIRSCH
VISUAL EFFECTS PRODUCTION
COORDINATOR ....SUSAN THURMOND
ASSISTANT ACCOUNTANT ....BEKKI MISIOROWSKI
DIGITAL EFFECTS COORDINATORS .....LISA HARRIMAN SCOTT
LISA SPENCE LISSAK, LAURA McDERMOTT
MIKELLA KIEVMAN, ALLYSE MANOFF, MELISSA DARBY
BEST BOY GRIP ....RICK "SLICK" RADER
COLOR GRADING SUPERVISOR ....JEFFREY KALMUS
STAGE PRODUCTION COORDINATOR .....CHRISTINA MUSREY
MOTION CONTROL OPERATORS ....JAMES RIDER
TIM CONWAY
ROTOSCOPE ARTISTS ....MIKE FRICK
TONIA YOUNG-BILDERBECK, BYRON WERNER
MECHANICAL ENGINEER ....SCOTT SALSA
ACCOUNTANT ....RAY WELKER
MOTION CONTROL GAFFER ....TONY ANDERSON
BEST BOY ELECTRIC ......ROBERT "GERN" TROWBRIDGE
SCANNING AND RECORDING ....JOSEPH GOLDSTONE
CHRISTOPHER HOLSEY
COORDINATOR ....CYNTHIA HALLIBURTON
MODEL MAKERS ....TOM NICOLAI, ALAN PILKINGTON
TOM WOESSNER, SCOTT LUKOWSKI
DON MARIANO, CAROLYN DALEY
DOTTIE STARLING
LEAD ROTOSCOPE ARTIST ....HOWIE MUZIKA
SPECIAL EFFECTS TECHNICIANS ....JOHN DOWNEY
TERRY KING, NATHAN ARBUTHNOTT
DON HASTINGS
ASSISTANT PRODUCTION
COORDINATORS ....LAUREN PRITCHARD
RACHEL FONDILLER
KEY GRIP ....DAVID NOVAK
MOTION CONTROL KEY GRIP ....GEORGE PALMER
ASSISTANT EDITOR ....LINDA RENAUD
LEAD MODEL MAKERS ....GORDON FORKERT
BRIAN RIPLEY, TED VAN DOORN
STAGE PRODUCTION MANAGER ....MARK KATCHUR
LOCATION MANAGER ....HARRY O'CONNOR
ADDITIONAL MODELS ....BRAZIL FABRICATION AND DESIGN
LIFEBOATS & LARGE SCALE SINKING

MINIATURES BY ....DONALD PENNINGTON INC.
FRANK AYRE, MITCH BRYAN, GARY YOUNG
MIKE WHEELWRIGHT, KATHLEEN MYERS
CHRIS NAKAYAMA, TOM GLEASON
SCOTT ALEXANDER, MILES CLAYTON
JON CRAIG, MIKE HOLDRIDGE

ADDITIONAL VISUAL EFFECTS BY VIFX
VISUAL EFFECTS SUPERVISOR ....RICHARD HOLLANDER
VFX PRODUCER ....JOYCE WEISIGER
CG SUPERVISORS ....CHERYL BUDGETT, EDWIN RIVERA
VFX PRODUCTION MANAGER ....DAN FOSTER

DIGITAL EFFECTS PRODUCTION MANAGER ....GENE KOZICKI
LEAD INFERNO ARTISTS ....MARK FELT, CHRIS RYAN
LEAD 2D COMPOSITORS ....SEAN McPHERSON
MARY LEITZ
INFERNO ARTISTS .....SCOTT BOGUNIA, WALT CAMERON
JOHN HELLER, CHRIS HOWARD
SEAN HYUN-IN LEE, CANDACE LEWIS
CESAR ROMERO, JON TANIMOTO
DIGITAL ARTISTS ....HUNTER ATHEY, DENNIS BENNETT
RAFAEL COLON, GREGORY ELLWOOD
KELLY FISCHER, GLORIA J. GEARY
UEL HORMANN, JENNIFER HOWARD
CHRISTOPHER IVINS, RIMAS JUCHNEVICIUS
GARRETT LAM, JAMES DO YOUNG LEE, LIZ LORD
KEITH McCABE, MIKE ROBY, MARC RUBONE
RICK SANDER, ANDREW TAYLOR, JONATHAN WOOD
TSZ "GEE" YEUNG, CYBELE SIERRA
SERKAN ZELEZELE, DAVID GUTMAN
DIGITAL ROTOSCOPING .....MIKE LAMB, MARIAN RUDNYK
DAVID SULLIVAN, ANTONIO TORRES
CHIEF TECHNOLOGIST ....MARK A. BROWN
MODEL SHOOT PRODUCER ....LEE BERGER
GAFFERS ....ROGER SAASEN, MICHAEL EVERETT
AVID EDITOR ....JIM THOMSON
MODEL MAKER FOREMAN ....PATRICK DENVER
SCRIPT SUPERVISOR ....JANE SLATER
ASSISTANT CAMERAMAN ....CHRISTOPHER PEARSON
3D TRACKING ....NICK ILYIN, MICHAEL LaFAVE
MARK de SOUSA
SYSTEMS MANAGER ....BOB FROEHLIG
DIRECTORS OF PHOTOGRAPHY ......DAVE DRZEWIECKI
JIM WEISIGER
PRODUCTION MANAGER ....GARY NOLIN
MOTION CONTROL OPERATORS ....PAUL JOHNSON
BILL McGILL
MOTION CONTROL CAMERA
ASSISTANTS ....TOM SHAUGHNESSY
JIM THIBO, ED NOTTOLI
DIGITAL DEPARTMENT MANAGER ....CRAIG NEWMAN
AVID SUPPORT ....GIAN GANZIANO
FILM COORDINATORS ....GUS DURON, ZEKE MORALES
1ST ASSISTANT DIRECTOR ....MARK OPPENHEIMER
KEY GRIP ....DON McCALL
PHYSICAL FX COORDINATOR ....ED FELIX
VIDEO ASSIST ....CHARLIE MAY, KEVAN JENSEN
PRODUCTION COORDINATOR ....ALICIA POWERS
2ND ASSISTANT CAMERAMAN ....KEVIN IVEY

INDUSTRIAL LIGHT & MAGIC, A DIVISION OF LUCAS DIGITAL LTD.
VFX SUPERVISOR ....DAVE CARSON
DIGITAL EFFECTS COMPOSITING
SUPERVISOR ....JON ALEXANDER
DIGITAL EFFECTS MATCHMOVER ....DAVID HANKS

COLOR TIMING SUPERVISOR ....KENNETH SMITH
VFX PRODUCER ....TOM KENNEDY
DIGITAL EFFECTS ARTISTS ....TIM ALEXANDER
DONALD S. BUTLER, JEFF DORAN
CRAIG HAMMACK
MARSHALL RICHARD KRASSER
VFX EDITOR ....TIM EATON
ASSOCIATE VFX PRODUCER ....HEATHER SMITH
ROTOSCOPE LEAD ARTIST ....JACK MONGOVAN
ROTOSCOPE ARTISTS ....CATHY M. BURROW
SUSAN GOLDSMITH
SCANNING SUPERVISOR ....JOSHUA PINES

CINESITE
DIGITAL VFX SUPERVISOR ....JERRY POOLER .
DIGITAL VFX PRODUCER ....AARON DEM
DIGITAL COMPOSITORS ....ABRA GRUPP, NICOLE HERR
MARCEL MARTINEZ, CRISTIN PESCOSOLIDO
LISA POLLARO, LISA DACKERMANN
DIGITAL ARTISTS .....CORRINE POOLER, MIKE CASTILLO
HILERY JOHNSON, JOE DUBBS, MARK LEWIS
JAMES VALENTINE, GEORGE OLIVER
EDITOR ....STEVE MATE .
ROTOSCOPE SUPERVISOR ....KAREN KLEIN
DIGITAL IMAGING SUPERVISOR ....BOB FERNLEY
DIGITAL VFX COORDINATOR ....CHRIS DEL CONTE .
PRODUCTION ASSISTANT ....KIMBERLY SPEAR

BANNED FROM THE RANCH
VISUAL EFFECTS SUPERVISOR ....VAN LING
DIGITAL ARTIST ....JORDAN HARRIS
TECHNICAL OPERATIONS ....DERICK TORTORELLA
TRAVIS LANGLEY
VISUAL EFFECTS EDITOR ....HITOSHI INOUE
COMPOSITE ARTISTS ....YUKIKO ISHIWATA
BRIAN HOLDEN
VISUAL EFFECTS PRODUCER ....CASEY CANNON
VISUAL EFFECTS COORDINATOR ....CRYSTAL FOTH

POP FILM & POP ANIMATION
DIGITAL COMPOSITING SUPERVISORS ....ADAM HOWARD
KEN LITTLETON
DIGITAL COMPOSITORS ....JENNIFER GERMAN
DAVID CRAWFORD, CANDICE SCOTT
CG TECHNICAL SUPERVISORS ....BARRY ROBERTSON
MATT HIGHTOWER
VFX PRODUCER ....ANDREA D'AMICO
COMPUTER ANIMATORS ....KIRK CADRETTE
SOM SHANKAR

4-WARD PRODUCTIONS, INC.
VFX SUPERVISOR ....ROBERT SKOTAK
PRODUCER / DIRECTOR OF PHOTOGRAPHY ....MARK SHELTON
PRODUCTION COORDINATOR ....KATHY DRAPER
SHOP SUPERVISOR ....JORGE FUENTES
SUPERVISOR DIRECTOR OF PHOTOGRAPHY .....DENNIS SKOTAK
VFX EDITOR ....BILL BLACK
RIGGING SUPERVISOR ....JAMES COOK
STAGE TECHNICIAN ....HOWARD HARNETT
EXECUTIVE PRODUCER ....ELAINE EDFORD
MODEL MAKER ....JIM DAVIDSON
CAMERA OPERATOR ....BRYAN GREENBERG

CIS HOLLYWOOD
VFX SUPERVISOR ....DR. KEN JONES
TECHNICAL SUPERVISOR ....BILL FEIGHTNER
DIGITAL SYSTEM COORDINATOR ....BOB PEISHEL
SENIOR PRODUCER ....JOE MATZA
DIGITAL COMPOSITING SUPERVISOR ....JEFF HEUSSER

VFX EDITOR ....DAWN LLEWELLYN
EXECUTIVE PRODUCER ....C. MARIE DAVIS
DIGITAL ARTISTS ....DANNY MUDGETT
GREGORY OEHLER, SUZANNE MITUS-URIBE

LIGHT MATTERS, INC.
VISUAL EFFECTS SUPERVISOR ....MAT BECK
VISUAL EFFECTS ASSOCIATE PRODUCER ....CHRIS HOLT
3D SUPERVISOR ....COLIN STRAUSE
COMPOSITORS ....JODI CAMPANARO, ERIK LILES
COMPOSITING SUPERVISORS ....GREG STRAUSE
EDSON WILLIAMS

HAMMERHEAD PRODUCTIONS, INC. ....JAMIE DIXON
REBECCA MARIE, THAD BEIER, EDIE PAUL

MATTE WORLD DIGITAL
VFX SUPERVISOR ....CRAIG BARRON
CHIEF DIGITAL MATTE ARTIST ....CHRIS EVANS
VFX PRODUCER ....KRYSTYNA DEMKOWICZ
DIGITAL COMPOSITOR ....CHRISTOPHER HORVATH

ADDITIONAL VISUAL EFFECTS BY ....PACIFIC TITLE DIGITAL
DIGISCOPE, PERPETUAL MOTION PICTURES

ADDITIONAL PRODUCTION SUPPORT
STUDIO DOCTOR ....NORA ALVAREZ, M. D.
FILTRATION MANAGER ....MARTIN VERDUGO
WATER SYSTEM ENGINEER ....JEFF DUDA
LIFEGUARD SUPERVISOR ....PATRICK RICHARDSON
DIVER ....GREGG TASH
AMBULANCE SERVICES ....DELTA HALCONES
TANK TECHNICIAN ....JOSE REYES
UNION DOCTOR ....ERNESTO TREJO, M. D.
FILTRATION TECHNICIAN ....MANUEL NIETO
DIVER MASTER ....DAMIAN FITZPATRICK
LIFEGUARDS ....JAMES B. ANDERSON
TRAVIS GLEASON, MATTHEW JACKSON
BENJAMIN LEWIS, ERIC MEECH
LANCE MENDOZA, FRANK POWELL
TONY BIXBY, WILLIAM RUSSELL
STRUCTURAL ENGINEER ....PETER HIGGINS & ASSOCIATES
ATTORNEY ....KAREN FAIRBANK
STORYBOARD ARTISTS ....RICK NEWSOME
PHIL KELLER, ERIC RAMSEY
CATERER ....DELUXE CATERING
CATERER - MEXICO .....ANA BALLESTEROS CATERING
LOS ANGELES PRODUCTION SECRETARY .....MELISSA RUDMAN
ANIMAL TRAINERS ....SLED REYNOLDS
DEANN ZARKOWSKI, ELIZABETH McMULLEN
JACKING SYSTEMS BY ....ALMAS INTERNATIONAL
M. INDUSTRIAL MECHANICAL, INC.
HYDRAULICS BY ....MAYO HYDRAULICS, INC.
HOUSING COORDINATORS ....FERNANDA ECHEVERRIA
FRAN SAIDMAN
ASSISTANT TO INDIG / MANN ....FLORISSE VAZQUEZ
PRODUCTION BUYER ....MOISES PINEDA
DELUXE CATERERS ....RICK EGGERS
RICHARD KATZENSON, SETH LIEBERMAN
KEVIN WHITE, LARRY BABBITZ
UNION PRODUCTION CHIEF ....MARIO A. REBOREDA
UNION PRODUCTION ASSISTANTS ...JUAN CARLOS GARRIDO
FELIPE L. MARISCAL
ASSISTANT TO KAREN FAIRBANK ....BEBE REYNOLDS
RENAULT REPLICA BY ....ADAMS CUSTOM ENGINES, INC.
ROSARITO HELICOPTER
SUPPORT ....CORPORATE HELICOPTERS OF SAN DIEGO
TRAVEL COORDINATORS ....MARK FLAHERTY
STEPHANIE CRAMER

RECEPTIONIST ....ANA MARIA LOMELI
ASSISTANT TO MARTY KATZ ....CAMPBELL KATZ
CONSTRUCTION OFFICE COORDINATOR .....LUCIA CASTANEDA
CRAFT SERVICE ....KAREN MERTZEL
ANDRE COMBS, PATRICK HIBLER
LOCAL LABOR COORDINATOR ....FRANCISCO YAÑEZ
SHIPPING ASSISTANT ....CHRISTIAN LOBOS
ASSISTANT TO SIMON CRANE ....ANA MANUELA TORRES
FREIGHT SHIPPING ....FILM FREIGHT
AKELA CRANE ....FLUID IMAGES, INC.
ELECTRICAL EQUIPMENT .......A.C. POWER DISTRIBUTION
SET PRODUCTION ASSISTANTS ....LOUIS TOCCHET
KERI BRUNO, YVETTE GURZA
GEORGE A. CASSELL
FERNANDO "BOOGIE" URIEGAS
ANDREI MAHANKOV, RICK COURTNEY
PRODUCTION ASSISTANTS ....DINAH ENGLUND
MATT BILSKI, ESTEBAN SANCHEZ FOCIL
SAMUEL LUGO GOMEZ, STACY PERSKIE KANISS
VANESSA ARMANINO LOPEZ
JULIO DIAZ ROSADO, IRAM COLLANTES LOPEZ
JUAN PABLO NOVAL MORGAN
HUGO BAYLON PAYAN, CHRISTOPHER HYSSONG
MATTHEW GOODMAN, DAWN HIGGINBOTHAM
PAUL LITTLETON, TODD COGAN
PRODUCTION ASSISTANTS (cont'd) ....MATTHEW JOHNSON
WAYNE LAMKAY, NICOLE WILDER
EMILIO VIDAURRETA, JORGE ACOSTA
CHRISTOPHER MAYHEW, SHERYL BENKO
STUNTS ....STEVE GRIFFIN, JOEY BOX
SARAH FRANZL, DAVID CRONNELLY
GARY POWELL, TOM STRUTHERS
LAURIE CRANE, SY HOLLANDS
STEVE CRAWLEY, JAMIE EDGELL
LEOS STRANSKY, DIMO LIPITKOVSKI
DUSAN HYSKA, MARTIN HUB
ALISTAIR SUTHERLAND
PAUL HEASMAN, PAUL HERBERT
GABOR PIROCH, MARC CASS, PAVEL CAJZL
BILL WESTON, EUNICE HUTHART
IGNACIO CARREÑO LOPEZ, JAN HOLICEK
JAROSLAV PSENICKA, KLAUS JINDRICH
PAVEL KRATKY, TIM TRELLA
CRIS THOMAS-PALOMINO
GABRIELA MORENO FLORES, KIRAN SHAH
MARK HENSON, RAY L. NICHOLAS
SEAN McCABE, ANDY BENNETT
DANA DRU EVENSON, JANI D. DAVIS
JAROSLAV PETERKA
RICARDO CRUZ MORAL, ALEJANDRO De La PENA
JAMIE LANDAU, JORGE CASARES
RAUL LOPEZ ARTEAGA, RAY DE-HAAN
TROY GILBERT, GERARDO MORENO FLORES
ERIK STABENAU, JIM PALMER
ROBERT INCH, DANE FARWELL
JOHN C. MEIER, TERRY FORRESTAL
ANNIE ELLIS, DEBBY LYNN ROSS
JORGE LUIS CORZO ROSALES
LEE SHEWARD, NANCY LEE THURSTON
RICHARD BRADSHAW, GEORGE FISHER
NOBY-ARDEN, CHUCK HOSACK, DEREK LEA
GARY L. GUERCIO, GLENN BOSWELL
JOHNNY HALLYDAY, LEON DELANEY
VINCENT P. DEADRICK, JR.

APX
5

LAWRENCE WOODWARD

MICHAEL PAPAJOHN, JOHNNY MARTIN

LINCOLN SIMONDS, GLEN YRIGOYEN

TIM RIGBY, CHARLIE BREWER

MARIO ROBERTS, DAVID LISTVAN

GUSTAVO CAMPOS HERNANDEZ

TERRY JACKSON, ALFREDO GUTIEREZ

BERNABE PALMA, WILEBALDO BUCIO

LYNN SALVATORI, MAURICIO MARTINEZ RAMOS

PAUL ELIOPOULOS, JOSH KEMBLE

STUNTS (cont'd) .... JILL BROWN, LANCE GILBERT

DOC D. CHARBONNEAU, DUSTIN J. MEIER

JUAN MANUEL VILCHIS SOSA

JULIO MARTINEZ, SIMONE BOISSEREÉ

MARK DeALESSANDRO, DIANE PETERSON

RALIEGH WILSON, CLARKE C. COLEMAN

DANNY ROGERS, JOHN CASINO

JUSTIN CROWTHER, TERRI RIPPENKROEGER

JAMIE A. KEYSER, JANET S. BRADY

DEBBIE LEE CARRINGTON, KIM K. KAHANA, JR.

MIC RODGERS, MIKE JUSTUS

TRISHA LANE, NANCY L. YOUNG

RUSTY HANSON, SANDRA BERUMEN

VICTORIA VANDERKLOOT

ANITA HART, DENISE LYNNE ROBERTS

JONI AVERY, JULIE MICHAELS

MATT JOHNSTON, RICK AVERY

SVETLA KRASTEVA, JULIE LAMM

MIKE AVERY, STEVEN LAMBERT

CINDY FOLKERSON, KURT LOTT

LARRY RIPPENKROEGER

MARCIA HOLLEY, BOBBY ANDREW BURNS

JOHANNA McLAREN-CLARK

ALEJANDRO AVENDAÑO LUHRS

LISA DEMPSEY, LUIS M. GUTIEREZ SANTOS

LUCY ALLEN, PAVEL VOKOUN

RAFAEL VALDEZ GARCIA CONDE

DANCERS .... KRIS ANDERSSON, BOBBIE BATES

AARON JAMES CASH, ANNE FLETCHER

ED FORSYTH, ANDIE HICKS

SCOTT HISLOP, STAN MAZIN

LISA RATZIN, JULENE RENEE

HALIFAX (CONTEMPORARY) SHOOT

DIRECTOR OF PHOTOGRAPHY ...... CALEB DESCHANEL, A.S.C.

2ND ASSISTANT DIRECTOR .... KRISTY SILLS

1ST ASSISTANT CAMERA .... JAMIE BARBER

1ST ASSISTANT CAMERA B .... TONY GUERIN

FORBES MacDONALD

CAMERA OPERATOR B .... HARALD ORTENBURGER

ELECTRIC BEST BOYS .... PAUL BOLTON, JAKE CLARKE

SOUND MIXER .... DOUG GANTON

PROPMASTER .... DANIEL BRADETTE

KEY GRIP .... RANDY TAMBLING, JEFF ADAMS

ASSISTANT COSTUMER .... JIM WORTHEN

GRIPS .... JOHN ADAMSON

CAROLYN ADAMS, KEVIN McNEIL

LEADMAN .... JOHN BROWN

KEY SCENIC .... BRENARD FAYE

CAMERA HELICOPTER PILOT .... CHUCK TAMBURRO

TRANSPORTATION CAPTAIN .... LORNE TAYLOR

MARINE SAFETY OFFICER .... JIMMY MAYO

SET DECORATOR .... ALI RUBENSTEIN

ASSISTANT COORDINATORS .... LAUREL ROBINSON

LEISA ETTINGER

3RD ASSISTANT DIRECTOR .... CRAIG CAMERON

LOADER .... ALBERT HENNEN

WESCAM OPERATOR .... STEVE KOSTER

VIDEO TECHNICIANS ...... JOE UNSINN, MICHAEL FOWLER

GENNY OPERATOR .... ALLAN ANGUS

GAFFERS .... SCOTTY ALLEN, JIM MacCAMMON

COSTUMER .... JEANIE KIMBER

DOLLY GRIP .... RON RENZETTI

KEY HAIRSTYLIST .... ANN TOWNSEND

ART DEPARTMENT ASSISTANT .... PIERETTE PRETTY

CONSTRUCTION COORDINATOR .... SCOTT McFARLANE

LOCATION MANAGER .... ANDREW McINNES

EXTRAS CASTING .... JOHN DUNSWORTH

MARINE COORDINATOR .... RICHARD FRASER

COAST GUARD .... KEN WALSH

PRODUCTION COORDINATOR .... KARLA MORASH

2ND 2ND ASSISTANT DIRECTOR .... MANDY KETCHESON

2ND ASSISTANT CAMERA .... YVONNE COLLINS

CYLVAN DesROULEAUX

2ND ASSISTANT CAMERA B .... JAYSON CLUTE

DARCY GASPAROVIC

VIDEO PLAYBACK .... SCOTT WARNER

RIGGING GAFFER .... TODD MURCHIE

ELECTRICIANS .... CHUCK LAPP

ALLAN VINCENT, WARD SWAN

BOOM OPERATOR .... REYNALD TRUDELL

ASSISTANT PROPS .... ANN FULLER, SASHA SERGETEWSKI

BEST BOY RIGGING .... PAUL MITCHELLTREE

KEY MAKE-UP .... LAURA BORZELLI

ART DEPARTMENT COORDINATOR ...... CHARLOTTE HARPER

CONSTRUCTION FOREMEN .... PETER WILLIAMS

ROBERT EAMES, GRAHAM BLINCO

SET DECORATORS .... CLAUDE ROUSSEL, JASON SHURKO

ESCONDIDO TANK SHOOT

PRODUCTION SUPERVISOR .... DANA BELCASTRO

KEY GRIP .... TONY MARRA

UNDERWATER LIGHTING .... J. P. GABRIEL

KELLY MYRSTOL, VINCE PACE, RANDY WIMBERG

ART DIRECTOR .... BILL REA

ROV TECH .... SCOTT MILLARD

LLOYD WELDER, JOHN ROSS

ROV PILOT .... JEFFREY N. LEDDA

GAFFER .... MARK GOODWIN

UNDERWATER COMMUNICATIONS .... MARK THURLOW

THE PRODUCERS WISH TO THANK:

ROBERTO CURIEL, Y CIA • MINISTER OF TOURISM MEXICO, SILVIA HERNANDEZ ENRIQUEZ • GOVERNOR OF THE STATE OF BAJA CALIFORNIA, HECTOR TERAN TERAN • MAYOR HUGO TORRES CHABERT • SECRETARY OF TOURISM, JUAN TINTOS
NATIONAL FILM COMMISSION OF MEXICO • MINISTRY OF THE ENVIRONMENT OF MEXICO • MINISTRY OF COMMUNICATION AND TRANSPORTATION OF MEXICO • GORDON & WILLIAMS • AMAYA CURIEL, Y CIA • YOLANDA & ESAUL LOPEZ
POPOTLA FISHERMAN'S VILLAGE • TOM McCLUSKIE • HARLAND & WOLFF • THE AUTHORITIES & CITIZENS OF THE STATE OF BAJA CALIFORNIA AND THE NOVA SCOTIA FILM COMMISSION

SPACECAM AERIAL CAMERA SYSTEM PROVIDED BY SPACECAM SYSTEMS, INC. • DIVING EQUIPMENT PROVIDED BY DACOR CORPORATION • FOOTAGE COURTESY OF WARNER BROS.
DIAMOND NECKLACE BY ASPREY LONDON • LIGHTING AND GRIP EQUIPMENT BY HOLLYWOOD RENTAL, A MATTHEWS GROUP COMPANY

"MY HEART WILL GO ON"
PERFORMED BY CELINE DION
MUSIC BY JAMES HORNER
LYRIC BY WILL JENNINGS
PRODUCED BY JAMES HORNER
AND SIMON FRANGLEN
CELINE DION PERFORMS COURTESY OF
550 MUSIC/SONY MUSIC ENTERTAINMENT
(CANADA) INC.

TITANIC ORCHESTRA MUSIC PERFORMED BY
I SALONISTI
PRODUCED BY JOHN ALTMAN

"VALSE SEPTEMBRE" BY FELIX GODIN
"WEDDING DANCE" BY PAUL LINCKE
"SPHINX" BY FRANCIS POPY
"VISION OF SALOME" BY ARCHIBALD JOYCE
"ALEXANDER'S RAGTIME BAND" BY IRVING
BERLIN

I SALONISTI
VIOLIN: LORENZ HASLER
VIOLIN: THOMAS FÜRI
CELLO: FERENC SZEDLÁK
DOUBLE BASS: BÉLA SZEDLÁK
PIANO: WERNER GIGER

STEERAGE BAND MUSIC PERFORMED BY
GAELIC STORM
PRODUCED BY RANDY GERSTON

"OH YOU BEAUTIFUL DOLL"
BY SEYMOUR BROWN AND NAT D. AYER
PRODUCED AND ARRANGED BY WILLIAM ROSS

**"COME, JOSEPHINE, IN MY FLYING
MACHINE"**
BY ALFRED BRYAN AND FRED FISHER
PRODUCED AND ARRANGED BY WILLIAM ROSS

"NEARER MY GOD TO THEE"
BY LOWELL MASON AND SARAH ADAMS
PERFORMED BY I SALONISTI
ARRANGED BY JONATHAN EVANS-JONES
PRODUCED BY LORENZ HASLER

NEGATIVE CUTTING MARY NELSON-DUERRSTEIN, EXECUTIVE CUTTING • NEGATIVE BREAK-DOWN SCOTT BEEBE • CFI COLOR TIMER DAN MUSCARELLA
MICRO THEATER SERVICE BY TMH CORPORATION • TITLES AND OPTICALS BY PACIFIC TITLE • PRE-MIX PLAYBACK SYSTEM THS • FILMED ON LOCATION AT FOX STUDIOS BAJA

CFI Color   KODAK Film Stock   Prints by DELUXE® LABORATORIES   Filmed in PANAVISION®   No. 35593   MOTION PICTURE ASSOCIATION OF AMERICA   IATSE

www.titanicmovie.com

These credits are subject to change as of 10/29/97.

scene 69
(rewritten)

This line was improvised by DiCaprio in rehearsals.

CAMERON: "I thought it pretty well summed up his character. Then later, Leo second-guessed it, maybe because he realized he heard it before, but the line seemed organic to his character, and I didn't want to remove it."

Jack and Rose walk side by side. They pass people reading and talking in steamer chairs, some of whom glance curiously at the mismatched couple.

                    JACK
          So I've been on my own since I was fifteen,
          since my folks died. I have no brothers and
          sisters, or close kin in that part of the
          country, no reason to stay, so I lit out
          an' never been back since.

                    ROSE
          So you don't have a home of any kind?

                    JACK
          Naw, I'm like a tumbleweed, blowin' in the
          wind. Listen, Rose, we've walked about a
          mile around this boat deck and we've chewed
          over how I grew up and how great the
          weather's been, but I reckon that's not
          why you came to talk to me.

There is an awkward pause.

                    ROSE
          Mr. Dawson, I—

                    JACK
          Jack.

                    ROSE
          Jack... I feel like such an idiot. It
          took me all morning to get up the
          nerve to face you.

                    JACK
            (he looks her in the eye)

                    ROSE
          (taking a deep breath) I... I want to
          thank you for what you did. Not just
          for... for pulling me back. But for
          your discretion.

                    JACK
          You're welcome. Rose.

                    ROSE
          Look, I know what you must be thinking!
          Poor little rich girl. What does she
          know about misery?

                    JACK
That's not what I was thinking. What I was
thinking was... what could have happened to
hurt this girl so much she thought she had
no way out.

                    ROSE
I don't... you see, it wasn't just <u>one</u> thing.
It was <u>everything</u>. It was my whole world and
all the people in it. And the inertia of my
life, plunging ahead and me powerless to
stop it.

She holds up her engagement ring.

                    JACK
Gawd look at that thing! You would have gone
straight to the bottom.

                    ROSE
500 invitations have gone out. All of
Philadelphia society will be there. And
all the while I feel like I'm standing
in the middle of a crowded room screaming
at the top of my lungs and no one even
looks up.
     (in a rush)
Last night I felt so trapped. I just had
to get away...just run and run and run...
and then I was at the back rail and there
was no more ship...even the <u>Titanic</u> wasn't
big enough. And before I'd really thought
about it, I was over the rail. I was so
furious. *I'll teach them not to listen.
They'll be sorry.*

                    JACK
They'll be sorry. 'Course you'll be dead.

                    ROSE
     (embarrassed)
Oh God, I am such an utter fool.

                    JACK
So you're stuck on a train you can't get
off cause you're marryin' this fella.
So don't marry him.

                    ROSE
If only it were that simple.

                    JACK
It <u>is</u> that simple.

                              ROSE

No, Jack. No, no, no, no. I'm sorry, I can't expect
you to understand how things work in my life.

                              JACK

Do you love him?

                              ROSE
    (shocked)
Pardon me?

                              JACK

Do you love him?

                              ROSE
    (flustered by his directness)
You're being very rude. You shouldn't
be asking me this.

                              JACK

Well it's simple. Do you love him or not?

                              ROSE

This is not a suitable conversation.

                              JACK

Why can't you just answer the question?

                              ROSE

This is absurd. You don't know me and I don't know
you and we are not having this conversation at all.
You are rude and uncouth and presumptuous and I'm
leaving now. Jack...<u>Mr.</u> Dawson... it's been a plea-
sure. I sought you out to thank you and now I <u>have</u>
thanked you—

                    JACK (OVERLAPPING)
And you've insulted me—

                              ROSE

Well, you deserve it.

                              JACK

Right. Right. (grinning) I thought you
were leaving.

                              ROSE
    (starts to laugh in spite of herself)
I am. You are <u>so</u> annoying. Wait! I don't have to
leave. This is my part of the ship. You leave!

                              JACK

Well, well, well. Now who's being rude?

> ROSE
> What's that stupid thing you're carrying around?

The question is rhetorical because she has already grabbed the sketchbook. She opens it.

> ROSE
> What are you, an artist or something?

ON JACK'S sketches... each one an expressive little bit of humanity: an old woman's hands, a sleeping man, a father and daughter at the rail. The faces are luminous and alive. His book is a celebration of the human condition.

> ROSE
> Well these are rather good.
> (looks at some more)
> They're very good actually.

> JACK
> They didn't think too much of 'em in old Paree.

> ROSE
> Paris? You do get around. For a...a person of...well...limited means.

> JACK
> Go on, go on. A poor guy. You can say it.

Some loose sketches fall out and are taken by the wind. Jack scrambles after them...catching two, but the rest are gone, over the rail.

> ROSE
> Oh no! Oh, I'm so sorry. Truly!

> JACK
> Don't worry about it. Plenty more where they came from.

He snaps his wrist, shaking his drawing hand in a flourish.

> JACK
> I just seem to spew 'em out. Besides, they're not worth a damn anyway.

For emphasis he throws away the two he caught. They sail off.

> ROSE
> (laughing)
> You're deranged!

She goes back to the book, turning a page.

> ROSE
> *Well, well*...well.

She has come upon a series of nudes. Rose is transfixed by the languid beauty he has created. His nudes are soulful, real, with expressive hands

Deleted in post